Karen Brown's
England, Wales & Scotland
Charming Hotels & Itineraries

Written by

JUNE BROWN and KAREN BROWN

Illustrations by Barbara Tapp
Cover Painting by Jann Pollard

Karen Brown's Guides, San Mateo, California

Karen Brown Titles

Austria: Charming Inns & Itineraries
California: Charming Inns & Itineraries
England: Charming Bed & Breakfasts
England, Wales & Scotland: Charming Hotels & Itineraries
France: Charming Bed & Breakfasts
France: Charming Inns & Itineraries
Germany: Charming Inns & Itineraries
Ireland: Charming Inns & Itineraries
Italy: Charming Bed & Breakfasts
Italy: Charming Inns & Itineraries
Mexico: Charming Inns & Itineraries*
Mid-Atlantic: Charming Inns & Itineraries
New England: Charming Inns & Itineraries
Pacific Northwest: Charming Inns & Itineraries*
Portugal: Charming Inns & Itineraries
Spain: Charming Inns & Itineraries
Switzerland: Charming Inns & Itineraries

*Now on our website, *www.karenbrown.com*, soon to be in print

To Simon and Clare
in the hope that they will
discover Britain for themselves

Editors: Anthony Brown, Karen Brown, June Brown, Clare Brown, Iris Sandilands, Lorena Aburto Ramirez.
Illustrations: Barbara Tapp; Cover painting: Jann Pollard; Web designer: Lynn Upthagrove.

Maps: Susanne Lau Alloway—Greenleaf Design & Graphics; Inside cover photo: W. Russell Ohlson.

Distributed by Fodor's Travel Publications, Inc., 280 Park Avenue, New York, NY 10017, USA.

Distributed in Canada by Random House Canada, 2775 Matheson Boulevard. East, Mississanga, Ontario, Canada L4W 4P7, phone: (905) 624 0672, fax: (905) 624 6217.

Distributed in the United Kingdom, Ireland, and Europe by Random House UK, 20 Vauxhall Bridge Road, London, SW1V 2SA, England, phone: 44 20 7840 4000, fax: 44 20 7840 8406.

Distributed in Australia by Random House Australia, 20 Alfred Street, Milsons Point, Sydney NSW 2061, Australia, phone: 61 2 9954 9966, fax: 61 2 9954 4562.

Distributed in New Zealand by Random House New Zealand, 18 Poland Road, Glenfield, Auckland, New Zealand, phone: 64 9 444 7197, fax: 64 9 444 7524.

Distributed in South Africa by Random House South Africa, Endulani, East Wing, 5A Jubilee Road, Parktown 2193, South Africa, phone: 27 11 484 3538, fax: 27 11 484 6180.

A catalog record for this book is available from the British Library.

ISSN 1535-7333

Contents

Introduction

This guide falls into three sections: practical information useful in planning your trip; driving itineraries that take you deep into the countryside through idyllic villages full of thatched-roofed cottages and flower-filled gardens, exploring ancient castles and traversing vast purple moorlands; and lastly, but most importantly, our personal recommendations for outstanding hotels in England, Scotland, and Wales. Every hotel included in this guide is one that we have seen and enjoyed—our personal recommendation written with the sincere belief that where you lay your head each night makes the difference between a good and a great vacation. If you prefer to travel the bed and breakfast way, you may prefer to select places to stay from our companion guide, *England: Charming Bed & Breakfasts*. We encourage you to buy new editions of our guides and throw away old ones—you will be glad you did because we add new listings, update prices, phone, and fax numbers, and delete places that have not maintained standards.

Eilean Donan Castle, Scotland

About England, Wales & Scotland

The following pointers are given in alphabetical order, not in order of importance.

CURRENCY

The pound sterling (£) is the official currency of Great Britain. An increasingly popular and convenient way to obtain pounds is simply to use your bankcard at an ATM machine. You pay a fixed fee for this but, depending on the amount you withdraw, it is usually less than the percentage-based fee charged to exchange currency or travelers' checks. Be sure to check with your bank or credit card company about fees and necessary pin numbers prior to departure. Visit our website (*www.karenbrown.com*) for an easy-to-use online currency converter.

CAR RENTAL

If you are coming from overseas, it is frequently less expensive to arrange and prepay a car rental before arriving in Britain. If you plan on a visit to London, we strongly recommend that you make it either at the beginning or end of your trip. One option is to fly into London, pick your car up at the airport, tour the countryside, drop the car back at the airport, and take public transportation or a taxi into the city. If you are starting your vacation with sightseeing in London, collect your car from the airport at the end of your stay in the city. The trick is to avoid driving in London.

Readers frequently ask our advice on car rental companies. We always use Auto Europe, a car rental broker that works with the major car rental companies to find the lowest possible price. They also offer motor homes and chauffeur services. Auto Europe's toll-free phone service from every European country connects you to their U.S.-based, 24-hour reservation center (ask for the card with European phone numbers to be sent to you). Auto Europe offers our readers a 5% discount, and occasionally free upgrades. Be sure to use the Karen Brown ID number 99006187 to receive your discount and any special offers. You can make your own reservations online via our website, *www.karenbrown.com* (select Auto Europe from the home page), or by phone (800-223-5555).

DRIVING

Just about the time overseas visitors board their return flight home, they will have adjusted to driving on the "right" side which is the left side in England. You must contend with such things as roundabouts (circular intersections); flyovers (overpasses); ring roads (peripheral roads whose purpose is to bypass city traffic); lorries (trucks); lay-bys (turn-outs); boots (trunks); and bonnets (hoods). Pedestrians are permitted to cross the road anywhere and always have the right of way. Seat belts must be worn at all times.

MOTORWAYS: The letter "M" precedes these convenient routes for covering long distances. With three or more lanes of traffic either side of a central divider, you should stay in the left-hand lane except for passing. Motorway exits are numbered and correspond to numbering on major road maps. Service areas supply petrol (gas), cafeterias, and "bathrooms" (the word "bathroom" is used in the American sense—in Britain "bathroom" means a room with a shower or bathtub, not a toilet—"loo" is the most commonly used term for an American bathroom).

"A" ROADS: The letter "A" precedes the road number. All major roads fall into this category. They vary from three lanes either side of a dividing barrier to single carriageways with an unbroken white line in the middle indicating that passing is not permitted. These roads have the rather alarming habit of changing from dual to single carriageways at a moment's notice.

"B" ROADS AND COUNTRY ROADS: The letter "B" preceding the road number or the lack of any lettering or numbering indicates that it belongs to the maze of country roads that crisscross Britain. These are the roads for people who have the luxury of time to enjoy the scenery en route and they require your arming yourself with a good map (although getting lost is part of the adventure). Driving these narrow roads is terrifying at first but exhilarating after a while. Meandering down these roads, you can expect to spend time crawling behind a tractor or cows being herded to the farmyard. Some lanes are so narrow that there is room for only one car.

ELECTRICITY

The voltage is 240. Most bathrooms have razor points (American style) for 110 volts. If you are coming from overseas, it is recommended that you take only dual-voltage appliances and a kit of electrical plugs. Often your host can loan you a hairdryer and an iron.

INFORMATION

The British Tourist Authority is an invaluable source of information. You can visit their website at *www.visitbritain.com.* Its major offices are located as follows:

AUSTRALIA–SYDNEY: BTA, Level 16, Gateway, 1 Macquarie Place, Sydney NWS 2000, tel: (02) 9377-4400, fax: (02) 9377-4499

CANADA–TORONTO: BTA, 5915 Airport Road, Suite 120, Mississauga, Ontario L4V 1T1, tel: (888) VISITUK

FRANCE–PARIS: BTA, Maison de la Grand Bretagne, 19 Rue des Mathurins, 75009 Paris, tel: (1) 4451-5620, fax: (1) 4451-5621

GERMANY–FRANKFURT: BTA, Westendstrasse 16–22, 60325 Frankfurt, tel: (069) 97-112-446, fax: (069) 97-112-444

NEW ZEALAND–AUCKLAND: BTA, Suite 305, 17th Floor, Fay Richwhite Building, 151 Queen Street, Auckland 1, tel: (09) 303-1446, fax: (09) 377-6965

USA–CHICAGO: BTA, 625 North Michigan Avenue, Suite 1001, Chicago, IL 60611— walk-in inquiries only

USA–NEW YORK: BTA, 551 Fifth Avenue, Suite 701, New York, NY 10176, tel: (800) 462-2748, email: travelinfo@bta.org.uk

Introduction–About England, Wales & Scotland

If you need additional information while you are in Britain, there are more than 700 official Tourist Information Centres identified by a blue-and-white letter "I" and "Tourist Information" signs. Many information centers will make reservations for local accommodation and larger ones will "book a bed ahead" in a different locality. In London at the British Visitor Centre at 1 Regent Street, London SW1Y 4PQ (near Piccadilly Circus tube station) you can book a room, hire a car, or pay for a coach tour or theatre tickets. It is open 9 am to 6:30 pm, Monday to Friday; 10 am to 4 pm Saturday and Sunday, with extended hours from mid-May to September.

THE NATIONAL TRUST

The National Trust works for the preservation of places of historic interest or national beauty in England, Wales, Northern Ireland, and Scotland. Its care extends to stately homes, barns, historic houses, castles, gardens, Roman antiquities, moors, fells, woods, and even whole villages. During the course of a driving itinerary, whenever a property is under the care of the National Trust we state (NT). You can check times and location with the current edition of *The National Trust Handbook* available from many National Trust shops and overseas from the British Tourist Authority, or utilize their website, *www.nationaltrust.org.uk*. If you are traveling to Scotland, you will need a copy of *The National Trust for Scotland Guide* or log on to *www.nts.org.uk*. A great many National Trust properties have excellent shops and tea rooms. If you are planning on visiting several sites, consider joining the National Trust as a member, thus obtaining free entry into all properties. In the UK contact: The National Trust, PO Box 39, Bromley, Kent BR1 3XL, tel: (020) 7315-1111. In the USA contact: The Royal Oak Foundation, 285 West Broadway, #400, New York, NY 10013, tel: (800) 913-6565 or (212) 966-6565.

SHOPPING

Non-EU members can reclaim the VAT (Value Added Tax) that they pay on the goods they purchase. Not all stores participate in the refund scheme and there is often a minimum purchase price. Stores that do participate will ask to see your passport before completing the VAT form. This form must be presented *with the goods* to the customs officer at the point of departure from Britain within three months of purchase. The customs officer will certify the form. After having the receipts validated by customs you can receive a refund in cash from the tax-free refund counter. Alternatively, you can mail your validated receipts to the store where you bought the goods. The store will then send you a check in sterling for the refund.

WEATHER

Britain has a tendency to be moist at all times of the year. The cold in winter is rarely severe; however, the farther north you go, the greater the possibility of being snowed in. Spring can be wet but it is a lovely time to travel: the summer crowds have not descended, daffodils and bluebells fill the woodlands, and the hedgerows are filled with wildflowers. Summer offers the best chance of sunshine but also the largest crowds. Schools are usually closed the last two weeks of July and all of August—this is the time when most families take their summer holidays. Travel is especially hectic on the weekends in summer—try to avoid major routes and airports at these times. Autumn is also an ideal touring time: the weather tends to be drier than in spring and the woodlands are decked in their golden fall finery.

Introduction–About England, Wales & Scotland

Overview Map of Driving Itineraries

Scotland

Edinburgh

The Dales and Moors of North Yorkshire

The Lake District

York

Chester

Derbyshire Dales and Villages

Chesterfield

Ashbourne

Cambridge and East Anglia

Wales

Coventry

Cambridge

Oxford

In and Around the Cotswolds

Bath

LONDON

Winchester

Southwest England

Exeter

Portsmouth

Southeast England

7

About Itineraries

Nine driving itineraries map a route through the various regions of England, Wales, and Scotland. At the beginning of each itinerary we suggest our recommended pacing to help you decide the amount of time to allocate to each region. Often all, or a large portion, of an itinerary can be enjoyed using one hotel as a base and staying for several days.

Most sightseeing venues operate a summer and a winter opening schedule, changing over around late March/early April and late October/early November. If you happen to be visiting at the changeover times, be sure to check whether your chosen destination is open before making plans. We try to give an indication of opening times, but there is every possibility that these dates and times will have changed by the time you take your trip, so before you embark on an excursion, check the dates and hours of opening.

MAPS

At the beginning of each itinerary a map shows the itinerary's routing, places of interest along the way, and towns with recommended hotels. These are drawn by an artist and are not intended to replace commercial maps. Our suggestion is to purchase a large-scale road atlas of England where an inch equals 10 miles. We use the Michelin Tourist and Motoring Atlas of Great Britain–1122. To outline your trip you might want to consider the one-page map of Britain, Michelin Map 986. We sell these and regional Michelin green guides in our website store at *www.karenbrown.com*.

About Hotels

The third section of this guide contains our recommendations for outstanding places to stay in England, Scotland, and Wales. Each listing is very different and occasionally the owners have their eccentricities, which all adds to the allure of these special hotels. We have tried to be candid and honest in our appraisals and attempted to convey each hotel's special flavor so that you know what to expect and will not be disappointed. All hotels are places that we have inspected, or stayed in—places that we enjoy. Our recommendations cover a wide range: please do not expect the same standard of luxury at, for example, the lovely Hotel du Vin in Winchester as at the luxurious Chewton Glen—there is no comparison—yet each is outstanding in what it offers. We have tried to mention major sightseeing attractions near each countryside listing to encourage you to spend several nights in each location. Few countries have as much to offer as Great Britain—within a few miles of most listings there are places of interest to visit and explore—lofty cathedrals, quaint churches, museums, and grand country houses.

CHILDREN

Places that welcome children state *Children welcome*. The majority of listings in this guide do not "welcome" children but find they become tolerable at different ages over 5 or, more often than not, over 12. In some cases places simply do not accept children. However, these indications of children's acceptability are not cast in stone, so if you have your heart set on staying at a listing that states *Children over 12* and you have an 8-year-old, call them, explain your situation, and they may well accept you. Ideally, we would like to see all listings welcoming children and all parents doing their bit by making sure that children do not run wild.

CREDIT CARDS

Whether hotels accept payment by credit card is indicated using the terms AX—American Express, MC—MasterCard, VS—Visa, or simply—all major. If credit cards are not accepted, an increasingly popular and convenient way to obtain cash is simply to use your bankcard at an ATM machine.

CHRISTMAS PROGRAMS

Several listings offer Christmas getaways—if the information section indicates that the listing is open during the Christmas season, there is a very good chance that it offers a festive Christmas package.

FINDING HOTELS

At the back of the book is a key map of Great Britain plus nine regional maps showing each recommended hotel's location. The pertinent regional map number is given at the right on the top line of each hotel's description. To make it easier for you, we have divided each location map into a grid of four parts—a, b, c, and d—as indicated on each map's key. We give concise driving directions to guide you to the listing, which is often in a more out-of-the-way place than the town or village in the address. We would be very grateful if you would let us know of cases where our directions have proved inadequate.

HANDICAP FACILITIES

We list all the places to stay that have ground-floor rooms, or rooms specially equipped for the handicapped, at the back of the book. Please discuss your requirements when you call hotels to see if they have accommodation that is suitable for you.

RATES

Rates are those quoted to us for the 2002 summer season. We have tried to keep rates uniform by quoting the 2002 rate for a standard double room and for a suite. Not all places conform, so where dinner is included, or the listing quotes only per person rates, we have stated this in the listing. Prices are always quoted to include breakfast (except in London where breakfast is not usually included in the rate), Value Added Tax (VAT), and service (if these are applicable). Please use the figures printed as a guideline and be certain to ask what the rate is at the time of booking. Many listings offer special terms, below their normal prices, for "short breaks" of two or more nights.

RELAIS & CHÂTEAUX

Several of our listings are members of Relais & Châteaux, in which cases we note *Relais & Châteaux Member* at the bottom of the descriptions.

RESERVATIONS

When making your reservations, be sure to identify yourself as a "Karen Brown traveler." The hoteliers appreciate your visit, value their inclusion in our guide, and frequently tell us they take special care of our readers, and many offer special rates to Karen Brown members (visit our website at *www.karenbrown.com*). We hear over and over again that the people who use our guides are such wonderful guests!

It is important to understand that once reservations for accommodation are confirmed, whether verbally by phone or in writing, you are under contract. This means that the proprietor is obligated to provide the accommodation that was promised and that you are obligated to pay for it. If you cannot, you are liable for a portion of the accommodation charges plus your deposit. Although some proprietors do not strictly enforce a cancellation policy many, particularly the owners of the smaller properties in our book, simply cannot afford not to do so. Similarly, many airline tickets cannot be changed or refunded without penalty. We recommend insurance to cover these types of additional expenses arising from cancellation due to unforeseen circumstances. A link on our website (*www.karenbrown.com*) will connect you to Access America, which offers a variety of insurance policies to fit your needs.

Reservations can be confining and usually must by guaranteed with a deposit. July and August are the busiest times and it is advisable to make reservations during this period. When making a reservation be specific as to what your needs are, such as a ground-floor room, en-suite shower, twin beds, or family room. Check the prices, which may well have changed from the guidelines given in the book (summer 2002). Ask what deposit to send or give your credit card number. Tell them about what time you intend to arrive and request dinner if you want it. Ask for a confirmation letter with brochure and map to be sent to you. There are several options for making reservations:

EMAIL: This is our preferred way of making a reservation. If the hotel/bed and breakfast is on our website, we have included their email address in the listing and added a direct link on their Karen Brown web page. (Always spell out the month as the British reverse the American month/day numbering system.)

FAX: If you have access to a fax machine, this is a very quick way to reach a hotel. If the place to stay has a fax, we have included the number in the listing. (See comment above about spelling out the month.)

LETTER: If you write for reservations, you will usually receive your confirmation and a map. You should then send your deposit. (Be sure to spell out the month.)

TELEPHONE: By telephoning you have your answer immediately, so if space is not available, you can then decide on an alternative. If calling from the United States, allow for the time difference (Britain is five hours ahead of New York) so that you can call during their business day. Dial 011 (the international code), 44 (Britain's code), then the city code (dropping the 0), and the telephone number.

WEBSITE

Please visit the Karen Brown website (*www.karenbrown.com*) in conjunction with this book. It provides comments and discoveries from you, our readers, information on our latest finds, post-press updates, the opportunity to purchase goods and services that we recommend (rail tickets, car rental, travel insurance), and one-stop shopping for our guides and associated maps. Most of our favorite places to stay are featured on our website (their web addresses are on their description pages in this book) with color photos and, through direct links to their own websites, even more information. For the properties not participating in our online booking program, you can e-mail them directly, making reservations a breeze.

In & Around The Cotswolds

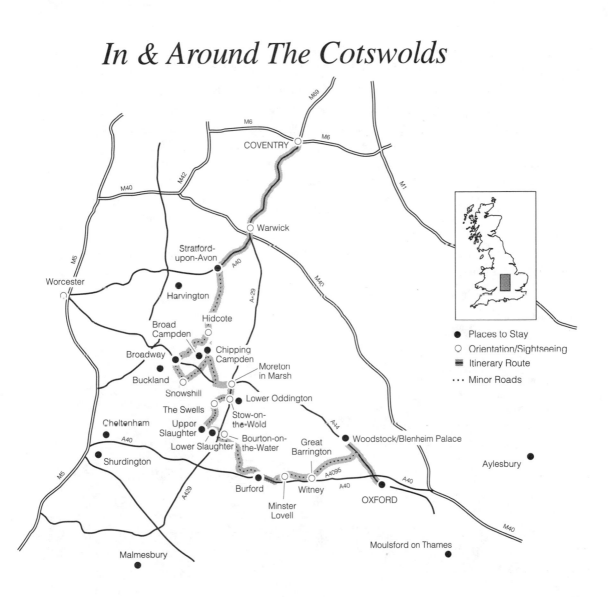

In & Around The Cotswolds

From the gracious university town of Oxford through the quintessentially English Cotswold villages to Shakespearean Stratford and the grand fortress of Warwick Castle, this itinerary covers famous attractions and idyllic countryside nooks and crannies. The Cotswolds is a region of one sleepy village after another clad in the local soft-gray limestone or creamy-golden ironstone, where mellow stone walls, manor houses, and churches cluster along riverbanks, perch on steep-sided hills, or scatter independently in a pocket of a pretty valley. In Shakespeare's day this was sheep country and the center of England's wool industry. By the mid-1800s the area had fallen into decline, its wool trade usurped by Australia and New Zealand. Thus the area slept, by-passed by the factories and cities of the Industrial Revolution. Now tourists flock to the Cotswolds and yet the region remains remarkably unspoilt: in fact, it appears to thrive on the attention.

Lower Slaughter

Recommended Pacing: Spend a night in Oxford or in nearby Woodstock. Follow this with two nights in a countryside hotel as a base for exploring the beautiful Cotswold villages (consider going into Stratford one night to see a play).

Oxford is a beautiful university town graced by spacious lawns, pretty parks, lacy spires, honey-colored Cotswold stones, romantic pathways, and two picturesque rivers—the Cherwell and the Thames. Follow signs for the city center, park in any of the well signposted, multi-story car parks, and foray on foot to explore. You may want to make your first stop the **Oxford Information Centre** on Gloucester Green, off George Street, to obtain a map. Walking tours of the town start from here. Much of the sightseeing in this the oldest university town centers on its colleges whose open times depend on whether the students are "up" (there) or "down" (not there). Particularly worth visiting are **Christ Church College** with its superb quad and tower designed by Wren to hold the bell Great Tom; **Magdalen College**, the most beautiful college, with its huge gardens making you feel as if you are in the countryside; and **Merton College**, whose chapel contains 13th- to 14th-century glass. Apart from the colleges, visit **St. Mary's Church** where you can climb the spire for a marvelous view of the city; the **Ashmolean Museum** with its remarkable collection of paintings, tapestries, and sculptures; the riverside **Botanical Gardens** opposite Magdalen College; **Blackwell's**, the most famous of Oxford's many bookstores; and **The Bear**, on Alfred Street, a marvelous old pub dating from 1242. Punts can be rented on the River Cherwell from beside Magdalen Bridge.

Leaving Oxford, take the A44 (Stratford-upon-Avon) to **Woodstock**, one of England's prettiest country towns. On the outskirts of Woodstock are the famous gates of **Blenheim Palace**, Sir John Vanbrugh's masterpiece, which was built for John Churchill, the 1st Duke of Marlborough. The construction of the house was a gift from Queen Anne to the Duke after his victory over the French and Bavarians at Blenheim in 1704. However, before its completion, Queen Anne's gratitude had waned and the Marlborough family had to pay to have the house finished. The gardens and parklike grounds were landscaped by Capability Brown. Sir Winston Churchill, the grandson of the 7th Duke, was born here on November 30, 1874, and associations with him have accentuated the historical interest of the Palace. (Winston Churchill, his wife, father, Lord Randolph Churchill, and mother, Jenny Jerome, the beautiful daughter of an American newspaper owner, are buried in St. Martin's churchyard in Bladon, 2 miles away.) You drive through the grounds to the house, park on the grass, and either tour the sumptuous rooms with a group or wander independently. A narrow-gauge railway takes you through the park to the butterfly farm and plant center. (*Open mid-March–October.*) In contrast to the immense palace and spacious grounds are the compact streets of the little town of Woodstock with its coaching inns, delightful hotel (**The Feathers**), and interesting shops.

Blenheim Palace

In & Around The Cotswolds

Retrace your steps for a short distance on the A44 in the direction of Oxford and take the A4095 for 7 miles to the mellow-stone town of **Witney** where blankets have been made for over a thousand years and which still preserves its Cotswold market-town atmosphere. The 18th-century **Blanket Hall** was used for weighing blankets and has an unusual one-handed clock.

Minster Lovell is a few miles to the west along the B4047: to reach the old part of the village, follow the brown signs for **Minster Lovell Hall**. Park at the end of the lane and walk through the churchyard to see the ruined home of the Lovell family in a field by the river's edge. Leave the village by the road to the side of the prettiest building in the village, The Swan, following signs through Astall Leigh and Astall to the A40, which you take in the direction of Cheltenham for a short distance to Burford.

Follow Tourist Information signs down the hill into the lovely old-world Cotswold town of **Burford**. The broad High Street sweeps down the hillside, bordered by numerous antique and gift shops, to the bridge spanning the River Windrush. Branching off are delightful, narrow residential streets with flower-filled cottage gardens. In the days when coach and horses were the main form of transport, Burford was a way station. The coaches are long gone but the lovely inns remain: two with the most atmosphere are **The Bay Tree** and the adjacent **Lamb Inn** (see listing).

Explore Burford and leave town following the road over the River Windrush. Go left at the mini-roundabout, directing yourself down country lanes to **Taynton** with its adorable thatched and golden-stone cottages and on up the valley to Great Barrington and **Little Barrington**, a village of quaint cottages. Turn right along the A40 towards Cheltenham and first right to Windrush where you pick up signs for the drive down country lanes through Sherbourne to Bourton-on-the-Water. (When you come to the A429 turn right and then right into Bourton-on-the-Water.)

Bourton-on-the-Water is a lovely village with a number of riverside greens and low bridges spanning the River Windrush. Go early in the morning, just before sunset, or in the winter to avoid the crowds that overrun this peaceful (albeit somewhat over-commercialized) spot.

Leave Bourton-on-the-Water by going down the main street and turning right for a very short distance on the A429 (in the direction of Cheltenham) to a left-hand turn that directs you down country lanes to the more peaceful side of the Cotswolds. This is typified by the outstandingly lovely villages of **Lower and Upper Slaughter** (see listings) with their honey-colored stone cottages beside peaceful streams—just the names on the signpost are enough to lure you down their lanes. From Upper Slaughter follow signs for Stow-on-the-Wold down country lanes through "the Swells," **Lower and Upper Swell**, further picturesque examples of villages with whimsical names.

Stow-on-the-Wold, its market square lined by mellow, old, gray-stoned buildings, was one of the most prosperous wool towns in England. Most of the 17th-century buildings around the square now house interesting shops. Two of Stow's main thoroughfares—Sheep Street and Shepherds Way—are reminders that selling sheep was once the town's main livelihood. Cromwell converted the 12th-century church into a prison and used it to hold 1,000 Royalists captive after a Civil War battle in 1646.

Nearby **Moreton in Marsh's** broad main street, once part of the Roman road known as the Fosse Way, is lined with interesting shops. At the crossroads take the A44 towards Evesham to **Bourton-on-the-Hill**, an appropriately named village whose houses climb a steep hillside. At the top of the hill turn right for Blockley and follow signs for the village center until you pick up signs for Broad Campden and **Chipping Campden** (see listings), with its High Street lined with gabled cottages and shops topped by steep tile roofs. **Woolstaplers Hall** is now a museum of photographic and medical equipment and home of the tourist information center.

Cross the A44 and a country lane brings you to **Snowshill** and **Snowshill Manor** (NT), a Tudor manor packed with collections of musical instruments, clocks, toys, and bicycles. (*Open April–October, closed Mondays, Tuesdays 12–5.*)

Just down the lane, flowers dress the lovely weathered-stone houses of **Broadway,** a town that is often described as the perfection of Cotswold beauty. The **Lygon Arms** (see listing) is as famous as the town, a magnificent 14th- to 16th-century hotel whose public rooms are exquisitely furnished with antiques. In summer the town is thronged with tourists so it is best to visit early or late in the day.

Turn right up the main street and first left on the B4632 (signposted Stratford), through peaceful **Willersey,** where ducks sail serenely on the village mere, and Weston-sub-Edge, to the outskirts of Mickleton where you turn right for **Hidcote Manor Gardens** (NT), one of the most delightful gardens in England. Created early this century by Major Lawrence Johnston, it is a series of individual gardens each bounded by sculpted hedges and linked by paths and terraces. Each "mini garden" focuses on a specific theme or flower. There are stunning displays of old roses and in summer the perennials are a blaze of color. (*Open April–October, closed Tuesdays and Fridays, except June–July closed Fridays only.*) Next door, another outstanding garden, **Kiftsgate Court,** has exquisite displays of roses. (*Open April–September, Wednesdays, Thursdays, and Sundays.*)

Leaving Hidcote, return to Mickleton and turn right onto the B4632 into **Stratford-upon-Avon** (see listing), the birthplace of the greatest poet in the English language, William Shakespeare. Stratford-upon-Avon is always impossibly crowded with visitors—if crowds are not to your liking, give it a miss. William Shakespeare was born in 1564 in a half-timbered house on Henley Street, educated at the King's New Grammar School, and, in 1597, six years before his death, retired to **New Place,** one of the finest and largest houses in Stratford. Simply engraved stones in front of the altar of the **Holy Trinity Church** mark the burial spot of Shakespeare and some other members of his family. It is a fairly large town, with beautifully renovated timbered buildings and lovely shops. The town's glory, however, is brought expertly to the stage at the **Royal Shakespeare Theatre** and at its associate theatre, **The Other Place.** (*Open all year.*)

Warwick Castle

Anne Hathaway married William Shakespeare in 1582, but until then she lived in a darling thatched cottage at **Shottery**, a small village just a stone's throw from Stratford-upon-Avon. You will see paintings and photographs of this picture-book cottage all over the world. (*Open all year.*)

When you leave Shottery head back towards the center of Stratford and take the A46 to Warwick. **Warwick Castle** is a magnificent, 14th-century fortress of formidable towers

In & Around The Cotswolds

and turrets. The fortress dominates a choice spot on the riverbank and its striking structure is beautifully preserved. Climb the towers, explore the armory and torture chamber below, then visit the Manor House. As you walk through the house you see what it was like to attend a house party given by the Earl and Countess of Warwick in 1898. The house has retained its period furniture and Madame Tussaud's has populated the rooms with wax figures from the past. Here a servant pours water into a bath for a guest while downstairs guests listen to a recital being given by Dame Clara Butt. The gardens are decorated by arrogant, strutting peacocks. (*Open all year.*)

Wander into **Warwick** with its mixture of Georgian and old timber-framed houses. At the town's west gate stands the **Leycester Hospital**, for 400 years an almshouse for crippled soldiers. (*Closed Mondays.*) In the **Beauchamp Chapel** lies the tomb of Elizabeth I's favorite, the Earl of Leicester.

The large industrial city of **Coventry** lies just to the north—it is worth a visit to see **Coventry Cathedral**, one of Europe's finest examples of modern architecture. On a night in 1940 Hitler's bombers destroyed 40 acres of the city center, including the cathedral. A new city center and a new cathedral were built after the war. The blackened ruins of the old cathedral form the approach to the new, with a cross made of two charred roof timbers on the old altar, inscribed "Father Forgive." In the new cathedral magnificent stained-glass windows by modern artists lead the eye to the massive stone altar with its abstract cross and crucifix. Behind it is a 75-foot tapestry of "The Redeeming Savior of the World." From Coventry fast motorways will connect you to all parts of Britain.

Southwest England

Places to Stay
Orientation/Sightseeing
Itinerary Route
Minor Roads

Boscastle
Tintagel
Padstow
Rock
A39
A30
Lostwithiel
The Eden Project
Talland-by-Looe
St Austell
Fowey
A390
A30
Truro
Lost Gardens
of Heligan
Mevagissey
St Ives
Veryan
Trelissick
Gardens
Portloe
A394
Portscatho
Cape
Cornwall
Marazion
St Just in Roseland
St Just
St Mawes
Falmouth
Lands End
St Michael's
Mount
Penzance
Gillan

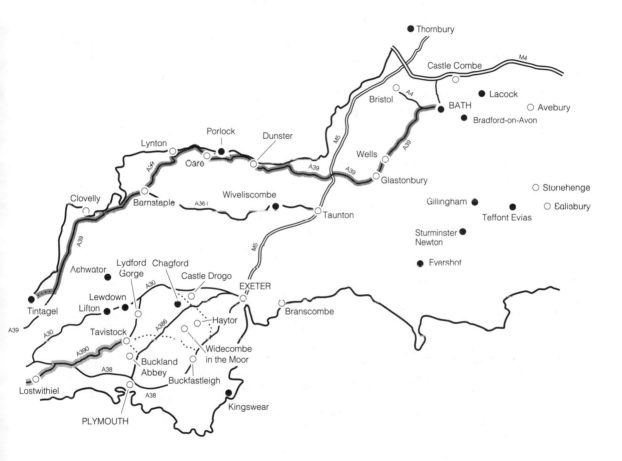

23

Southwest England

Scenery changes noticeably as this itinerary traverses England southwest from Bath through Somerset and along its unspoilt coast, outlining Cornwall, into the heart of Devon. Wild ponies gallop across the expanses of Exmoor. Along the northern coastline, the scenery changes dramatically from wooded inlets dropping to the sea to wild rollers crashing on granite cliffs, giving credence to old tales of wreckers luring ships onto rocky shorelines. Picturesque villages surround sheltered harbors, their quays strewn with nets and lobster pots. Southern ports present a gentler scene: bobbing yachts dot wooded estuaries and gentle waves lap the shoreline. Hedgerow-lined lanes meander inland across Dartmoor's heather-clad moorlands to picturesque towns nestling at her edge. Relax and enjoy your explorations of this westernmost spur of land jutting out into the Atlantic Ocean.

St. Michael's Mount

Recommended Pacing: Spend two full days in Bath to give you time to appreciate the flavor of this lovely city. Use Tintagel or Rock as a base for exploring the northern coast of the peninsula, and Penzance, St. Mawes, Fowey, or Talland-by-Looe as a base for exploring the south of Cornwall. Complete the itinerary with a couple of nights in south Devon to enable you to enjoy the wild beauties of Dartmoor.

The elegant city of **Bath** (see listings) with its graceful, honey-colored buildings, interesting museums, and delightful shopping area is best explored on foot over a period of several days. Bath, founded by the Romans in the 1st century around the gushing mineral hot springs, reached its peak of popularity in the early 1700s with the arrival of Beau Nash, who opened the first Pump Room where people could take the water and socialize. Architects John Wood, father and son, used the local honey-colored stone to build the elegant streets and crescents in neoclassical Palladian style.

Maps are available from the Tourist Information Centre near the abbey (corner of Cheap and Stall streets). Entry into the **Roman Baths** is via the **Pump Room,** which was the place to gather in the 18th and 19th centuries. The Great Bath, a large warm swimming pool built around a natural hot spring, now open to the sky, was once covered. Mosaics, monuments, and many interesting artifacts from the town can be seen in the adjacent museum. (*Open all year.*)

Nearby, tucked into a narrow passageway between Abbey Green and North Parade, is **Sally Lunn's House**, a museum and a tea shop. The museum, in the cellar, has the kitchen preserved much as it was in the 1680s when Sally's buns and other baked goods were the favorites of Bath society. Upstairs you can try a freshly baked Sally Lunn bun.

Eighteenth-century society came to be seen at balls and gatherings at the **Assembly Rooms** and authors such as Austen, Smolett, and Fielding captured the social importance of these events. The **Museum of Costume**, in the Assembly Rooms basement, should not be missed. (*Open all year.*)

From the Museum of Costume it is an easy walk via **The Circus**, a tight circle lined with splendid houses designed by John Wood I, and Brock Street to the **Royal Crescent**, a great arc of 30 terraced houses that epitomize the Georgian elegance of Bath. **One Royal Crescent** has been authentically restored to the 18th-century style and contains an interesting kitchen museum and a gift shop. (*Open mid-February–November. Closed Mondays.*)

Bath has some wonderful restaurants and delightful shops and boutiques: whether you are in the market for antiques or high fashion, you will find shopping here a real joy.

While our itinerary takes us south and west from Bath, there are a great many interesting places to the east, listed below, that can easily be visited as day trips from this lovely city.

The village of **Avebury** (NT), made up of a church, several houses, shops, and an old pub, lies within a vast circle of standing stones surrounded by earthworks. The site covers 28 acres. Unlike Stonehenge, where the stones are larger, the site smaller, and the crowds sometimes overwhelming, Avebury is a peaceful spot. Here, armed with a map, you can wander amongst the stones and wonder why about 4,000 years ago Bronze Age man spent what has been estimated at 1½ million man-hours to construct such a temple. (Just off the A4 between Calne and Marlborough.) (*Open all year.*)

Castle Combe is the most photogenic collection of warm, honey-stone cottages snuggled along a stream's edge. (Just south of the M4 motorway between exits 17 and 18.)

Claverton Manor is the American museum in the United Kingdom. Furniture, household equipment, and period rooms show home life in the United States from the 17th to 19th centuries. (3 miles east of Bath.) (*Open April–October, closed Mondays.*)

Lacock (NT) is an exquisite village where no building dates from later than the 18th century, many dating from much earlier. Be sure to visit the **Fox Talbot Museum** of early photographs and **Lacock Abbey**. The abbey was converted to a manor house in the 16th century but retains its 13th-century cloisters. **At The Sign of The Angel** is a delightful 15th-century inn, easily distinguished by being the only black-and-white building in the village. (Between Chippenham and Melksham on the A350.) (*Closed November–February.*)

Salisbury has been a prosperous Hampshire market town since the 13th century. Park your car in one of the large car parks on the edge of town and wander through the bustling town center to **Salisbury Cathedral**, the only ancient English cathedral built to a single design. Completed in 1258, it sits gracefully isolated from the busy town, surrounded by a large green field.

Salisbury Cathedral

Britain's most famous ancient monument is **Stonehenge**. Built over a period of almost 1,000 years up to 1250 B.C., this circular arrangement of towering stone slabs was probably meant either to mark the seasons or to be used as a symbol of worship. It is intriguing to ponder what prompted a society thousands of years ago to drag these immense stones many miles and erect them in just such a formation, isolated in the middle of flat Salisbury Plain. Understandably, Stonehenge attracts many visitors. Your visit will be more enjoyable if you are prepared for coachloads of tourists. (On the A303 about 10 miles from Salisbury.) (*Open all year.*)

When it is time to leave Bath, take the A4 following signs for Bristol until you come to the A39 Wells road. **Wells** is England's smallest cathedral city and the cathedral is glorious. Park you car in one of the well-signposted car parks on the edge of town and walk through the bustling streets to **Wells Cathedral**. The cathedral's west front is magnificently adorned with 400 statues of saints, angels, and prophets. The interior is lovely and on every hour the Great Clock comes alive as figures of four knights joust and one is unseated. From the cathedral you come to Vicars Close, a cobbled street of tall-chimneyed cottages with little cottage gardens built over 500 years ago as housing for the clerical community. On the other side of the cathedral regal swans swim lazily in the moat beneath the Bishop's Palace where at one time they rang a bell when they wanted to be fed—now visitors' picnics provide easier meals.

Nearby **Glastonbury** is a quiet market town steeped in legends. As the story goes, Joseph of Arimathea traveled here and leaned on his staff, which rooted and flowered, a symbol that he should build a church. There may well have been a primitive church here but the ruins of **Glastonbury Abbey** that you see are those of the enormous abbey complex that was begun in the 13th century and closed by Henry VIII just as it was completed. The abbey is in the center of town. Legend also has it that Glastonbury (at that time surrounded by marshes and lakes) was the Arthurian Isle of Avalon. Arthur and Guinevere are reputedly buried here and it is said that Arthur only sleeps and will arise when England needs him. (*Open all year.*)

Cross the M5 near Bridgwater, detouring around the town, and follow the A39, Minehead road, to **Dunster**, a medieval town dominated by the battlements and towers of **Dunster Castle** (NT). Constructed by a Norman baron, it has been inhabited by the Luttrell family since 1376. While much of the castle was reconstructed in the last century, it has a superb staircase, halls, and dining room. (*Open April–October, closed Thursdays and Fridays.*) Park before you enter the town and explore the shops and ancient buildings (including a dormered Yarn Market) on the High Street. On Mill Lane you can tour 18th-century **Dunster Watermill** (NT), which was restored to working order in 1979. (*Open April–October, closed Fridays April–June, September–October.*)

Continue your drive along the A39, watching for a sign directing you to your right to the hamlet of **Selworthy** (NT). Its pretty green, surrounded by elaborate thatched cottages, makes this a very picturesque spot. The National Trust has a small visitors' center and excellent tea shop.

Porlock is a large, quaint, bustling village with narrow streets. As the road bends down to the sea, the hamlet of **Porlock Weir** appears as a few picturesque cottages and the Ship Inn facing a pebble beach and a tiny harbor dotted with boats.

Retrace your steps towards Porlock for a short distance and take the first road to the right, a private toll road that rises steeply out of Porlock Weir. It is a pretty, forested drive along a narrow lane with views of Porlock Bay. The toll road returns you to the A39, which you take for a short distance before turning left for the village of **Oare**. R. D. Blackmore who wrote about the people, moods, and landscape of Exmoor used the little church that you see in the valley below for Lorna Doone's marriage to John Ridd. Continue into the village where you can park your car behind the village shop and take a 3-mile walk along the river to Badgworthy Valley, the home of the cutthroat outlaw Doone family.

Continue to Brenden where you turn right, signposted Lynton and Lynmouth, and regain the A39. A short drive through squat red and green hills brings you to the coast where the road dips steeply and you see the neighboring villages of **Lynton** and **Lynmouth.** Victorian Lynton stands at the top of the cliff and Lynmouth, a fishing village of old-style houses, nestles at its foot. Park by the harbor and take the funky old cliff railway, which connects the two villages.

Leaving Lynmouth, proceed up the hill into Lynton, following signs for the alternative route for light vehicles to Valley of the Rocks. Wend your way through the town and continue straight. Beyond the suburbs the road tapers and you find yourself in a narrow valley with large, rugged rock formations separating you from the sea, then in a more pastoral area with seascapes at every dip and turn.

Deposit your road toll in the honesty box and follow signs along narrow lanes for **Hunters Inn**, a lovely old pub set in a peaceful valley. From here direct yourself back towards the A39, which bends inland across the western stretches of Exmoor and south through **Barnstaple**, a market center for the area. Continue along the A39 to Bideford where a bridge sweeps you high above the old harbor.

Just beyond Bucks Cross you see a small signpost for **Hobby Drive**. This narrow coastal road winds through woodlands, provides panoramic views of Clovelly, and brings you out on the road above the village. **Clovelly** is an impossibly beautiful spot, its whitewashed cottages tumbling down cobblestone lanes to boats bobbing in the harbor far below. However, to be able to walk through this picturebook village you have to pay an entrance fee and pass through a very commercial visitors' center, a real tourist trap.

Leave the A39 at the B3263 and detour on narrow country lanes leading to the picturesque little village of **Boscastle**. Braced in a valley 400 feet above a little harbor, the town was named after the Boscastle family who once lived there, rather than an actual castle.

Nearby, **Tintagel Castle** clings to a wild headland, exposed to coastal winds, claiming the honor of being King Arthur's legendary birthplace. The sea has cut deeply into the slate cliffs, isolating the castle. Climb the steep steps to the castle and gaze down at the sea far below. Prince Charles, as Duke of Cornwall, owns the castle whose interior is more attractive than the exterior. The town itself (see listing), while it is quite touristy, has charm and the most adorable, and certainly most photographed, **Post Office** (NT) in Britain.

Leaving Tintagel, follow signs for the A39, in the direction of Truro, to the A30, which takes you around Redruth, Cambourne, and Hayle to the A3074 to **St. Ives**, about an hour-and-a-half's journey if the roads are not too busy. St. Ives is a former fishing town with cobbled streets and old cottages that has spread to suburban sprawl—it's very crowded in summer, so visit in the off season if you can. With the decline of fishing came the artists, who have done much to preserve its quaint cobbled streets and picturesque old cottages, and the town is now home to a branch of the Tate Gallery.

The most attractive, windswept stretch of Cornwall's coastline lies between St. Ives and Land's End. Stone farm villages hug the bare expanse of land and are cooled by Atlantic Ocean breezes that wash up over the cliff edges. Abandoned old tin mine towers stand in ruins and regularly dot the horizon. On the western outskirts of **St. Just** lies **Cape Cornwall**: rather than visit over-commercialized Land's End, consider visiting here to enjoy a less crowded, more pastoral western view. Pull into **Sennen Cove** with its long, curving crescent of golden sand and the powerful Atlantic surf rolling and pounding.

The expression "from John O'Groats to Land's End" signifies the length of Britain from its northeasternmost point in Scotland to England's rocky promontory, **Land's End**, in the southwest. Many visitors to Cornwall visit Land's End, but be prepared to be disappointed—you have to pay to enter a compound of refreshment stands, exhibits, and children's rides to get to the viewpoint.

As the road rounds the peninsula from Land's End, it is exposed to the calmer Channel waters, far different from the Atlantic rollers. Mount's Bay is just around the bend from Land's End with the pretty village of **Mousehole** (pronounced "mowzle") tucked into a niche on its shores. With color-washed cottages crowded into a steep valley and multi-colored fishing boats moored at its feet, this adorable village is crowded in summer but worth the aggravation endured in finding a parking spot.

Pirates from France and the Barbary Coast used to raid the flourishing port town of **Penzance** (see listing) until the mid-18th century. Now it is quite a large town, a real mishmash of styles from quaint fishermen's cottages to '60s housing estates, where long, peaceful, sandy beaches contrast with the clamor and activity of dry-dock harbors.

Leave Penzance on the A30 following the graceful sweep of Mount's Bay and turn right onto a minor road that brings you to **St. Michael's Mount** (NT). Its resemblance to the more famous mount in France is not coincidental, for it was founded by monks from Mont St. Michel in 1044. A 19th-century castle and the ruins of the monastery crown the island, which is reached at low tide on foot from the town of Marazion. If you cannot coincide your arrival with low tide, do not worry—small boats ferry you the short distance to the island. The steep climb to the top of this fairy-tale mount is well worth the effort. (*Open April–October, closed Saturdays and Sundays, limited winter opening.*)

To the east lies **Falmouth**. Overlooking the holiday resort, yachting center, and ancient port are the ruins of **Pendennis Castle**. Built in 1540 to guard the harbor entrance, it was held during the Civil War by the Royalists and withstood six months of siege before being the last castle to surrender to Cromwell's troops in 1646. (*Open all year.*) Falmouth is a bustling town whose narrow, shop-lined streets have a complex one-way system—parking is an additional problem. Unless you have shopping to do, avoid the congestion of the town center and follow signposts for Truro.

The road from Falmouth to St. Mawes winds around the river estuary by way of Truro. A faster and more scenic route is to take the **King Harry Ferry** across the river estuary. If you love wandering around gardens, you will enjoy **Trelissick Gardens** (NT), filled with subtropical plants, located on the Falmouth side of the estuary. (*Open April–September.*)

St. Mawes (see listing) is a charming, unspoilt fishing harbor at the head of the Roseland Peninsula. Its castle was built by Henry VIII to defend the estuary.

The 20 miles or so of coastline to the east of St. Mawes hide several beautiful villages located down narrow, winding country lanes. **Portscatho** is a lovely fishing village that has not been overrun with tourists. **Veryan** is a quaint village where thatched circular houses were built so that "the devil had nowhere to hide." **Portloe** is a pretty fishing hamlet. The most easterly village is **Mevagissey** whose beauty attracts writers, artists, and throngs of tourists.

Overlooking this quaint port lie the expansive estates of the Tremayne family, centered at one time on Heligan House and vast acres of gardens and woodlands. There used to be 20 staff in the house and 22 in the garden but all this ended in the 1914–18 war when two-thirds of the gardeners died fighting in Flanders. After that the garden went into decline and when in 1970 the Tremaynes sold the house for apartments it simply went to sleep—a sleep from which it emerged in the 1990s when two professional gardeners hacked their way through the undergrowth and were inspired to begin the largest garden restoration project in Europe. Evoking images of *The Secret Garden,* the **Lost Gardens of Heligan** have emerged from their slumber. A magnificent complex of walled gardens, vegetable gardens, and melon yards shows how pineapples and melons were grown in Victorian times. To the south of the main garden are vast acres of palms and tree ferns know as The Jungle, which leads to the Lost Valley with its woodland walks. (*Open all year.*)

Drive through St. Austell on the A390 and turn left up into the hills above the town, following signs to **The Eden Project,** set in a former china clay pit. This global garden terraces down the quarry sides to its floor where two massive geodesic conservatories house thousands of beautiful plants in two different environments: Humid Tropics (rainforest and oceanic islands plants) and Warm Temperate (Californian, Mediterranean, and Southern African plants). The outdoor gardens include a section telling the stories of plants that have changed the world, started wars, and inspired artists and that clothe, feed, and shelter. There is plenty of convenient parking and enough hands-on exhibits and restaurants to make this a fun visit rather than an academic experience. (*Open all year.*)

Returning to the A390, drive northwest to **Lostwithiel,** the 13th-century capital of Cornwall. Twenty miles to the east, **Liskeard** is crowded in summer, but fortunately much of the traffic has been diverted around the town. Between Liskeard and Tavistock you find **Cotehele** (NT), built between 1485 and 1627, the home of the Edgecumbe family. The house contains original furniture, armor, and needlework. A highlight is the kitchen with all its wonderful old implements. The gardens terrace steeply down to the lovely River Tamar. (*Open April–October, closed Fridays.*)

The A390 crosses the River Tay and brings you into Tavistock. Turn right at the first roundabout in town signposted B3357 Princetown (then the B3212 Mortenhampstead road), which brings you up, over a cattle grid, and into **Dartmoor National Park**. Vast expanses of moorland rise to rocky outcrops (tors and crags) where ponies and sheep graze intently among the bracken and heather, falling to picturesque wooded valleys where villages shelter beneath the moor. From Mortenhampstead it's a half-hour drive to Exeter and the motorway. But, saving the best for last, linger on Dartmoor and enjoy some of the following sights.

The view from atop **Haytor Crags** on the Bovey to Widecombe road is a spectacular one—there is a feel of *The Hound of the Baskervilles* to the place. Softer and prettier is the walk down wooded **Lydford Gorge** (NT) to White Lady Waterfall (between Tavistock and Okehampton). (*Open all year.*) A cluster of cottages and a tall church steeple make up **Widecombe in the Moor**, the village made famous by the *Uncle Tom Cobbleigh* song: the famous fair is still held on the second Tuesday in September. The pretty town of **Chagford** (see listing) at the edge of the moor has attractive houses and hostelries grouped round the market square. **Buckland-in-the-Moor** is full of picturesque thatched cottages. **Buckland Abbey** (NT), a onetime Cistertian abbey and home of Sir Francis Drake, is now a museum with scale model ships from Drake's time to today among its exhibits (*Open April–October, closed Thursdays.*) At **Buckfastleigh** you can take a steam train 7 miles alongside the river Dart. Nearby is **Buckfast Abbey**, famous for its tonic wine and colorful stained-glass windows. **Castle Drogo** (NT) is a fanciful, castlelike home designed by Edward Lutyens overlooking the moor near Drewsteignton. (*Open April–October, closed Fridays.*)

Leaving Dartmoor National Park, A roads quickly bring you to **Exeter**, a city that was much damaged by German bombs in 1942. Happily, the cathedral, which was begun in 1260, survived. The old town towards the River Exe has many fine old buildings including the Custom House and a maze of little streets with old inns and quaint shops. On Town Quay is a fascinating **Maritime Museum**. (*Open all year.*) The rebuilt center is a modern shopping complex. From Exeter the M5 will connect you to all parts of Britain.

Southeast England

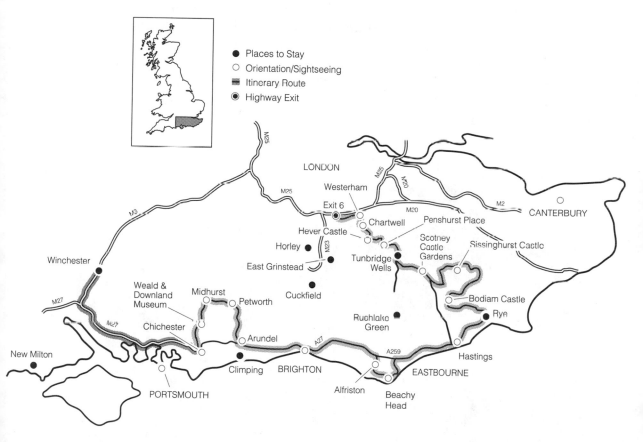

- ● Places to Stay
- ○ Orientation/Sightseeing
- ▦ Itinerary Route
- ◉ Highway Exit

LONDON

Westerham

Exit 6

Hever Castle

Chartwell

Penshurst Place

M25

M20

M2

CANTERBURY

Scotney
Castle
Gardens

Sissinghurst Castle

Horley

Tunbridge
Wells

Winchester

East Grinstead

M23

Bodiam Castle

Rye

Weald &
Downland
Museum

Midhurst

Petworth

Cuckfield

M27

M3

Chichester

Ruchlake
Green

Arundel

Hastings

New Milton

M27

Climping

BRIGHTON

A27

A259

EASTBOURNE

PORTSMOUTH

Alfriston

Beachy
Head

Southeast England

Southeast from London through Kent and Sussex to England's southern coast, the land is fertile and the climate mild. Scores of narrow country lanes twist and turn among the gentle slopes of the pleasant countryside, leading you from Chartwell, Churchill's home, through castles, manors, and some of the most exquisitely beautiful gardens in England to Rye, a town full of history and rich in smugglers' tales. Along the busy, crowded coast you come to Brighton where seaside honky-tonk contrasts with the vivid spectacle of the onion domes of the Royal Pavilion, Arundel with its mighty fortress, and Portsmouth with its historic boats.

Scotney Castle Gardens

Recommended Pacing: Spend two nights in southeast England to enable you to accomplish the first part of this itinerary. Allow a day's drive, with sightseeing, along the coast and into Winchester. Spend two nights in Winchester to give you a complete day for sightseeing.

Chartwell, your first sightseeing destination, is signposted from exit 6 of the M25, through Westerham and onto country lanes. Chartwell was the home of Winston Churchill from 1924 until his death in 1965, when Lady Churchill gave the house and its contents to the nation. To visit this large home and Churchill's studio, full of his mementos and paintings, is to have a glimpse into the family life of one of Britain's most famous politicians. (*Open April–October, closed Mondays and Tuesdays except July–August, closed Mondays only.*)

Leaving Chartwell, retrace your steps the short distance to the main road and follow signs for **Hever Castle**, a small 13th-century moated castle that was at one time home to the Boleyn family. Anne Boleyn was Henry VIII's second wife and Elizabeth I's mother. At the turn of the century vast amounts of money were poured into the castle's restoration by William Waldorf Astor, an extremely wealthy American who forsook his native country and became a naturalized British citizen. Because the castle was far too small to provide accommodation for his family and friends, Mr Astor built an adjacent village of snug, Tudor-style cottages and joined it to the castle. While the village is not open to the public, the restored castle, its rooms full of antiques that span the last 800 years, and the parklike grounds are open to visitors. (*Open March–November.*)

Leave the castle heading left in the direction of Tunbridge Wells, turning left down a small country road to **Chiddingstone**, a National Trust village, whose short main street has several 16th- and 17th-century half-timbered houses, a church, and a tea shop. Park by the old houses and follow a footpath behind the cottages to the Chiding Stone, from which the village gets its name: nagging wives were brought here to be chided by the villagers.

Just beyond the village, branch left at the oast house for Penshurst Station and **Penshurst Place**, a 14th-century manor house with an Elizabethan front surrounded by magnificent parkland and gorgeous gardens. Here Sir Philip Sidney—poet, soldier, and statesman—was born and his descendant, Viscount de l'Isle, lives today. The enormous, 14th-century great hall with its stone floor and lofty, ornate, beamed ceiling contrasts by its austerity with the sumptuously furnished state rooms. There is also a fascinating collection of old toys. The gardens are a delight, full of hedges and walls that divide them into flower-filled alleyways and rooms—each garden with a very different character. (*Open March–November, closed Mondays.*)

Tunbridge Wells (see listing) lies about 7 miles to the south. In its heyday Royal Tunbridge Wells rivaled Bath as a spa town. The Regency meeting place, The Pantiles, a terraced walk with shops behind a colonnade, is still there as are the elegant Regency parades and houses designed by Decimus Burton. Central parking is well signposted to the rear of the Corn Exchange, which contains an exhibit, *Day at the Wells*, which traces the town's growth from the time the spring water became fashionable for its curative powers to its popularity with wealthy Victorians.

Leave Tunbridge Wells on the A267 following signposts for Eastbourne till you are directed to the left through Bells Yew Green to cross the A21 (Hastings road) and enter **Scotney Castle Gardens** (NT), a gorgeous, romantic garden surrounding the moated ruins of a 14th-century castle. (*Open April–October, closed Mondays and Tuesdays.*)

Leave Scotney Castle Gardens to the left, taking the A21 (Hastings road) for a short distance to Flimwell where you turn left on the A268 to Hawkshurst and from here left on the A229 Maidstone road to **Cranbrook**. While it is not necessary to go through Cranbrook to get to Sissinghurst Gardens, it makes a very worthwhile detour because it is a delightful town whose High Street has many lovely, white-board houses and shops, a fine medieval church, and a huge, white-board windmill with enormous sails. On the other side of town you come to the A262 where you turn right for the short drive to Sissinghurst Castle Gardens.

Sissinghurst Castle (NT) was a jail for 3,000 French prisoners in the Seven Years' War. Its ruined remains were bought by Vita Sackville-West and her husband, Harold Nicolson, in 1930 and together they created the most gorgeous gardens with areas divided off like rooms and each room a distinctly different, beautiful garden. They also rescued part of the derelict castle where you can climb the tower in which Vita wrote her books. At the entrance to the garden an old barn has been tastefully converted into a tea room and shop. (*Open April–October, closed Mondays.*)

Continue along the A262 to Biddenden and take the A28 through **Tenterden** with its broad High Street of tiled and weather-boarded houses to the A268 (Hawkshurst road) where you turn right for the short drive to the village of Sandhurst. Here you turn left onto country lanes to **Bodiam Castle** (NT), a small, picturesque, squat fortress with crenelated turrets surrounded by a wide moat and pastoral countryside. Richard II ordered the castle built as a defensive position to secure the upper reaches of the Rother against French raiders who had ravaged nearby towns, but an attack never came. (*Open mid-February–October daily, November–mid-February weekends only.*)

Turn left as you leave the castle, following a country lane to Staple Cross where you turn left on the B2165, which brings you into **Rye**, a fortified seaport that was often attacked by French raiders. However, the sea has long since retreated, leaving the town marooned 2 miles inland. Find the quaintest street in Rye, **Mermaid Street**, with its weatherboard and tile-hung houses and up one cobblestoned block you find yourself on the doorstep of **The Mermaid Inn**. Opened in 1420, The Mermaid Inn is a fascinating relic of the past. As late as Georgian days, smugglers frequented this strikingly timbered inn and used to sit drinking in the pub with their pistols on the table, unchallenged by the law. Near the Norman Church is the 13th-century **Ypres Tower**—formerly a castle and prison, it is now a museum of local history. **Lamb House** (NT) (on West Street near the church) was the home of American novelist Henry James from 1898 to 1916. (*Open April–October, Wednesdays and Saturdays 2–6.*) To learn more about Rye's fascinating history attend the sound and light show at the **Rye Town Model**. (*Open all year.*)

Rye

Leave Rye on the A259, taking this fast road around Hastings and Bexhill to **Eastbourne** where you follow signs for the seafront of this old-fashioned holiday resort and continue on to the B2103, which brings you up and onto the vast chalk promontory, **Beachy Head**, which rises above the town. It is a glorious, windswept place of soaring seagulls and springy turf, which ends abruptly as the earth drops away to giant chalk cliffs plummeting into the foaming sea. This is the starting point for the **South Downs Way**, a popular walking path. Passing the Belle Tout Lighthouse, you come to **Birling Gap**, a beach once popular with smugglers but now favored by bathers. The most dramatic scenery, the **Seven Sisters**, giant, white, windswept cliffs, are an invigorating walk from the tiny village of Friston.

From Friston take the A259 to Westdean where you turn right for **Alfriston**, an adorable village on the South Downs Way which traces its origins back to Saxon times. Behind the main village street in a little cottage garden facing the village green sits the **Clergy House** (NT) with its deep thatched roof, the first building acquired by the National Trust, in 1896.

Either the fast A27 or the slower coastal road (A259) will bring you into **Brighton**, a onetime sleepy fishing village transformed into a fashionable resort at the beginning of the 19th century when the Prince Regent built the fanciful, extravagant **Royal Pavilion** with its onion domes and gaudy paintwork. Follow signs for the town center and park near the pavilion, an extravaganza of a place full of colorful, rather overpowering decor. (*Open all year.*)

Very near the Royal Pavilion are **The Lanes**, narrow streets of former fishermen's cottages now filled with restaurants and antique and gift shops. The seafront is lined by an almost 3-mile-long promenade with the beach below and gardens and tall terraces above. Many of the once-fashionable townhouses are now boarding houses and small hotels but this does not detract from the old-fashioned seaside atmosphere of the town. Stretching out into the sea, the white, wooden **Palace Pier** harks back to an earlier age. At the end is a delightful, old-fashioned funfair with a helter-skelter and carousel horses along with other rides.

Leave Brighton along the seafront in the direction of Hove to join the A27 at Shoreham-by-Sea. This section of the A27 passes through suburb after suburb and is the least interesting part of this itinerary. On the outskirts of **Arundel** the massive keep and towers of **Arundel Castle** rise above the town. Built just after the Norman Conquest to protect this area from sea pirates and raiders, the castle contains a collection of armor, tapestries, and other interesting artifacts. (*Open April–October, closed Saturdays.*)

From Arundel take the A284 inland towards Pulborough and then follow signs through the narrow, winding old streets of **Petworth**, proffering several antique stores, to **Petworth House** (NT), an enormous, 17th-century house in a vast deer park with landscaping by Capability Brown. The house, completed by the 6th Duke of Somerset in 1696, retains the 13th-century chapel of an earlier mansion and houses a proud art collection, which includes a series of landscapes by Turner and also paintings by Holbein, Rembrandt, Van Dyck, Gainsborough, Titian, Rubens, and Reynolds. (*Open April–October, closed Thursdays and Fridays except July–August, closed Thursdays only.*)

Retrace your route the short distance into Petworth and take the A272 through Midhurst to reach the A286 (Chichester road). **Midhurst** has some fine old houses and attractive inns. Knockhundred Row leads from North Street to Red Lion Street and the old timbered market. Curfew is faithfully rung each evening at 8 pm in the parish church. Legend has it that a rider, lost in darkness, followed the sound of the church bells and found his way to the town. To show his gratitude he purchased a piece of land in Midhurst, now called Curfew Garden, which he presented to the town as a gift and made money available for the nightly ringing of the bells.

Across the South Downs the A286 brings you to the **Weald and Downland Museum**, an assortment of old, humble buildings such as farmhouses and barns brought to and restored on this site after their loss to demolition was inevitable. Inside several of the structures are displays showing the development of buildings through the ages. (*Open March–October daily, November–February Wednesday–Sunday.*)

Leaving the museum, take the A286 around Chichester to the A27 Portsmouth road, which leads you onto the M275 to the historic center of **Portsmouth** and your goal, the *H.M.S. Victory* and *Mary Rose*. The ***H.M.S. Victory***, Nelson's flagship at the Battle of Trafalgar in 1805, has been restored to show what life was like on board. Nearby, the ***Mary Rose***, Henry VIII's flagship, is housed in a humidified building that preserves its remains, which were raised from the seabed several years ago. The **Naval Museum** has a display of model ships, figureheads, and a panorama depicting the Battle of Trafalgar. (*Open all year.*)

Retrace your steps up the M275 and onto the M27, which quickly brings you to the A33/M3 and **Winchester** (see listings) where a magnificent **cathedral** stands at the center of the city. Park in one of the car parks on the edge of town and walk into the pedestrian heart of the city, which was the capital of England in King Alfred's reign during the 9th century and stayed so for 200 years. Construction of the 556-foot-long cathedral began in 1079 and finished in 1404. Treasures include a memorial window to Izaak Walton, a black marble font, seven chancery chapels for special masses, medieval wall paintings, stained glass, and tombs of ancient kings including King Canute. Close by is **Winchester College**, founded in 1382, one of the oldest public (i.e., private) schools in England. At the top of the High Street is a fascinating area that has formed an important part of the city's defenses since Roman times. Here you find the 13th-century **Great Hall**, the only surviving part of Winchester Castle and home to the legendary Round Table, which has hung on the wall here for 600 years. (*Open all year.*). Military history buffs will enjoy the five **military museums**, which offer guided tours by arrangement.

Leaving Winchester, the M3 will quickly take you back to London.

Cycling through Suffolk

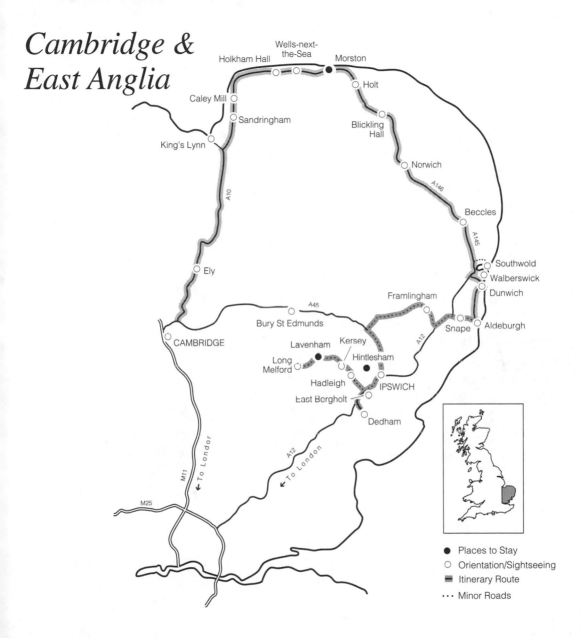

Cambridge & East Anglia

Holkham Hall

Wells-next-the-Sea

Morston

Caley Mill

Holt

Sandringham

Blickling Hall

King's Lynn

A10

Norwich

A146

Beccles

A145

Ely

Southwold

A45

Walberswick

Framlingham

Dunwich

Bury St Edmunds

A12

Snape

Aldeburgh

CAMBRIDGE

Lavenham

Kersey

Long Melford

Hintlesham

Hadleigh

IPSWICH

East Bergholt

Dedham

M11

To London

M25

A12

To London

● Places to Stay
○ Orientation/Sightseeing
▰ Itinerary Route
··· Minor Roads

45

Cambridge & East Anglia

Many visit the famous university town of Cambridge, but few travelers venture beyond to explore the bulge of England's eastern coastline with its sky-wide landscapes, stunning sunsets, lofty windmills, and unspoilt villages. This itinerary takes you from the vast fenlands, drained by the Dutch in the 17th century, along the pancake-flat Norfolk coastline with the sea often just out of sight beyond fields and marshes, into Norwich with its ancient streets and vast cathedral, through sleepy Suffolk villages full of quaint cottages to "Constable Country" where John Constable painted so many of his famous works. Be sure to visit Cambridge, but expand your trip to explore this quiet corner of Britain.

Kersey

Recommended Pacing: Spend one night in Norfolk, two if you have the luxury of time, and two in Suffolk, which gives you ample time to explore its quaint villages.

Leaving London, navigate yourself onto the M11 for the fast, two-hour drive to **Cambridge**, a city with much new building, but at whose heart is a fascinating university complex whose history spans over 700 years. Park your car in one of the well-marked car parks near the town center, buy a guidebook, and set out to explore, for this is a city for strolling and browsing.

At most times visitors can go into college courtyards, chapels, dining halls, and certain gardens. **King's College Chapel** is one of the finest buildings in England, with Rubens's masterpiece, the *Adoration of the Magi*, framing the altar. Be sure not to miss **Clare College**, **Trinity College**, and **St. John's College**, which backs onto the enclosed stone "Bridge of Sighs." Explore the various alleys and streets on foot, row, or punt, drifting under the willow trees that line the River Cam. Boats are for hire at Silver Street Bridge and Quayside.

Leaving Cambridge on the A10 towards **Ely**, you come to open countryside offering sky-wide horizons of flat farmland that are soon punctuated by the soaring mass of **Ely Cathedral**, a building so large that it seems to dwarf the little market town that surrounds it. Until the surrounding fens were drained, Ely was an island, surrounded by water, and the cathedral must have appeared even more magnificent than it does today. This awesome structure was built in 1083, awesome not only for its sheer size but because it is an amazing piece of engineering, its huge tower held up by eight massive oak timbers each more than 60 feet in length.

Leaving Ely, regain the A10 following it around Downham Market to **King's Lynn**, a large, bustling town with a well-marked historic core. A market is held every Saturday and Tuesday and the port has many fine old buildings: the **Guildhall** (1421), the **Customs House** (1683), and **St. Margaret's Church**. The father of George Vancouver, who explored the northwestern coast of North America and after whom the Canadian city and island are named, was a customs officer hereabouts.

Leaving King's Lynn, follow signs for the A149 in the direction of Hunstanton. After several miles turn right for **Sandringham**, one of the Royal Family's homes, and almost immediately first left to take you on a scenic drive through the woodlands that surround it. Edward VII, at that time Prince of Wales, bought this huge Victorian house in 1861 because he did not like Osborne House on the Isle of Wight. From mid-April to the end of September from 11 am (all week except Fridays and Saturdays) the grounds and several rooms in the house are open to the public—provided that the Royal Family is not in residence.

Leave the car park to your left, and passing the main gates (the Norwich gates, a wedding gift to Edward from the city of Norwich), go left through Dersingham to regain the A149. In summer the air is heavy with the scent of lavender and the fields surrounding **Caley Mill** are a brilliant purple for this is one of the country's centers for the cultivation of lavender. There is a gift shop selling every imaginable lavender product.

After bypassing Hunstanton, the A149 becomes narrower, pottering along through attractive villages of pebble-and-red-brick cottages (Thornham, Titchwell, Brancaster, Staithe, and Overy Staithe) as it traces the flat Norfolk coast with the sea often just out of sight beyond fields and marshes. This is not a coastline of dramatic cliffs and headlands—the land merely ends and the sea begins.

On the outskirts of **Holkham** you follow the wall surrounding **Holkham Hall** to its driveway. This magnificent, 18th-century Palladian mansion, the seat of the "modern" Earls of Leicester, contains paintings by Rubens, Van Dyck, Poussin, and Gainsborough; 17th- and 18th-century tapestry and furniture; thousands of items of bygone days, such as steam engines, kitchen equipment, smithy tools, ploughs, and fire engines; and Greek and Roman statuary. (*Open June–September, closed Fridays and Saturdays.*) Detour into **Wells-next-the-Sea**, one of the few villages along this coast to have a waterfront. Leave the coast behind and turn inland following the B1156 into Holt then continuing in the direction of Norwich (B1354) to **Blickling Hall** (NT), a grand, 17th-century red-brick house set in acres of parkland. The house if full of fine pictures, tapestries, and gracious furniture. (*Open April–October, closed Mondays and Tuesdays.*)

Following signs for Norwich, join the A140, which takes you to the heart of this sprawling city. **Norwich** is rich in historic treasures including a beautiful Norman cathedral, topped by a 15th-century spire, with a huge close running down to the River Wensum. The castle, built by one of William the Conqueror's supporters, is now the **Castle Museum**. (*Open all year.*) **Strangers Hall**, a 14th-century home, has its rooms furnished in the styles of different periods and **Elm Hill** is a cobbled street with shops and houses from the 14th to the 18th centuries. **Colman's Mustard Shop** in Bridewell Alley is a major tourist attraction. Norwich has an interesting market (*closed Sundays*) and some very nice shops and restaurants.

From the ring road surrounding Norwich take the A146 in the direction of Lowestoft. Turn on the A145 through Beccles to the A12 where you turn left and first right on the A1095 into **Southwold**, a quiet, sedate Victorian/Edwardian seaside resort, with its most attractive houses lining the seafront and its narrow rows of shops forming the town center. Across the river estuary lies **Walberswick**, a pretty little fishing/holiday village of cottages and a pub, reached by a little ferry that plies back and forth (or the longer road route that traces the estuary).

Regaining the A12, turn left, towards Ipswich, for a short distance to the village of **Blythburgh** and visit its church, so imposing in size that hereabouts it is referred to as **Blythburgh Cathedral**. The size of the church is indicative of the community's importance in years gone by when it was a thriving port, with its own mint, on the estuary of the River Blyth. Its prosperity declined and the church was neglected until it was restored this century. Carvings of the Seven Deadly Sins decorate the pew-ends and the rare, wooden Jack-o'-the-Clock.

A short distance farther along the A12 you come to the left-hand turn for **Dunwich**—cross the heathlands and go through the village to the car park in front of the **Flora Tea Rooms**, which serves excellent fish and chips, beneath the pebbly bank which separates it from the sea. The fish comes fresh from the fishermen who draw their boats up on the beach. Along the headlands lie the few remains of the medieval port of Dunwich, which was almost completely swept out to sea in 1326 by a great storm. What was left has continued to be eroded by the sea. Local legend has it that before a storm the bells of Dunwich's 15 submerged churches can be heard ringing.

A short drive brings you to **Minsmere Nature Reserve**, a celebrated place for birdwatching, and through Westleton to **Aldeburgh**, a charming town whose streets are lined with Georgian houses and whose High Street has antique and other interesting shops. The local council still meets in the half-timbered **Moot Hall** (1512). Benjamin Britten, who directed the Aldeburgh music festival for 30 years until his death in 1976, based his opera *Peter Grimes* on a poem by local poet George Crabbe.

Head inland on the A1094, turning left onto the B1069 into **Snape** to arrive at **Snape Maltings**, a collection of red-brick granaries and old malthouses, which has been converted into a riverside center with interesting garden and craft shops, art galleries, tea rooms, and a concert hall, home of the Aldeburgh music festival every June. From here you can take a boat trip on the River Alde which meanders through the marshes to the sea.

Continue inland and map a quiet country route through sleepy Suffolk villages and rolling farmland to **Framlingham**, a quiet market town where Mary Tudor was proclaimed queen of England in 1553. The town is dominated by 12th-century **Framlingham Castle** with tall, gray-stone walls linking its towers. (*Open all year.*)

Two miles away at **Saxtead Green** a 200-year-old **Post Mill**, one of Suffolk's few remaining windmills, stands guard over the green. (*Open April–September, closed Sundays.*)

From Saxtead Green follow the A1120 towards Ipswich and the A14 as it skirts Ipswich and joins the A12 (in the Colchester direction) at a large roundabout (busy dual carriageways like these keep the small roads quiet and peaceful). Leave the A12 at the third exit, following signs to your left for **Dedham**, a pretty village settled along the banks of the lazy River Stour made famous by John Constable who painted its mill and church spire on several occasions. (Even though it is just a river bend away from East Bergholt, Constable's birthplace, today you have to go between the two villages by way of the busy A12.) Sir Alfred Munnings, the painter of horses, lived in **Castle House**, which is now a museum containing examples of his work.

Retrace your steps to the A12 and return in the direction of Ipswich, following signs for **Flatford** and **East Bergholt** where John Constable was born in 1776, the son of the miller of Flatford Mill. The little hamlet of Flatford, now a National Trust property, is signposted in East Bergholt. A one-way lane directs you to the car park above the hamlet (it is not well signposted and you may have to stop and ask the way). The collection of cottages has been restored to the way it was in Constable's time and a tea room serves scrumptious afternoon teas and sandwiches. If the weather is fine, you can take a picnic, hire a rowing boat, or simply while away an afternoon on the river. The National Trust shop sells a packet that includes a map identifying where Constable painted some of his most famous pictures and postcards of the paintings so you can wander along the riverbank and pinpoint the very spot where he painted his father's mill, Willy Lott's cottage, or the boatbuilders at work. The scene has changed little since those times— apart from the tourists. Constable said of the area, "Those scenes made me a painter." (*Open all year.*)

Leaving the Constable complex, the road returns you to East Bergholt where you turn right to go through the village and take the B1070 to **Hadleigh**, a large market town whose High Street has some lovely old houses. On the edge of the town cross the A1071 and then take the first left and first right to bring you onto the main street of **Kersey**, the most picture-book-perfect of all Suffolk villages. Its narrow main street is lined with ancient weavers' cottages, grand merchants' houses, and old pubs, all jostling one another for roadside space and each colorwashed a different color. In the middle of the village a stream runs across the road and drivers must take care to avoid the local ducks.

Join the A1141 for a short drive through **Monks Eleigh** with its thatched cottages and large craft shop selling traditional corn dollies to **Lavenham** (see listings), which in Tudor times was one of England's wealthiest towns. Now it is a sleepy village where leaning timbered houses line its quiet street and continue into the market square with its 16th-century cross and **Guildhall** (NT), which houses displays of local history and the medieval wool industry. (*Open April–October*.) If you are captivated by the serenity of Lavenham, morning coffee or afternoon tea at the lovely **Swan Hotel** (see listing) serves as a pleasurable excuse to linger.

Country lanes take you the 5 miles to **Long Melford** whose long, broad, tree-lined main street houses many antique shops and leads to the village green, which is overshadowed by the magnificent, 15th-century Holy Trinity Church. A short walk away, the red-brick, turreted **Melford Hall** (NT) contains a wealth of porcelain, paintings, and antiques and a display of Beatrix Potter's paintings—she was a frequent visitor here. (*Open May–September, closed Mondays, April and October weekends only*.)

Leaving Long Melford, you can go south to the A12 or west to the M11, which quickly return you to London.

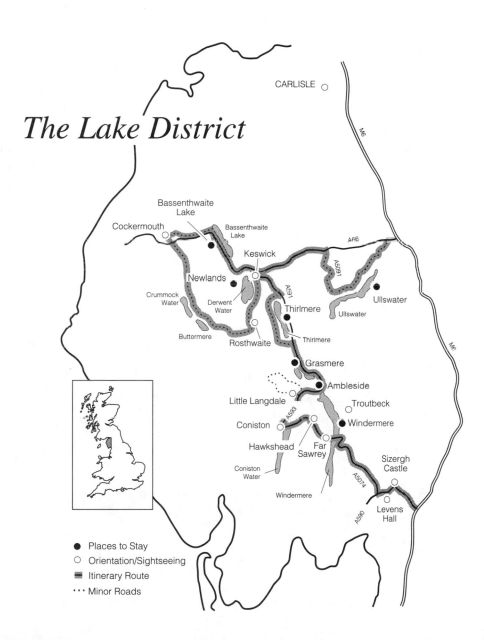

The Lake District

CARLISLE ○

M6

Bassenthwaite
Lake

Cockermouth ○

Bassenthwaite
Lake

Keswick

A66

A5091

Newlands

Crummock
Water

Derwent
Water

Thirlmere

Ullswater

Ullswater

A591

Buttermere

Rosthwaite

Thirlmere

M6

Grasmere

Little Langdale

Ambleside

Troutbeck

Coniston

A593

Hawkshead

Far
Sawrey

Windermere

Sizergh
Castle

Coniston
Water

Windermere

A5074

Levens
Hall

A590

● Places to Stay
○ Orientation/Sightseeing
▨ Itinerary Route
••• Minor Roads

53

The Lake District

For generations the beauty of the Lake District has inspired poets, authors, and artists. It is a land of tranquil lakes of all shapes and sizes, quiet wooded valleys, and awesome bleak mountains, a land where much of the natural beauty is protected by the National Trust who work hard to keep this a working community of sheep farmers and to keep man in harmony with nature. One of the most determined preservers of the Lake District was Beatrix Potter, who used much of her royalties from her famous children's books to purchase vast tracts of land and donate them to the nation. It is a region to be explored not only during the summer when the roads are more heavily traveled and the towns crowded, but also in the early spring when the famous daffodils brighten the landscape and well into the autumn when the leaves turn to gold and dark storm clouds shadow the lakes.

The Lake District

Recommended Pacing: Base yourself at one of the hotels we recommend in the Lake District. If you cover all of our sightseeing recommendations, you will need four nights, though three might just suffice.

From junction 36 on the M6 motorway take the A590 in the direction of Barrow then a few minutes' drive along the A591 brings you into the grounds of **Sizergh Castle** (NT), not a mighty fortress but a lovely, mostly Tudor house, the home of the Strickland family for over 700 years. The house is fully furnished—just as though the family has gone out for the day and you are a visitor to their home. There is an excellent tea shop in the old cellar and a portion of the grounds presents an impressive rock garden. (*Open June–October, closed Fridays and Saturdays.*)

Return to the A590 and in just a minute you are at another fine Tudor manor house, **Levens Hall**. The property is most famous for its topiary gardens, which have remarkably remained unchanged since 1690, when they were landscaped by a Frenchman, Guillaume Beaumont. (*Open April–mid-October.*)

Join the A5074 Windermere road and on the outskirts of the town follow signs to the ferry, which takes you across the broad expanse of **Windermere** (see listings) for the short drive to the tiny villages of **Near Sawrey** and **Far Sawrey**, discovered by Beatrix Potter on childhood holidays. She was so charmed by the villages that out of the royalties from *Peter Rabbit* she bought **Hill Top Farm** (NT) in Near Sawrey. It was here in a vine-covered stone cottage set among trees and a garden of flowers that she dreamed up childhood playmates such as Jemima Puddleduck, Mrs Tiggy Winkle, the Flopsy Bunnies, Cousin Ribby, and Benjamin Bunny. Because of its popularity the house is open on a very limited basis, but the National Trust shop by the roadside is open more often and you can walk through the garden to the front door. (*Open April–October, closed Thursdays and Fridays.*)

In nearby **Hawkshead**, a pretty village with a pedestrian center, there is a delightful **Beatrix Potter Gallery** (NT) containing an exhibition of her original drawings and illustrations of her children's books, together with a display of her life as author, farmer, and preserver of her beloved Lake District. (*Open April–October, closed Fridays and Saturdays.*) A short drive brings you to **Coniston**, a delightful village of gray-stone buildings at the head of **Coniston Water**. John Ruskin, the eloquent 19th-century scholar, lived on the east side of the lake at **Brantwood.** His home contains many mementos and pictures. (*Open mid-March–mid-November, rest of the year Wednesday–Sunday.*) You will find a small **Ruskin Museum** with drawings and manuscripts in the village. (*Open Easter–October.*)

Travel a short distance along the A593 Ambleside road and turn left to wind along a country lane up into a quiet, less touristy part of the Lake District. Stop for refreshment in **Little Langdale** at the **Three Shires**, a delightful walkers' pub that also offers accommodation. Leaving the village, you enter a wild, bleak, and beautiful area. The lane brings you to Blea Tarn and just as you think you are in the absolute midst of nowhere and contemplate turning around, you come to a cattle grid and a fork in the road. Take the right-hand fork signposted Great Langdale and follow the narrow road through wild and lonely countryside, down a steep pass, and through a lush valley into **Great Langdale**, another off-the-beaten-path village popular with walkers. Leaving the village, the road winds you up onto the moor and drops you back onto the A593 where a left-hand turn quickly brings you into Ambleside.

Ambleside (see listing) is a bustling, busy town at the head of Lake Windermere with lots of shops selling walking equipment and outdoor wear, and gray Victorian row houses huddling along its streets. Leave town in the direction of Keswick (A591), watching for a right-hand turn to **Rydal Mount,** the home of William Wordsworth, the poet, from 1813 to his death in 1850. The house is furnished and contains many family portraits and possessions. A keen gardener, Wordsworth laid out the 4½ acres of informal gardens. (*Open March–November, closed Saturdays and Sundays.*)

Wordsworth fans will also want to stop at **Dove Cottage** where Wordsworth lived from 1799 to 1808 and the adjacent **Wordsworth Museum**. (*Open March–December.*) Park by the tea room on the main road and walk up to the museum to buy your ticket. Try to visit early in the day as they restrict a tour to the number of people who can comfortably fit into Wordsworth's tiny living room. The docent who led our tour was a true Wordsworthian, mixing together lots of "juicy" information on Wordsworth, his family, and friends with many insights into his poetry. As you tour the few meager rooms, which housed six adults and three children, it is hard to believe that this was home to one of the leading poets of the era. Poet laureates write poems on royal events, but not Wordsworth: he was the only poet laureate to write not a word on such occasions—but he relished the royal stipend. Just off the busy main road, the adjacent village of **Grasmere** is full of charming shops and galleries.

Dove Cottage, Grasmere

The A591 is a delightful drive into Keswick through in turn wild, rugged, and pastoral scenery. Take small roads to the west of **Thirlmere** (see listing) as the views from the west of the lake are much better than from the A591. The lively market town of **Keswick**, cozily placed at the northern end of **Derwent Water**, is full of bakeries, sweet shops (selling fudge and Kendal mint cake), pubs, restaurants, and outdoor equipment suppliers. There are plenty of car parks near the town center, though on a busy summer afternoon you may have to drive around for a while before you secure a spot. The **Moot** (meeting) **Hall** at the center of the square is now the National Park Information Centre— full of maps, books, and good advice.

Returning to your car, head towards Derwent Water, taking the B5289 to Borrowdale for a spectacular drive between Keswick and Cockermouth, a journey not to be undertaken in bad weather. Follow Derwent Water to **Grange** where inviting woodlands beckon you to tarry awhile and walk, but desist because the most spectacular walking country lies ahead. Passing through the village of Rosthwaite, the narrow road begins to climb, curving you upwards alongside a tumbling stream to the high, treeless fells before suddenly tipping you over the crest of the mountain and snaking you down into the valley to **Buttermere** and **Crummock Water** whose placid surfaces mirror the jagged peaks surrounding this wooded, green valley. The mountains here are over 500 million years old, among the oldest in the world. Walking paths beckon in every direction—though these are not paths to be trod without equipment and maps, for the fickle weather can turn from sun to storm in just a short while. Leaving this lovely spot, the narrow road quickly brings you into the center of bustling **Cockermouth** where Wordsworthians have the opportunity to visit **Wordsworth House**, his birthplace on Main Street. (*Open April–October, closed Saturdays and Sundays except June–August, closed Sundays only.*)

From Cockermouth follow signs for the A66 and Keswick along a country road that parallels the A66 to the head of **Bassenthwaite Lake**. At the junction cross the busy A66 onto a quiet country side road to visit **The Pheasant** (see listing), a superb example of the very best of traditional pubs. From here the A66 quickly speeds you alongside Bassenthwaite Lake, around Keswick, and to the M6 motorway. However, if you have time for one more idyllic lake, take the A5091 through Troutbeck to **Ullswater** (see listing) where you turn left to trace the lake to **Aira Force** (NT), a landscaped Victorian park with dramatic waterfalls, arboretum, and rock gardens (there is also a café). After a walk along the shores of Ullswater Wordsworth wrote his poem *Daffodils*. The dramatic scenery is still very much as it was in his day. Leaving Ullswater, return to the A66 and join the M6 at junction 40, with convenient connections to all parts of Britain.

Derbyshire Dales & Villages

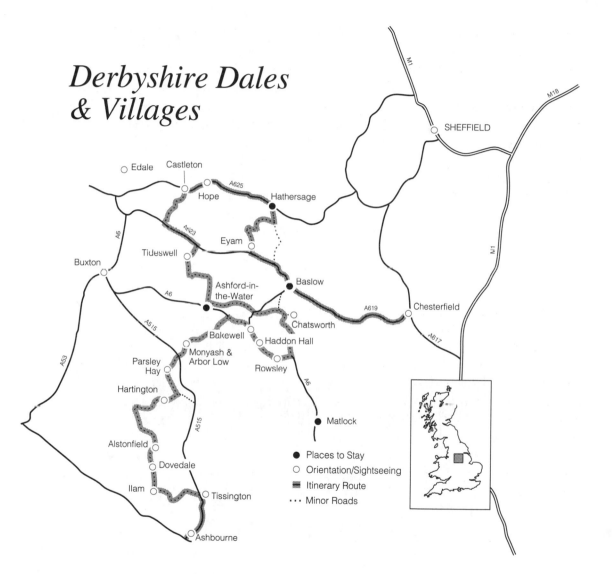

Edale

Castleton

Hope

A625

Hathersage

A623

Eyam

Tideswell

Buxton

A6

Ashford-in-
the-Water

Baslow

Chatsworth

A619

Chesterfield

Bakewell

Haddon Hall

Monyash &
Arbor Low

Parsley
Hay

Rowsley

A515

Hartington

A53

A6

Alstonfield

Matlock

Dovedale

Ilam

Tissington

Ashbourne

A515

A617

SHEFFIELD

M1

M18

M1

● Places to Stay

○ Orientation/Sightseeing

▬ Itinerary Route

⋯ Minor Roads

Derbyshire Dales & Villages

Every structure in this itinerary—manor houses, churches, cottages, farmhouses, shops—even the walls that edge the fields, making a patchwork of the landscape—is built of gray stone. This is the Peak District, a National Park, where you can enjoy the beauty of a wild landscape of rolling rocky pastures, sheltered valleys, and windswept moors laced by swift rivers tumbling through deep dales—Monks Dale, Monsal Dale, Miller Dale, and, the most beautiful of all, Dovedale where the River Dove flows through a rocky, wooded ravine and is crossed by stepping stones. While this is a driving itinerary, to really appreciate the wild beauty of this area you have to forsake your car and proceed on foot—on the many miles of well-marked footpaths—or rent a bike and pedal the cycle routes that travel disused railway lines and quiet country lanes.

Chatsworth House

Recommended Pacing: Select a base for this itinerary. To cover all our sightseeing suggestions will take two full days.

This itinerary begins in **Ashbourne**, a small market town just south of the Peak District National Park where on Thursdays and Saturdays market stalls crowd the town square. Close by, on St. John Street, visit the **Gingerbread Shop**, which sells aromatic Ashbourne gingerbread and baked goods from a restored 15th-century timber-framed shop that gives you a glimpse of how beautiful Ashbourne must have been during its heyday. (*Cycle hire for the Tissington Trail: Ashbourne Cycle Hire, Mapleton Lane, Ashbourne, Derbyshire.*)

Leave Ashbourne on the A515, Buxton road, and watch for a discreetly signposted right-hand turn that brings you through a broad avenue of trees to **Tissington** with its Jacobean manor house, Norman church, limestone cottages, and ducks swimming on the village pond. Tissington is reputedly the birthplace of the Derbyshire village tradition of well dressing, giving thanks for the unfailing supply of fresh water that the village wells provided by creating intricate, large mosaic pictures from flower petals and placing them beside the village wells. These spectacular displays are very interesting to visit, so in the course of this itinerary, the dates that villages dress their wells is mentioned in parentheses, for example, "Tissington (*wells dressed for Ascension day*)." If you carry on through the village and across open farmland, you come to a ford where the road splashes through a brook.

Retrace your steps to the A515 and cross it, heading through **Thorpe** village and down into **Dovedale**. Dr. Johnston gave it a glowing testimonial: "He who has seen Dovedale has no need to visit the Highlands." Cars can go no farther than the car park whence you walk into the dale, crossing the River Dove on stepping stones and entering a rocky ravine. The farther you walk into the dale the more you are tempted to continue as round each river bend beautiful scenery unfolds—fantastic rock formations, steeply wooded hillsides, and the noisy, tumbling water. The length of the dale is a delightful 4-mile walk. Walkers can be dropped at the car park and picked up in Milldale by Viators Bridge.

At a bend in the road sits **Ilam** (pronounced "I lamb"), a picture-postcard estate village, built to house the workers on what was once a shipping magnate's vast holdings. On to **Alstonfield** (pronounced "Alstonfeld") and the **Post Office Tea Shop**, which serves scrumptious scones and cream. (Turn right here if you are picking walkers up in nearby Milldale.)

Well Dressing

Drive into **Hartington** (*wells dressed on second Saturday in September*) with its white limestone cottages, shops, and pubs. Admire the mallards waddling by the village pond and visit the **cheese shop**, an outlet for the last of Derbyshire's cheese factories producing Hartington Stilton and Buxton Blue.

Leave Hartington on the B5054, Ashbourne road, and take the first left, signposted Crowdicote, following the narrow dale. As the dale widens, turn right to **Parsley Hay**. (*Parsley Hay Cycle Hire, Parsley Hay near Buxton, Derbyshire.*) From here you can cycle the **Tissington Trail** towards Ashbourne or the **High Peak Trail** to Cromford. At the main road turn left (towards Buxton) and immediately right towards Monyash then right again following discreet signposts for **Arbor Low**, Derbyshire's answer to Stonehenge. The huge monoliths have all fallen to the ground and you will probably be one of only a few visitors. The stones are set atop a bare hill, swept by cold winds, and reached by tramping across fields from a lonely farm. Pause and wonder why man built here 4,000 years ago. (*Open all year.*)

Retrace your path to the Monyash road, turning right in the village onto the B5055 which leads you into **Bakewell** (*wells dressed on last Saturday in June*), a lovely market town ringed by wooded hills where a picturesque, 700-year-old arched and buttressed bridge spans the swiftly flowing River Wye. The Tourist Information Centre in the splendid, 17th-century **market hall** has displays on the Peak District and information pamphlets. Behind it are set the market stalls where every Monday a farmers' market is held— offering everything from lengths of dress fabric to underwear and pigs. You can buy the original Bakewell tarts (known as puddings in Bakewell) from **Ye Olde Original Pudding Shop** and the splendid **Bakewell Pudding Factory** on Granby Arcade. The town has some excellent shops (china, antiques, clothing, and hardware). Up the hill, just behind the church, is The **Old House Museum**, a folk museum displaying kitchen and farm equipment. (*Open April–October.*)

Three miles along the A6 in the direction of Matlock lies **Haddon Hall**, a 14th-century manor, home of the Duke of Rutland. In my opinion, this house is more interesting to tour than the opulent Chatsworth House (your next stop) because it lacks the vastness and grandeur of Chatsworth and you can really imagine people living in these aged rooms hung with threadbare tapestries and decorated with magnificent woodcarvings. Parts of the chapel walls are covered with barely discernible frescos that date back to the 11th century. In summer the gardens are a fragrant haven, with a profusion of climbing roses and clematis decorating the house and the stone walls of the terraces. (*Open April–September.*)

Continue along the A6 to **Rowsley** where you can tour **Caudwell's Mill**, a water-powered flour mill, and visit the craft shops. Leaving Rowsley, take the first left (B6012). Pass the edge of Beeley, cross the River Derwent on a narrow humpbacked bridge, and enter the vast Chatsworth estate. Immediately on your left is the **Chatsworth Garden Centre,** which, in addition to an expansive array of all things garden, has a gift and coffee shop. The road leads you through rolling green parkland to **Chatsworth House**, the enormous home (the roof alone covers 1.3 acres) of the Duke and Duchess of Devonshire. While the Duke and Duchess occupy a portion of the house, you can walk through the opulent halls admiring priceless paintings, furnishings, silver plate, and china. Best of all, though, are the acres and acres of landscaped gardens with the great fountain playing and the lawns above the house, laid down in 1760 and groomed ever since (except in wartime). The tea shop is a must. If you are traveling with children, they will enjoy a visit to the farm and the adventure playground. (*Open mid-March–October.*)

The picturesque village of **Edensor** (pronounced "Ensor"), mentioned in the Doomsday Book of 1086, was much rebuilt and moved here in the 19th century by a duke who did not want to see it from his park. Kathleen Kennedy, JFK's sister, lies buried near the handsome old church.

Leave the estate in the direction of Baslow and take the first left, B6048, to **Pilsley** where the farm shop sells an interesting variety of nifty gifts and produce from the Chatsworth estate. As the B6048 merges with the main road take the first right on the A6020 (Ashford) following it to **Ashford-in-the-Water** (see listing) and cross the river into this picturesque village strung along the River Wye. "Sheepwash" is the oldest and quaintest of the village's bridges. Built for packhorses and now closed to traffic, it gets its name from the adjacent stone enclosure in which sheep used to be washed.

Follow the narrow lanes upwards to **Monsal Head** where the ground seemingly falls away and opens up to a magnificent vista of the River Wye running through **Monsal**

Dale. Go straight across, beside the Monsal Head car park, and follow the road as it winds down into and along the dale to **Cressbrook Mill**, where the road climbs steeply past the terraces of mill cottages clinging precariously to the hillsides. The first terrace is where pauper apprentices lived and higher up are the more opulent foremen's houses. Emerging from the dale, the narrow road skirts stone-walled fields to **Litton** (*wells dressed in June*), a delightful stone village round a green where you turn left for Tideswell.

The magnificent, spacious, 14th-century church at **Tideswell** (*wells dressed on Saturday nearest John the Baptist day, June 24th*) is so impressive that it is often described as "the cathedral of the Peak." It was built between 1300 and 1370 when Tideswell was an affluent place and it is fortunate that Tideswell fell upon hard times so that parishioners could not afford to update their church as ecclesiastical fashions changed.

Leaving Tideswell, you come to the A623 and turn left in the direction of Chapel-en-le-Frith to Sparrowpit where you turn right at the Wanted Inn. Passing an enormous quarry, you see that half the mountain is missing—gone to build all the lovely stone houses and cottages. When you come to a brown-and-white country sign stating "Castleton Caverns, Peveril Castle, light traffic only," turn right into Winnats Pass, which drops you down a steep ravine between high limestone cliffs.

As the ravine opens up to the valley, **Speedwell Cavern** presents itself. This is one of several famous caverns (mixtures of natural cavities and lead-mine workings resplendent with stalagmites and stalactites) found around Castleton. Speedwell is reached by a 105-step descent to a motorboat that takes you along an underground canal to a cavern which was the working face of the former Speedwell Mine. Blue John (a corruption of the French *bleue-jaune,* blue-yellow), a translucent blue variety of fluorspar found only in this area, was mined here. (*Open all year.*)

Before you head off to explore other nearby caves (Blue John, Treak Cliff, and Peak), head into **Castleton**, a village huddled far below the brooding ruins of Norman **Peveril Castle** where Henry II accepted the submission of Malcolm of Scotland in 1157. (*Open March–November daily, Wednesday–Sunday the rest of year.*)

Castleton

Below the castle is the huge mouth of **Peak Cavern**, an enormous cave that once sheltered ropemakers' cottages. The soot from the chimneys of this subterranean village can be seen on the cave's roof. Regrettably, the entrance to the cave has been marred by the erection of a high wooden barrier giving access to the cave only to those willing to pay an entrance fee. In the village's streets you will find cafés, pubs, and several shops selling the polished Blue John set into bracelets, rings, and the like.

This is walking country and you might consider walking up **Mam Tor** (the big bulky mountain beside Winnats Pass) known hereabouts as "Shivering Mountain" because its layers of soft shale set between harder beds of rock are constantly crumbling. Those in search of a longer walk may wish to go to nearby **Edale** where the **Pennine Way** starts its 250-mile path north.

Leave Castleton on the A625 traveling along the broad Hope valley through **Hope** (*wells dressed last Saturday in June*) and Bamford to **Hathersage** (see listing), a thriving, non-traditional Derbyshire village strung out along the main road. Its tourist attractions center on its 14th-century church, St. Michael and All Angels, built by a knight named Robert Eyre. Memorial brasses to the Eyre family are in the church and Charlotte Brontë used the village as "Morton" in *Jane Eyre*. In the graveyard is the reputed grave of Little John, the friend and lieutenant of Robin Hood.

Leaving the churchyard, backtrack on the A625 for a short distance, taking the first left (B6001), signposted Bakewell, beyond the village where you turn right, opposite The Plough, up a narrow country lane signposted "Gliding Club." This country lane takes you through the hamlet of **Abney** past the gliding club and the historic **Barrel Inn** (offering views of the valley, good pub food, and refreshing ale) and brings you into **Eyam** (pronounced "Eem") (*wells dressed last Saturday in August*).

This large mining and quarrying village was made famous by its self-imposed quarantine when plague hit the village in 1665. It was thought that the virus arrived in a box of cloth from London brought by a visiting tailor. The rector persuaded the community to quarantine themselves to prevent the plague spreading to outlying villages and for over a year the village was supplied by neighboring villagers who left food and supplies at outlying points. Tragically 259 people from 76 families perished—little plaques on Eyam's cottages give the names of the victims who lived there. The church has a plague register and just inside the door is the letter written by the young rector when his wife succumbed (Katherine Mompesson is buried near the Saxon cross in the churchyard). The most poignant reminder of these grim days lies in a field about ½ mile from the village where within a solitary little enclosure, known as the **Riley Graves**, are the memorials to a father and his six children, all of whom died within eight days of each other.

Leave Eyam in the direction of Bakewell, traveling down a steeply wooded gorge that brings you to the A623. Following signs for Chesterfield, you drive down narrow **Middleton Dale**, whose limestone cliffs are so sheer they almost block the sunlight from the road, to **Stoney Middleton**, an appropriately named village huddling beneath the cliffs. It does not look at all inviting from the main road but its quiet side streets and pretty church are full of character.

Driving a few miles farther along the A623 brings you to the winding lanes of **Baslow** (see listings) where the River Derwent flows past tidy houses on the northern edge of the Chatsworth estate. From here fast roads will bring you to **Chesterfield** (visit the leaning spire and if it is a Monday, Friday, or Saturday, you will enjoy the interesting open-air market) where you can join the M1 at junction 29.

The Dales & Moors of North Yorkshire

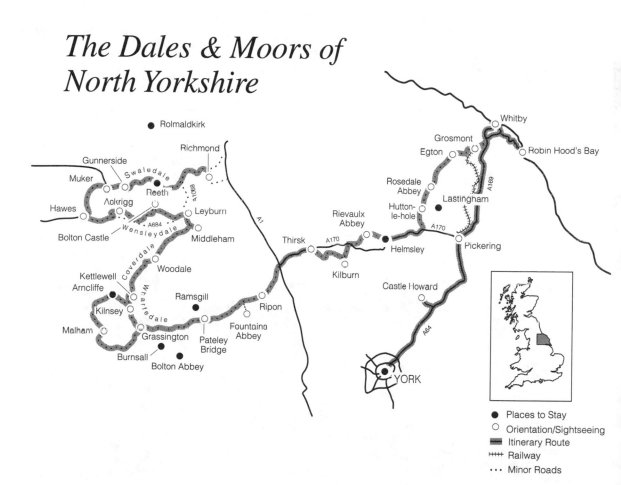

Rolmaldkirk

Richmond

Gunnerside

Muker

Swaledale

Reeth

Aokrigg

Hawes

Leyburn

Bolton Castle

Wensleydale

Middleham

Coverdale

Woodale

Wharfedale

Kettlewell
Arncliffe

Ramsgill

Kilnsey

Malham

Grassington

Pateley
Bridge

Ripon

Fountains
Abbey

Burnsall

Bolton Abbey

A1

Thirsk

Rievaulx
Abbey

Kilburn

Whitby

Grosmont

Egton

Robin Hood's Bay

Rosedale
Abbey

Hutton-
le-hole

Lastingham

Helmsley

Pickering

A170

A169

A170

Castle Howard

A64

YORK

● Places to Stay
○ Orientation/Sightseeing
▬ Itinerary Route
┼┼┼┼ Railway
••• Minor Roads

The Dales & Moors of North Yorkshire

After exploring historic York, this itinerary samples the wild and beautiful countryside of two National Parks: the North York Moors and the Yorkshire Dales. This is an area of rugged, untamed, harsh beauty in its landscape and its stout stone villages. With seemingly endless miles of heather-covered moorlands, few roads, and even fewer sturdy villages sheltering in green valleys, the North York Moors appear vast and untamed, dipping to the sea to embrace the villages and towns of the east coast. Across the flat expanse of the Vale of York lie the Yorkshire Dales, characterized by sleepy rivers weaving through peaceful valleys and by gray-stone walls bounding the fields and tracing patterns on the countryside to the moorlands above. Here every valley has a name and a very different character—Swaledale, Littondale, Coverdale, and Wharfedale. Scattered throughout Yorkshire are small gray-stoned villages with a cluster of stone houses, a hump-backed bridge, a friendly pub, and an ancient church.

Recommended Pacing: Spend two nights in York to appreciate the flavor of this historic city. Follow this with a minimum of one night on or near the North York Moors (Helmsley or Lastingham) and two nights in the Yorkshire Dales.

If you delight in historic towns, you will love **York** (see listings), a compact city brimful of history, encircled by 700-year-old walls with great imposing gates known as "bars." There has been a settlement here since Roman times and by the time of the Norman Conquest it was, after London, the principal city of England.

Your first stop in York should be the Tourist Information Centre on St. Leonards, near Bootham Bar. Avail yourself of a detailed city map and ask about walking tours that will, in the space of several hours, orient you to this historic city.

Walk the narrow, cobblestoned streets with such appealing names as The Shambles, Stonegate, and Goodramgate past timbered buildings whose upper stories lean out, almost forming a bridge over the streets. While interesting shops abound, the **National Trust Shop** on Goodramgate and **Betty's Bakery and Tearooms** on St. Helen's Square are ones to target.

York's magnificent cathedral is known simply as **The Minster**, a huge structure that towers above the skyline and dwarfs everything else around it. It was begun in 1220 and you can quickly appreciate why it took over 250 years to complete. Entering through the Great West Door, you see the vast nave stretching out in front of you and fluted pillars rising to flying buttresses reaching high above. There are more than 100 stained-glass windows and the huge east window is almost the size of a tennis court. Guided tours leave at regular intervals. Nearby the **Treasurer's House** (NT), a 17th/18th-century townhouse on the site of the former residence of the Treasurers of York Minster, has a fine collection of furniture and an exhibition showing the development of the house from Roman times. (*Open April–October, closed Fridays.*)

The **Jorvik Viking Centre**, Coppergate, is set below ground amidst the most complete Viking dig in England. Electric cars take you on a Disneyland ride backwards through history to a re-created Viking village—complete with sounds and smells of Viking

Jorvik. Then they move you forward to the dig itself and a display of the artifacts that have been recovered. Because there is often a long line, it is best to be there first thing in the morning for opening at 9 am. (*Open April–October.*)

Enjoy another trip back in time at York's outstanding **Castle Museum**. One section of the museum is a reconstructed Victorian cobbled street, with houses, shops, jail, and a hansom cab in recognition of inventor Joseph Hansom who was born in Mickelgate. (*Open all year.*) Opposite the museum you can climb to the ramparts of **Clifford's Tower**, a stubby, 13th-century keep set high on a mound. From its ramparts you have a panoramic view of York.

Located beyond York's walls, just a short walk from the magnificent Victorian railway station, is the **National Railway Museum**, Leeman Road, crammed with famous steam locomotives including the world's fastest (202 mph), *Mallard*, and a wealth of railway items. (*Open all year.*)

Depart York on the A64 Scarborough road for the fast drive to **Castle Howard**, which is well signposted to your left just 4 miles from Malton. Designed by Sir John Vanbrugh for the 3rd Earl of Carlisle, a member of the Howard family, Castle Howard was built between 1699 and 1726—one glimpse of this majestic building and you understand why it took 27 years to complete. Its immense façade reflects in a broad lake and it is surrounded by a vast parkland and approached down a long, tree-lined avenue. It isn't really a castle at all but one of England's grandest homes, as impressive inside as out, full of fine furniture and paintings. This grand setting is better known to many visitors as "Brideshead" from the television dramatization of Evelyn Waugh's *Brideshead Revisited*. It is still owned by the Howard family. (*Open mid-March–October.*)

From nearby Malton take the A169 through Pickering and across the vast expanse of the North York moors to **Robin Hood's Bay**, the most picturesque of villages situated beneath a cliff top, a maze of huddled houses clinging to the precipitous cliff. Park in the large car park above the village and follow the long, steep street down to the shoreline, peeping into little alleyways and following narrow byways until you emerge at the slipway. Pieces of Robin Hood's Bay have been washed away, and in an attempt to minimize further damage to this little fishing village, much of the cliff has been reinforced by a large sea wall.

The ruins of **Whitby Abbey** face the cold North Sea and the old seaside town of **Whitby**, built on either side of the River Esk. It's a lovely sight: majestic ruins high on a bleak, windy headland; rows of cottages climbing up the hillsides; and, gazing over the scene, a statue of the town's most famous mariner, Captain Cook. Cook circled the world twice, explored the coasts of Australia and New Zealand, and charted Newfoundland and the North American Pacific coast before being killed by natives in Hawaii. His home on Grape Lane is a small museum. Near Cook's statue is a whalebone arch commemorating this photogenic old town's importance as a whaling port. The whaling ships are a thing of the distant past: now just a few fishing boats bob in this large, sheltered harbor. Explore the area of the town that lies below the abbey, for this is the quaintest, most historic portion of Whitby. During the summer the town is filled with holidaymakers.

Leave Whitby on the A169, Pickering road, and follow signs to the right for the **North York Railway**, a road that winds you to **Grosmont**, the terminus of a glorious, 18-mile steam railway that runs to and from Pickering. The railway opened in 1863 with horse-drawn carriages—steam engines came 11 years later. The line was closed by British Rail in 1965 and reopened by train enthusiasts. The railway shed is full of steam locomotives of all colors and you can see engines being prepared for their daily shift and watch restoration from the viewing gallery.

From nearby Egton a narrow road leads you up from a lush valley and onto acres of gently rolling moorland, with a mass of purple heather stretching into the distance, a dramatically empty, isolated spot. It then drops you into another green valley where stone walls separate a patchwork of fields around the tiny village of Rosedale Abbey. Go straight across the crossroads, up the steep bank, and across another stretch of vast moorland, keep to your right at the fork in the road, and you arrive in the most picturesque village on the North York Moors, **Hutton-le-Hole**. A tumbling stream cuts through the village and children play on close-cropped grassy banks between the sturdy stone houses. At the heart of the village lies **Ryedale Folk Museum** where paths lead from a museum of domestic bygones through a collection of ancient Yorkshire buildings (from simple cottages to an elaborate cruck-framed house) rescued from demise and restored on this site. (*Open March–October.*)

Farther on from Hutton-le-Hole you join the A170, which brings you to **Helmsley**, a pretty market town beneath the southern rim of the moors. Around the market square (*market day Friday*) are interesting shops and the lovely **Black Swan** hotel (see listing). At the edge of town sits a ruined castle enclosed by Norman earthworks.

About 4 miles beyond Helmsley (take the B1257 towards Stokesley) lie the ruins of **Rievaulx Abbey** (pronounced "Ree-voh"), the delicate and beautiful remnants of York's

first Cistercian abbey, standing quietly beside a picturesque group of thatched cottages. The abbey fell into debt and declined until Henry VIII ordered its dissolution. Today it is a graceful, ghostly ruin, often shrouded in mist. Follow the narrow lane beside the cottages, turn right over the little humpbacked bridge, proceed through Scrawton, and turn right on the A170 (Thirsk road) for a short distance to a left-hand turn that zigzags you down **Sutton Bank**. On a clear day park in the car park at the top and enjoy the sky-wide view of the Vale of York before descending down the Hambleton Hills escarpment.

A delightful side trip can by taken by turning left at the bottom of the escarpment and following the narrow lane that brings you to **Kilburn**, a village known for its fine oak furniture. Quality oaken furniture found all over the world can easily be traced back here to the workshop of Robert Thompson. He died in 1955, but craftsmen he trained still use his carved signature, a small church mouse, signifying "poor as a church mouse" to identify their work. It is fun to tour the workshops and watch skilled craftsmen quietly hand-carving beautiful oaken objects with a wavy, adzed surface.

Returning to the main road, you soon come to **Thirsk**, its very pleasant cobbled market square overlooked by shops (*market day Monday*). Here you can visit the **Herriot Centre**, onetime veterinary surgery of James Herriot, quiet local vet turned author. (*Open all year.*)

From Thirsk the A61 traverses rich farmland, crosses the A1 and meanders you through **Ripon** to the market square (*market day Thursday*) where you follow well-marked signs for Fountains Abbey.

Cistercian monks arrived in sheltered **Fountains Abbey** (NT) in 1132, at about the same time they came to Rievaulx, but, unlike Rievaulx, this abbey prospered, so that by the end of the 13th century it had acquired vast estates and the abbey was home to over 500 monks. However, its prosperity did not save it from the axe of Henry VIII who sold the monastery, leaving the abbey to fall into majestic ruin. Considering that for hundreds of years it was used as a quarry for precut stone, the complex is remarkably intact. Wander over the closely cropped grass to the soaring walls of the church. Examine the few remaining floor tiles, gaze at the flying buttresses soaring high above, wander through the cloisters, and wonder at the glory that was Fountains Abbey so many years ago. (*Open all year, closed Fridays November–January.*) Walking paths abound: a particularly pretty path leads you across grassy meadows to the adjacent National Trust property of **Studley Royal**, an 18th-century deer park and water garden. (*Open all year.*)

Turn west (B6265) through Pateley Bridge and climb higher and higher onto bleak moorlands through Greenhow and down the fellside through fields trimmed with white stone walls to Hebden and into **Grassington**, a neat village of narrow streets and cobbled squares full of shops and cafés. It's this itinerary's introduction to the Dales National Park and very crowded in summer, so you may want to park at the National Park Information Centre (useful for maps and information) and walk into town.

To experience some magnificent scenery take a breathtaking circular drive from Grassington and back again through Littondale, over the fells to Malham Cove, and back to the B6160 on the outskirts of town. Leave Grassington on the B6265, cross the River Wharfe, and turn right onto the B6160, which leads you up **Wharfedale** towards Kettlewell. Just after passing the huge crags that hang above Kilnsey, turn left up a narrow lane for Arncliffe. The road meanders deep into **Littondale**, a narrow, steep-sided, very pretty dale. At the cluster of cottages that make up Arncliffe turn left for Malham and follow the narrow road as it zigzags you up the side of the dale. As the road reaches the top, there is a spectacular view back into Littondale. The high, bleak moorland suddenly ends and to your left lie immense curving cliffs that drop 240 feet into a green valley. This is **Malham Cove**, one of Yorkshire's most celebrated natural features. Huddled in the valley below lies the village of **Malham**. Country lanes direct you through Kirby Malham, Airton, Winterburn, Hetton, and Threshfield to rejoin the B6160, which takes you back into Wharfedale.

Retrace your steps and head north to **Kettlewell**, a pretty village at the foot of Great Whernside. In the 8th century this was an Anglican settlement, then after the Norman Conquest formed part of the estates of the powerful Percy family. A small road leads you to the right over Great Whernside and into quiet **Coverdale** through **Woodale**,

Horsehouse, and **Carlton**, little villages that shelter in this pretty valley with the moors looming above. Horses are a feature of **Middleham** for there are many famous racing stables in this attractive town of gray-stone houses beneath the ruins of Middleham Castle.

Cross the River Ure and follow the A6108 into Leyburn then turn left on the A648 and right on country lanes through Redmire to the crumbling ruins of **Bolton Castle**, which stands grim and square, dwarfing the adjacent village, overlooking distant Wensleydale. You can tour several restored rooms. The castle's most famous visitor was Mary, Queen of Scots, who was held prisoner here for six months in 1568.

Minor roads take you up Wharfedale through Carperby (detour into **Aysgarth** if you would like to walk to **Aysgarth Falls**, a series of spectacular waterfalls where the River Ure cascades down a rocky gorge) and Woodhall to the picturesque Dales village of Askrigg. Cross the river to Bainbridge and take the A648 into **Hawes**, a bustling village whose narrow streets abound with interesting shops, good pubs, and cafés. You can visit the **Wensleydale Creamery** to watch cheese being produced. After exploring, leave town in the direction of Muker. As the road climbs from the valley go right, following signs for Muker via **Buttertubs**. This is one of the highest mountain passes in England (1,682 feet), rising steeply from Wensleydale, crossing dramatic high moorlands, and depositing you in narrower, wilder **Swaledale**. The road gets its name "Buttertubs" from the deep, menacing, limestone pits some distance from the road near the summit.

At the T-junction follow the road to the right and cross the little bridge into **Muker**, the most charming of Swaledale's little villages—just the place to stop for a refreshing cuppa.

As you travel down Swaledale, there's a feeling of remoteness: sturdy, gray-stone barns dot the stone-walled fields that checker the valley floor and rise to the green fells. **Gunnerside**, Norse for "Gunner's pasture," where a Viking chieftain herded his cattle long ago, is now an appealing village.

Through Low Row, Feetham, and Healaugh the enchantment of being in a narrow, secluded valley continues till at **Reeth** the landscape opens up and the feeling of being in a wild and lonely place is gone. On the village green you will find **The Burgoyne Hotel** (see listing), a delightful place to stay. You continue on to Richmond through pretty countryside.

Richmond sits at the foot of Swaledale, a network of cobbled alleys and streets stretching from its cobbled square. At its center sits an ancient church with shops set into its walls. Overhanging the River Swale, **Richmond Castle** was built by Norman lords within 20 years of the Norman Conquest. Over the years only a few Scottish raiders tested the defenses of this guardian of North Yorkshire. Sweeping views across dales down to the Vale of York can be enjoyed from the top of its 11th-century ruins.

The nearby A1 will quickly guide you north into Scotland or return you south towards York.

Scotland

Inverewe
Gardens
Achiltibuie
Ullapool
A835
Poolewe
Loch Torridon
A852
Colbost
A855
Muir of Ord
Shieldaig
Nairn
Culloden
Portree
Glen Cannich
Bunchrew
Auldearn
Dunvegan
Cawdor
Castle
Dufftown
Inverness
Tallisker
Kyle of
Lochalsh
A850
Kildrummy
Castle
Castle
Fraser
A87
A82
Grantown-
on-Spey
A4
Sleat
A851
Loch Ness
Craigievar
Castle
A941
A37
ABERDEEN
Mallaig
Fort Augustus
A93
Ballater
Banchory
Genfinnan
Braemar
A830
A82
Spean Bridge
Balmoral
Castle
A9
Strontian
Fort William
Rannoch
Kirkmichael
Isle of
Eriska
Glencoe
A32
Killin
Pitlochry
A924
Port Appin
A9
Dunkeld
A984
Blairgowrie
Oban
A85
Kinclaven
Strachur
Auchterarder
Perth
A93
Ardrishaig
Kinbuck
Callander
A84
Stirling
M90
GLASGOW
M74
EDINBURGH

Places to Stay
Orientation/Sightseeing
Itinerary Route
Minor Roads

79

Scotland

This itinerary begins in Scotland's capital, Edinburgh, journeys to Inverness via Pitlochry, samples magnificent castles and portions of "The Whisky Trail," traces the shore of Scotland's most famous lake, Loch Ness, wends through the glens, and travels over the sea to Skye. It then takes you up into the beauties of Wester Ross where the gardens at Inverewe blossom in a harsh landscape, on to Fort William, Callander, and Glasgow with its magnificent Burrell Collection. At every turn there are echoes of history and romance—Nessie the legendary monster of Loch Ness, homes that sheltered Bonnie Prince Charlie and Flora Macdonald, and the lands where Rob Roy Macgregor roamed. The roads are few and often narrow and the long distances between villages and small towns add to the feeling of isolation. The fickle Scottish weather offers no guarantee that the dramatic scenery will be revealed, but what you can be assured of is a warm, friendly welcome from the hospitable Scots.

Eilean Donan Castle, Scotland

Recommended Pacing: Spend a full day (two if possible) sightseeing in Edinburgh. With an early-morning start you will find yourself at Kildrummy Castle by nightfall (skip Perth sightseeing). If you prefer a more leisurely pace, also include an overnight in Pitlochry. Stay overnight around Inverness because it's an all-day drive from Inverness to the Isle of Skye, then spend two nights on Skye—more if you prefer a more leisurely pace. If you are venturing up Wester Ross, plan on spending two nights there. A day-long drive from Skye will find you in Edinburgh by nightfall. If you are not a cities person, skip Glasgow and stay instead in or around Callander.

Edinburgh (see listings) is Scotland's beautiful capital, dominated by Edinburgh Castle sitting high above the city. Before the castle lies the long green band of gardens that separates Edinburgh's Old Town, with its narrow streets crowded with ancient buildings, and New Town where Edinburgh's shopping street, Princes Street, is backed by wide roads of elegant Georgian houses. The city's principal sights are easily explored on foot, but as an introduction to Edinburgh take one of the double-decker sightseeing buses from Waverley Bridge opposite the Tourist Information Office and railway station. The tours run every ten minutes and wind a circular route through the city with a commentary on the significance of the buildings along the route. Your ticket is valid for the whole day and the bus makes several stops so that you can take the entire tour for an overview of what there is to see and then later use it as transportation between the sights, hopping on and off to visit the places that interest you. Several guided walking tours are offered, some exploring the city's ancient underground chambers—purported to be haunted!

The most popular time to visit Scotland's capital is during the **Edinburgh Festival**. The city glows for the last three weeks of August: pipers dance down the streets and kilts are worn almost as a uniform. The hum of bagpipes sets the stage, and parades, flags, presentations, floodlights, and color appear everywhere. The Military Tattoo provides tradition, The Fringe offers everything from the avant-garde to the eccentric along with jugglers, mimes, and buskers, making this the most comprehensive international arts festival in the world.

Edinburgh Castle from the Princes Street Gardens

Some of Edinburgh's major sights are:

Princes Street, the elegant main thoroughfare, its north side lined by shops and its south side bordered by gardens.

Majestically perched on the edge of the city atop an extinct volcanic outcrop, **Edinburgh Castle** looms against the skyline. There has been a castle here throughout the city's history, with today's comprising a collection of buildings from the little 11th-century St. Margaret's chapel, through medieval apartments to more modern army barracks and the Scottish United Services Museum. A dramatically staged exhibition tells the tale of the Scottish Crown Jewels, the "Honours of Scotland," which dazzle the visitor from their glass case. From the castle ramparts the view over Edinburgh is spectacular. (*Open all year.*)

From the castle gates you enter a famous sequence of ancient streets, referred to as The Royal Mile, where you find **Gladstone's Land** (NT), a building which typifies the more pleasant side of what life must have been like in the crowded tenements of Old Town

Edinburgh. The house is arranged as a 17th-century merchant's house with the ground floor set up as a cloth merchant's booth and the upstairs as a home. (*Open April–October.*)

On the High Street is the great **St. Giles' Cathedral**, founded in the 1100s, whose role has been so important in the history of the Presbyterian Church. John Knox preached from its pulpit from 1561 until his death in 1572, hurling attacks at the "idolatry" of the Catholic Church.

John Knox's home is just a little farther down the High Street. (*Open all year.*)

At the end of The Royal Mile lies **The Palace of Holyroodhouse**, the historic home of the Stuarts, to which Mary, Queen of Scots came from France at the age of 18. The six years of her reign and stay at Holyrood made a tragic impact on her life. Shortly after marriage to a meek Lord Darnley, the happiness of the couple dissolved and their quarrels became bitter. Lord Darnley was jealous of Mary's secretary and constant companion, David Rizzio, and conspired to have him stabbed at Holyrood in the presence of the queen. Just a year later, Lord Darnley himself was mysteriously murdered and gossip blamed the Earl of Bothwell. Mary, however, married the Earl promptly after Lord Darnley's death and rumors still question the queen's personal involvement in the murder. Conspiracies continued and Scotland's young queen fled to the safety of the English court. However, considering her a threat to the English Crown, Queen Elizabeth I welcomed her with imprisonment and had her beheaded 19 years later. Bonnie Prince Charlie was the last Stuart king to hold court at Holyrood in 1745. Today Holyrood, whose apartments are lavishly furnished with French and Flemish tapestries and fine works of art from the Royal Collection, is used by the British monarch as an official residence in Scotland. (*Closed when Royal Family in residence. Guided tours only.*)

Not far from the palace, on Holyrood Road, **Our Dynamic Earth** takes you on a fantastic journey of discovery from the very beginning of time to the unknown future of Planet Earth. The special effects and dioramas are nothing short of amazing. (*Open all year, closed Mondays and Tuesdays November–Easter.*)

The **Museum of Scotland** on Chambers Street chronicles the variety and richness of Scotland's long and exciting history, bringing it all to life with the fascinating stories each object and every gallery has to tell. An added bonus is the spectacular view from its rooftop garden. (*Open all year.*)

The Georgian House (NT), at 7 Charlotte Square, is typical of the elegant Georgian homes found in New Town. From the kitchen through the drawing room to the bedrooms, the house is furnished and decorated much as it would have been when it was first occupied in 1796 and gives you an insight into the way the family and servants of the house lived. (*Open April–October.*)

Just outside the city, at the historic port of Leith, you can visit the royal yacht *Britannia*, which traveled to every corner of the globe as a floating residence for the royal family. A visitors' center and audio-visual presentation introduce you to the yacht's history then you can take a self-guided tour to every part of the ship. If you are driving, follow signs to Leith (North Edinburgh) and *Britannia*. There is a direct bus service from Waverley Bridge, next to the railway station. (*Open all year.*)

Leaving Edinburgh, follow signs for the **Firth of Forth Bridge** and Perth. After crossing the Firth of Forth, the M90 takes you through hilly farmland to the outskirts of Perth where you take the A93 following signs for Scone Palace.

Before reaching the palace you can detour off the main road to visit the city of **Perth**, known as the "Fair City," which straddles the banks of the Tay. A lovely city, it was the capital of Scotland until 1437 and the murder of James I. Following his death, his widow and young son, James II, moved the court to Edinburgh. One of Perth's most important historic buildings is **St. John's Kirk**, a fine medieval church that has been attended by many members of English and Scottish royalty. Also of interest are the **Perth Museum and Art Gallery** (*open all year*) and the **Museum of the Black Watch**, which is housed in **Ballhousie Castle**. (*Open Easter–October, closed Sundays.*)

Scone Palace is a 19th-century mansion that stands on the site of the Abbey of Scone, the coronation palace of all Scottish kings up to James I. By tradition, the kings were crowned on a stone that was taken from the abbey in 1297 and placed under the Coronation Chair in Westminster Abbey. This token of conquest did nothing to improve relations between Scotland and England. The present mansion is the home of the Earl of Mansfield and houses a collection of china and ivory statuettes. (*Open April–October.*)

Continuing along the A93, shortly after leaving the abbey you pass through **Old Scone**. This was once a thriving village but was removed in 1805 by the Earl of Mansfield to improve the landscape and only the village cross and graveyard remain to mark the site.

Continue through Guildtown to **Stobhall**, a picturesque group of buildings (*not open*) grouped round a courtyard. Once the home of the Drummond family, much of the structure dates back to the 15th century.

Cross the River Isla and continue alongside the enormous beech hedge that was planted in 1746 as the boundary of the Meikleour estate. At the end of the hedge turn left to the village of **Meikleour**. The focal point of the village is the 1698 mercat cross, opposite which is an old place of punishment known as the Jougs Stone. Driving through the village you join the A984 Dunkeld road.

Continue through Caputh to **Dunkeld**. Telford spanned the Tay with a fine bridge in 1809, but this picturesque town is best known for the lovely ruins of its ancient cathedral. Founded in the 9th century, it was desecrated in 1560 and further damaged in the 17th-century Battle of Dunkeld. The choir has been restored. Stroll to **Dunkeld Cathedral** by way of Cathedral Street where the National Trust has restored the little 17th- and 18th-century houses.

Leaving the town, cross Telford's bridge and take the A9 for the 11-mile drive to **Pitlochry** (see listings) where the Highlands meet the Lowlands of Scotland. The town owes its ornate Victorian appearance to its popularity in the 19th century as a Highland health resort. Now it is better known for its **Festival Theatre** whose season lasts from May to October and attracts some 70,000 theatergoers each year.

In the 1940s the local electricity company built a hydroelectric station and dam across the salmon-rich River Tummel on the outskirts of town. It is hard to imagine a power station being an asset to the town but this is certainly the case here. From the observation room at the dam you can watch fish as they climb the 1,000-foot **fish ladder** around the dam and fight their way upstream to spawn in the upper reaches of the river. A special exhibition is devoted to their life cycle and the efforts being made to conserve them. (*Open April–October.*)

The drive from Pitlochry to Braemar is spectacular. The A924 winds up from Pitlochry to the moorlands behind the town. Alternating lush green fields and heather-clad hills give way to heather-carpeted mountains as you approach the glorious Highland scenery of **Glen Shee** (A93). At the edge of the village of **Spittal of Glenshee** large orange gates are swung across the road when it is closed by winter storms. The road begins its steep climb across the heather up the Devil's Elbow to the ski resort at the summit and drops down to the green lush valley of the River Dee and **Braemar**.

Here in this picturesque valley the clans gather for Scotland's most famous Highland games, the **Braemar Gathering**. A brilliant spectacle of pipe bands, traditional Scottish sports, and Highland dancing, the event is usually attended by the Queen and her family. Also in the village of Braemar is the cottage in which Robert Louis Stevenson lived the year he wrote *Treasure Island*.

Following the River Dee, a short drive brings you to **Braemar Castle**, a doll-sized castle on a little knoll surrounded by conifers—a hint of the magnificent castles that wait you. Following the rushing River Dee, a turn in the road offers a splendid view of **Balmoral Castle**, the Royal summer residence. It's a very overrated Victorian pile of a building built in 1853 in the Scottish baronial style at the request of Queen Victoria and Prince Albert. When the Royal Family are not in residence, you can visit the gardens and view the exhibition in the castle ballroom. (*Grounds open May–July when Royal Family not in residence.*)

Coming into the tiny hamlet of **Craithe**, park in the riverside car park and stroll up to **Craithe Church** whose foundation stone was laid by Queen Victoria in 1895. The Royal Family attend services here when in residence at Balmoral just across the river.

Continue into **Ballater** (see listing), an attractive, small town internationally famous for its Highland games held in August. These include many old Scottish sports and the arduous hill race to the summit of Craig Cailleach. Continue along the A93, watching for the signpost that directs you left for a drive of several miles to **Craigievar Castle** (NT). This single-turret, pink-washed fortress surrounded by farmland is the most appealing of

Craigievar Castle

fairy-tale castles. Up the narrow spiral staircase the rooms are small and familial and furnished as though the laird and his family are still in residence. Willie Forbes, better known as Danzig Willie because he made his money trading with Danzig, bought an incomplete castle here in 1610. He wanted the best that money could buy and gave the master mason free reign with the castle's beautiful design. The best plasterers were busy, so Danzig Willie waited many years for the magnificent molded plasterwork ceilings that were completed the year before his death in 1627. (*Open May–September.*)

Twenty miles away lies **Castle Fraser** (NT), a grander, more elaborate version of Craigievar set in parklike grounds with a formal walled garden. Begun in 1575, the castle stayed in Fraser hands until the early part of this century. It contains a splendid Great Hall and what remains of an alleged eavesdropping device known as the "Laird's Lug." (*Open daily mid-April–September, weekends only in October.*)

Regain the A944, which takes you through Alford and on towards Rhynie. Detour from the main road to visit the romantic ruins of **Kildrummy Castle** (A97). Overlooking the ruins and surrounded by acres and acres of beautiful gardens is **Kildrummy Castle Hotel** (see listing), one of our favorite Scottish country house hotels.

The road from Kildrummy to **Dufftown** via the little Highland villages of Lumsden, Rhynie (where you leave A97 and turn left on A941), and Cabrach takes you across broad expanses of moorland. James Duff, the 4th Earl of Fife, laid out Dufftown in the form of a right-angled cross in 1817. Turn right at the Tolbooth tower in the center of the square and you come to the **Glenfiddich Distillery**, the only distillery in the Highlands where you can see the complete whisky-making process from barley to bottling. (*Closed last two weeks of December.*)

Malt whisky is to Scotland what wine is to France. The rules for production are strict: It must be made from Highland barley dried over peat fires. Water is gathered from streams that have run through peat and over granite. Distillation is carried out in onion-shaped copper stills with the final product aged and stored in oak vats before bottling. A map is available from the tourist office in Dufftown that gives details of which distilleries are open and when.

Once a Highland fortress but now sadly in ruins, **Ballathie Castle** stands on the hill overlooking the distillery.

Four miles down the A941 you come to **Craigellachie** village and distillery (the home of White Horse Whisky). Turn left on the A95 for Grantown-on-Spey and follow the Spey valley through pleasant countryside to **Ballindalloch Castle**, the beautiful home of the Macpherson-Grants. An interesting selection of tastefully furnished rooms and a tea shop are open to the public. This elegant home with its lovely gardens shows the transition from the tower house of Craigievar to the country mansion so idealized by the Victorians in the Highlands. (*Open Easter–September.*)

A short distance brings you to the **Glenlivet Distillery**. (*Open all year, closed weekends mid-October–Easter.*)

Cross the River Spey at Advie and continue into Grantown-on-Spey on the narrow road that follows the north bank of the river. From Grantown-on-Spey the A939 leads towards the holiday resort of Nairn. After about 15 miles take a small road to the left signposted for **Cawdor Castle**. This was the castle Shakespeare had in mind when he set the scene of Duncan's death in *Macbeth*. The present-day Thane of Cawdor shares his family home and gardens with the public. Portraits, tapestries, lovely furniture, and, of course, tales of romance and mystery blend to make this an interesting tour. (*Open May–September.*)

An 8-mile drive brings you to the cairn that marks the site of the battle of **Culloden** (NT) (see listing) where on a wet day in 1746 Bonnie Prince Charlie marched his tired, rain-soaked Highlanders into hopeless battle with the English: 1,200 Highlanders were killed. This was the last battle fought on British soil and Charles's defeat led to the decline of the Highlands and the destruction of the clan system. After the battle the British hunted Charles for five months before he escaped to France. A museum documents this sad incident and on the surrounding moorland red flags outline the Scots battle plan while yellow flags denote the English. (*Open all year.*)

Nearby **Inverness** (see listing) is known as the "Capital of the Highlands." Straddling the River Ness, the town takes its name from the river and the Gaelic word "inver" meaning river mouth. Leave the town on the A82 (Fort William road) and after a mile you come to the Caledonian Canal, which links the lochs of the Great Glen together to provide passage between the Irish and the North Seas. The canal splits Scotland in two and without it boats would have to risk the dangerous passage around the northernmost stretches of Scotland.

The road then follows the northern shore of Scotland's deepest (700 feet), longest (24 miles), and most famous lake, **Loch Ness**. This is the legendary home of the Loch Ness Monster or "Nessie," as she is affectionately known. So, keep an eye on the muddy gray waters of the lake and you may see more than the wind ruffling its surface. If she doesn't happen to surface for you, visit the **Loch Ness Monster Exhibition** at **Drumnadrochit**, which documents sightings that go back to the 7th century. Photographs of eel-like loops and black heads swimming give credence to the legends. (*Open all year.*)

Monster spotting is a favorite pastime around Loch Ness and visitors gaze from the ramparts of **Urquhart Castle** because some of the best sightings have been made from here. The ruined castle dates from the 14th century and has a long and violent history. (*Open all year.*)

Following the shores of Loch Ness, a 19-mile drive brings you to **Fort Augustus**, a village that stands at the southwestern end of the loch. Park your car by the **Caledonian Canal** and wander along its banks to see the pleasure craft being lowered and raised through the locks. Thomas Telford, the famous engineer, spent from 1803 to 1847 building the sections of this canal that connects the North Sea and the Atlantic without boats having to navigate around the treacherous Cape Wrath.

A few miles to the southwest, the little village of **Invergarry** is framed by spectacular mountain scenery. The village was burnt to the ground after the battle of Culloden because it had sheltered Bonnie Prince Charlie before and after the battle. Turn west in the village and follow the A87, through breathtaking Highland scenery, for 50 miles to

Kyle of Lochalsh. The wild, rugged scenery changes with every bend in the road as you drive high above the lochs across empty moorlands then descend into glens to follow the shores of lochs whose crystal-clear, icy waters reflect the rugged mountain peaks. Habitations are few and far between yet, until the Highland chiefs decided, in the 18th century, that sheep were more profitable than tenants, the hillsides held crofts, schools, and chapels.

As you trace the shore of **Loch Duich**, on the last lap of the journey to Skye, **Eilean Donan Castle** appears, linked to the rocky shore by a bridge. The castle is named for a saint who lived here in the 7th century. It is a massive, walled keep that during subsequent centuries defended the coast against Danish and Norse invaders. More recently it has been restored and it is fascinating to go into rooms with 14-foot-thick walls and to climb to the battlements to see the loch spread out before you. (*Open April–October.*)

From the busy fishing port of **Kyle of Lochalsh** the toll road bridge takes you "over the sea to Skye." There is an exhilarating feel to the often mist-shrouded shores of the **Isle of Skye** (see listings) where mystery and legends intermingle with dramatic scenery. Islanders still make a living crofting and fishing, though tourism is becoming ever more important. This is the home of the Scottish heroine Flora Macdonald who disguised Bonnie Prince Charlie as her maid and brought him safely to Skye after his defeat by the English at the battle of Culloden.

Set out to explore Skye's coastline where magnificent mountains rise from the rocky shore and sea lochs provide scenic sheltered harbors. Skye has very good roads, although often quite narrow, making it easy to tour portions of the island in a day. (A trip from Portree around the northern end of Skye, west to Dunvegan, and back to Portree by the hill road from Struan is all that you could expect to do comfortably in one day.) If the weather is inclement and mist veils the island, content yourself with a good book by the fireside, for what appears stunningly beautiful on a fine day can appear dreary when sheathed in fog.

Follow the A87 (signposted Portree) through the scattered village of Broadford set along a broad, sheltered bay. Skirting the shoreline, you pass the island of Scalpay before tracing the southern shoreline of Loch Ainort. The surrounding humped peaks of the Cullin Hills are spectacular as you follow the road through Sconser and Sligachan to Portree.

Portree, the capital of Skye, is its most attractive town. Pastel-painted houses step down to the water's edge, fishing boats bob in the harbor, and small boats arrive and depart from its pier. Climbing away from the harbor, the town's streets are lined with attractive shops. If you have not booked your ferry passage from Armadale to Mallaig, you can do so at the Caledonian MacBrayne ferry office behind the bus station. The town derives its name from *Port an Righ*, meaning "King's Haven," following the visit in 1540 of James V who made a vain attempt to reconcile the feuding Macleod and Macdonald clans. If you base yourself in Portree, there is no better place to stay than at the home of Hugh and Linda Macdonald, **Viewfield House** (see listing).

Leaving the town, turn right onto the A850, a narrow, single-lane road with passing places, which takes you north. As you approach the shores of Lochs Fada and Leathan, the jagged, craggy peaks of **The Storr** (mountains) come into view. Standing amongst them is the **Old Man of Storr**, one of the most challenging pinnacles for mountain climbers.

Around the island's northernmost headland the crumbling ruins of the Macdonalds' **Duntulm Castle** stand on a clifftop promontory overlooking the rocky shores of Duntulm Bay. A short drive brings you to the **Skye Croft Museum** where four traditional Highland crofts have been restored and appropriately furnished to show a family home, a smithy, a weaver's house, and a small museum. These little cottages with their thick stone walls topped by a thick straw thatch were the traditional island dwellings—very few good examples remain though, as you travel around the island, if you look very carefully, you can see several traditional cottages in various states of ruin. Flora Macdonald is buried in a nearby graveyard. (*Open May–October.*)

Returning to the main coastal route (A850), a short drive takes you through Kilmuir and down a steep hill into the scattered hamlet of **Uig** whose pier is used by ferries to the Outer Hebrides. It is here that Bonnie Prince Charlie and Flora Macdonald landed after fleeing the Outer Hebrides. Continue to Kensaleyre and half a mile beyond the village turn right onto the B8036. When this road meets a T-junction, turn right onto the A87 for the 22-mile drive to the village of **Dunvegan**.

Just to the north of the village is **Dunvegan Castle**, the oldest inhabited castle in Scotland and the home of the Macleod family for over 700 years. It stands amidst hills and moorlands guarding the entrance to a sheltered bay. After parking your car walk through rhododendron-filled gardens to the fortress. The castle's 15th-century section is known as the Fairy Tower after the threadbare Fairy Flag that hangs in one of the chambers. Legend has it that this yellow silk flag with crimson spots is the consecrated banner of the Knights Templar, taken as a battle prize from the Saracens. It is said to have the magical properties to produce victory in battle, the birth of sons, and plentiful harvests. Other relics include items relating to Bonnie Prince Charlie. During the summer you can take boat excursions to view the nearby seal colonies. (*Open April–October.*)

The A863 winds you down the western side of Skye. If you wish to visit the island's only distillery, take the B8009 to **Talisker** where the **Talisker Distillery** offers guided tours and a tasting. (*Open weekdays April–October.*)

Follow the narrow, single-track A851 across open moorland to **Sleat** (pronounced "Slate"), which refers to the complete southern peninsula of Skye where most of the land is divided into two estates: Clan Donald lands to the south and those of Sir Iain Noble to the north. Sir Iain is a great promoter of Gaelic, which is undergoing a revival in the western Highlands. On a rocky spit of land almost surrounded by water, the whitewashed **Eilean Iarmain** hotel (see listing), a shop, and a huddle of cottages face **Isle Ornsay**—a postage-stamp-sized island whose lighthouse was built by Robert Louis Stephenson's grandfather. (The lighthouse cottage's most famous occupant was Gavin Maxwell.) Across the sound mountains tumble directly into the sea adding a wild, end-of-the-earth feel to this hamlet.

A few more miles of narrow roads bring you to the **Clan Donald Centre** where the stable block serves as a tea room and gift shop whence you walk through the wooded **Armadale Castle** grounds to an exhibition on the Lords of the Isles and Gaelic culture. (*Open April–October.*)

Scotland

SKYE TO FORT WILLIAM VIA MALLAIG

If time or weather prevents you from following this itinerary north into Wester Ross, you can board the ferry for **Mallaig** in nearby **Armadale**. The ferry sails five to six times a day during the summer months and reservations should be made before sailing—it is suggested that you purchase your tickets from the Caledonian MacBrayne ferry offices in Portree (*tel: 01478-612075*). The ferry company requires that cars arrive half an hour before sailing time. It takes 1½ hours to drive from Portree to the ferry, so unless you are an insomniac, do not book the 9 am ferry. Leaving Mallaig, you cannot get lost for there is only one narrow road, "The Road to the Isles," that leads you out of town (A830).

If the weather is fine, you may want to pause at the spectacular white beaches that fringe the rocky little bays near **Morar**. The narrow road twists and turns and passing places allow cars going in opposite directions to pass one another. The village of **Arisaig** shelters on the shores of **Loch Nan Ceal** with views, and ferries, to the little islands of **Rhum** and **Eigg**.

From Arisaig your route turns eastwards following the picturesque shores of **Loch Nan Uamh**, best known for its associations with Bonnie Prince Charlie and the Jacobite Rising of 1745. The clan leaders met in a house nearby and after his defeat the prince hid near here before being taken to the Outer Hebrides—a cairn marks the spot where he left Scotland.

More than 1,000 clansmen gathered at **Glenfinnan** at the head of **Loch Shiel** to begin the 1745 Jacobite Rising. A tall castellated tower marks the place where they are said to have hoisted the Stuart standard. You climb the tower stairs to the statue of a Highlander overlooking the icy waters of the mountain-ringed loch. At the adjacent visitors' center the prince's exploits are portrayed.

Leaving the monument to Bonnie Prince Charlie's lost cause, follow the A830 for the 15-mile drive through Kinlocheil and Corpach to **Fort William** (see listings). As you approach the town, the rounded summit of Britain's highest mountain, **Ben Nevis**, appears before you.

Plockton on Loch Carron

SKYE TO FORT WILLIAM OR INVERNESS VIA WESTER ROSS

If you love Skye with her magnificent seascapes and mountains, then you will adore the Wester Ross coastline that stretches from Kyle of Lochalsh to Ullapool and beyond. It is a long day's drive from Kyle to Ullapool and the scenery is so magnificent that you may want to break the journey and spend several days in the area. Traditionally, **Wester Ross** has most sunshine in May and June, it rains more in July and August, then brightens up in September. Scottish weather is very fickle in May: we went from seven days of glorious sunshine to seemingly endless days of lashing rain. A great deal of the drive from Kyle of Lochalsh to Ullapool is on single-track road—one lane of tarmac just a few inches wider than your car (with passing places).

From **Kyle of Lochalsh** turn left to **Plockton** to see the hardy yucca palms growing bravely in the harborside gardens in this pretty village that hugs a sheltered spot of the wooded bay. Leaving Plockton, the road traces Loch Carron and after passing the Stratcarron Hotel, at the head of the loch, you turn left on the A896 for Tornapress and on to Shieldaig.

If the weather is sunny, rather than continuing along the A896 from Tornapress to Shieldaig, take the coastal road around the headland following signposts for Applecross. You will be rewarded by a most challenging drive and spectacular scenery. The narrow road twists and turns as it climbs ever higher up the **Bealach-na-Bo** pass with the mountains rising closer and taller at every turn. Crest the summit, cross a boulder-strewn moorland dotted with tarns (tiny lakes), and drop down into **Applecross**, a few whitewashed houses set in a lush green valley with salmon-pink sandy beaches. Grazing sheep fill the coastal fields and the occasional whitewashed croft faces across the water to the Isle of Raasay and, beyond that, the misty mountains of Skye. Rounding the peninsula you come to **Ardehslaig**, a few white cottages set round a rocky inlet with boats bobbing in the tiny sheltered harbor. Turn into **Shieldaig** where little cottages line the waterfront facing a nearby island densely forested with Scotch pines. It's an idyllic, peaceful spot and **Tigh an Eilean** (House by the Island) with its shop, pretty hotel, and pub makes an excellent place to break your journey (see listing).

A deceptive few yards of two-lane road quickly turn to single track as you travel along the south shore of **Loch Torridon** where the **Loch Torridon Hotel** (see listing) sits on its bank and through Glen Torridon to turn left on the A832, an arrow-straight, two-lane highway. After half a mile you find a whitewashed visitors' center on the left. The road traces **Loch Maree** with tempting glimpses of the glassy loch between groves of birch trees. The soft lushness and straight road give way to wild moorland and a single-track road to **Gairloch** with its wide bay of pink sand, scattered houses, cemetery, and golf course.

Heading inland to cross the peninsula you come to **Inverewe Gardens** (NT). Osgood Mackensie bought this little peninsula in 1862, a barren site exposed to Atlantic gales but with frosts prevented by the warmth of the Gulf Stream. He planted belts of trees for shelter, brought in soil, and began his garden, a lifetime project that was continued by his daughter who handed over Inverewe to the National Trust in 1952. The lushness of the gardens is a striking contrast to the miles of grandiose, barren scenery that surround it. The surprise is not so much what the garden contains as the fact that it exists at all on a latitude similar to that of Leningrad. The gardens, shop, and tea room are a venue that will occupy several hours. The National Trust brochure outlines a suggested route along the garden's pathways, but you can wander at will down the twisting paths through the azaleas, rhododendrons, and woodlands. Colorful displays are to be found in most seasons: in mid-April to May, rhododendrons; May, azaleas; June, rock garden, flower borders, and roses; September, heather; and November, maples. (*Open all year.*)

Leaving Inverewe, another 35 miles finds you at the head of **Loch Broom** at an impressive vantage point that offers magnificent views down the valley across lush farmland to the distant loch. Travel down the hill and turn left into the green valley for the 12-mile drive to Ullapool.

Ullapool has a beautiful setting: cottages line the quay and overlook a jumble of slipways, quays, vessels from huge international trawlers to small wooden fishing boats, fishing gear, and nets. On the distant shore heather-clad hills rise steeply from the waters of Loch Broom. The port is a bustle of freighters and foreign fishing boats and is the terminal for the car ferry to Stornoway on the Isle of Lewis. Summer visitors add to the throng. You can always find good food and a reviving cup of coffee (and accommodation) at **The Ceilidh Place** (see listing).

North of Ullapool there's a lot of heart-stopping scenery but beyond the Summer Isles there are no good places to stay. Journey to the **Summer Isles** (see Achiltibuie listing) by boat to see the seals and seabirds. Travel to **Lochinver** with its breathtaking views of beautiful coastline and visit the **Inchnadamph Caves** and the ruin of **Ardvreck Castle**.

Leaving Ullapool, a 60-mile drive (A835) will return you to Inverness from where it's a 3-hour drive down the A9 to Edinburgh. Or retrace your steps down the northern shore of Loch Ness and continue into Fort William (A82).

Bordering the shores of **Loch Linnhe, Fort William** (see listings) is the largest town in the Western Highlands. While the town itself cannot be described as attractive, it is the economic hub of the area and it is always crowded with tourists during the busy summer months.

From Fort William the A82 takes you southwest along the southern shore of Loch Linnhe, then turns you inland over the pass of **Glen Coe,** notorious for the massacre of the Macdonalds by the Campbells in 1692. After accepting their hospitality, the Campbells issued an order—written on the nine of diamonds playing card—to kill their hosts, the Macdonalds. The pass of Glen Coe is barren and rocky and the road south travels across this seemingly empty land. A short detour to **Killin** with its craft shops and impressive waterfalls provides an enjoyable break on a long drive.

The area of low mountains and serene lakes around **Callander** (see listing), a most attractive town, is known as **The Trossachs**. This is the country of Sir Walter Scott's novel *Rob Roy* and his poem *Lady of the Lake*. Robert MacGregor, "Rob Roy," existed as a romanticized 17th-century Robin Hood, who stole from the rich and gave to the poor. However, some regarded him more realistically as a thief and rustler! Scott's "lady" was Ellen Douglas, and her "lake" was **Loch Katrine**. (*Loch Katrine boat trips May–September.*) There are several lovely lakes to view in this area, such as **Loch Achray** and **Loch Venachar**.

A few miles distant lies **Stirling**, dominated by its imposing Renaissance castle. **Stirling Castle**, once the home of Scottish kings, is perched high on a sheer cliff overlooking the battleground of **Bannockburn** where the Scots turned the English back in their attempt to subdue the Highland clans. (*Open all year.*)

From Stirling the M80 will quickly bring you to **Glasgow**, Scotland's most populous city. Its established tradition as a port and industrial center has in recent years been surpassed by its reputation as a cultural center.

As in many large cities, the best way to get an overview of the major sights is to take a tour bus. Open-top double-deckers leave every half hour on two routes from George Square, where you also find the **Tourist Information Centre** (*closed Sundays*), and you can hop on and off wherever you like. This is a Victorian city with a particular pride in its architecture and architects of that time, notably Charles Rennie Mackintosh and Alexander "Greek" Thomson, whose buildings feature prominently on the tour. Be sure to visit the 13th-century **cathedral** with its open timber roof and splendid collection of stained-glass windows. Here you find the shrine of St. Mungo, patron saint of Glasgow who died in 603, which was an important medieval pilgrimage spot.

Glasgow is home to over 30 art galleries and museums including the **Kelvingrove Art Gallery and Museum**, the most popular in Scotland, **St. Mungo Museum of Religious Life and Art**, the only museum of its kind in the world, and **The Burrell Collection**, Scotland's most outstanding museum. The Collection is set in the delightful surroundings of Pollok Country Park, formerly the grounds of **Pollok House** (NT), and can be reached by bus, train, or car (take the M8 towards the airport to the M77). Sir William Burrell, a successful Glasgow shipping agent, amassed a magnificent collection of some 9,000 works of art, primarily in the areas of medieval European art (the tapestries are stunning), Oriental ceramics and bronzes, and European paintings. In 1944 he bequeathed his collection to the city, with the stipulation that it be housed away from the highly polluted city center and eventually, in 1983, it found the perfect setting here in a corner of the Pollok Estate in a custom-built, award-winning building. (*Open all year.*)

At the other end of the social spectrum, it is fascinating to get a glimpse of what life used to be like for working-class Glaswegians, as you can in the **Tenement House Museum** (NT), a Victorian apartment re-creating the poorest living conditions in the first half of the 20th century. (*Open March–October.*) **The People's Palace** opened in 1898 as a cultural center for the people of the East End, one of the unhealthiest and most overcrowded parts of the city. It is now the local history museum of Glasgow, telling the story of the people from 1750 to the present. (*Open all year.*)

Shopping is excellent in Glasgow and evenings are alive with every kind of entertainment from opera to nightclubs.

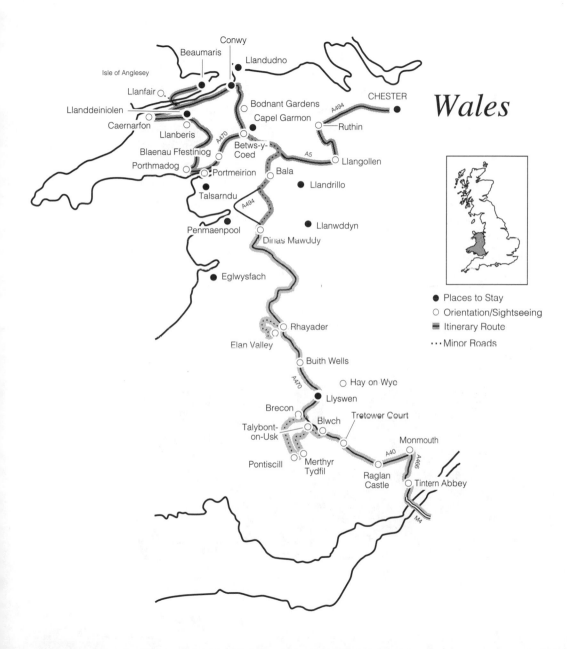

Wales

Conwy
Beaumaris
Llandudno
Isle of Anglesey
CHESTER
Llanfair
Bodnant Gardens
Llanddeiniolen
Capel Garmon
Caernarfon
Ruthin
Llanberis
Betws-y-
Coed
Llangollen
Blaenau Ffestiniog
Porthmadog
Bala
Portmeirion
Talsarndu
Llandrillo
A494
Penmaenpool
Llanwddyn
Dinas Mawddy
Eglwysfach
Rhayader
Elan Valley
Buith Wells
Hay on Wye
Llyswen
Brecon
Tretower Court
Blwch
Talybont-
on-Usk
Monmouth
Pontiscill
Merthyr
Tydfil
Raglan
Castle
Tintern Abbey

A494
A5
A470
A40
A466
M4

● Places to Stay
○ Orientation/Sightseeing
▨ Itinerary Route
··· Minor Roads

103

Wales

Wales has myriad towns and villages with seemingly unpronounceable names, its own language, an ancient form of Celtic, and its own prince, Charles. Narrow-gauge steam railways puff contentedly through glorious scenery, and there are more castles per square mile than anywhere else in Europe. The Welsh have always been fiercely independent. Consequently, they built fortifications to defend themselves while Edward I commissioned a series of mighty fortresses from which the English could sally forth to subdue the fiery Welsh. Today these mighty fortresses are some of Wales's greatest treasures. Smaller but beloved treasures are the "Great Little Trains," narrow-gauge steam railway lines with hard-working "toy" trains that once hauled slate and still steam through gorgeous countryside. And at journey's end there is bound to be a steaming cuppa to be enjoyed with *bara brith*, a scrumptious currant bread. As the signs say, *Croeso i Cymru*—Welcome to Wales.

Conwy Castle

Recommended Pacing: One night in southern Wales is all you need to accomplish the sightseeing outlined in this itinerary. In our opinion, Wales's most magnificent scenery and stunning castles lie to the north in and around Snowdonia National Park, so allow at least two nights in northern Wales.

Leave England on the M4 crossing the Severn toll bridge. The first indication that you are in another country is that all road signs appear in two languages, Welsh first, English second. As you leave the bridge take the first left turnoff signed A466 Monmouth and the Wye Valley. The road winds a course up the steep-sided, wooded valley to **Tintern Abbey**, a romantic ruin adored by the sentimental Victorians. Drive alongside the ruin to the car park at the rear by the tourist office. Stretch your legs with a quick walk round the ruin or, if you would like to visit the prettiest spot on the 168-mile length of **Offa's Dyke**, the tourist office will provide you with a detailed instruction sheet called *Offa's Dyke and the Devil's Pulpit Viewpoint*. Offa's Dyke was a great earthwork built over 1,200 years ago at the direction of King Offa to divide England and Wales. (*Open April–October.*)

Follow the river as it winds into Monmouth and turn left on the A40 towards Abergavenny. Traveling this dual carriageway quickly brings into view the substantial ruins of **Raglan Castle** in a field to your right. Because it is on the opposite side of a divided highway you need to do an about-face at the first roundabout. Raglan Castle is the last of the medieval castles, dating from the more settled later Middle Ages when its builders could afford to indulge in decorative touches. It was begun in 1431 and its Great Tower was rendered the ruin you see today by Oliver Cromwell's demolition engineers. A huge fireplace and the windows are all that remain of the Grand Hall but with imagination and the aid of a map you can picture what a splendid place this must have been. You can climb the battlements and picnic in the grassy grounds. (*Open April–October.*)

Stay on the ring road around Abergavenny and 2 miles after passing through **Crickhowell**, a one-time stagecoach stop for coach travelers on the way to Brecon, turn right on the A479 to **Tretower Court and Castle**. The castle, a sturdy keep, was usurped as a habitation in the 14th century by nearby Tretower Court, a grand mansion that was the home of the Vaughan family for three centuries. As you walk through the empty medieval hall and along the stone passageways, you can imagine how splendid a home it was. (*Open all year.*)

Leaving Tretower, continue down the lane, beside the house, and turn right on the A40. If the weather is fine, you can enjoy an almost circular driving tour through the **Brecon Beacons** by turning left towards Llangynidr and, after crossing the river, taking a right turn to Cwm Cronon and Talybont-on-Usk. Here you turn left and follow a beautiful wooded valley alongside lakes and over the hills to Pontiscill. On a fine day it is a spectacular drive along a narrow paved road, but this is not a trip to be appreciated when the clouds hang low over the mountains and visibility is not good. From Pontiscill the road weaves down to the outskirts of Merthyr Tydfil where you turn right on the A470 along another lovely valley and climb the stark, bare escarpment over the pass to Brecon.

If you do not deviate through the Brecon Beacons, remain on the A40 where views of the Usk Valley and the mountains present themselves as the road climbs to the village of Blwch. Bypass the market town of Brecon and take the A470 (Buith Wells) to **Llyswen** where you can enjoy an overnight stay at **Llangoed Hall** (see listing). From Llyswen an 18-mile round-trip detour will afford you the chance to explore the many bookstores and antique shops of **Hay-On-Wye**.

It's a lovely drive to Buith Wells as the road follows the River Wye through soft, pretty countryside. Crossing the river, head to **Rhayader** where an opportunity to enjoy a beautiful (in fair weather) drive through wild, rugged moorlands rising from vast reservoirs is afforded by turning left in the village for the **Elan Valley**. Your first stop lies beneath the looming dam at the information center where a small display outlines the importance and history of clean drinking water and gives details on the vast reservoirs that provide 76 million gallons of drinking water a day. Returning to the road, follow it as it traces the reservoir through fern-covered mountains. A right-hand turn returns you to the center of Rhayader and the A470.

From Rhayader the A470 quickly takes you north. After the junction with the A458 be on the lookout for a small sign that directs you into the pretty roadside village of Dinas Mawddy and along a narrow lane that climbs and climbs above the green fields into stark mountains. You crest the pass and wind down and around the lake to the outskirts of Bala. Here you make a right-hand turn then go immediately left on the A4212 (Trawsfyndd road) for a short distance to the B4501, which quickly brings you to Cerrigydrudion. There you turn left on the A5 to **Betws-y-Coed**, set in a narrow, densely wooded valley at the confluence of three rivers. Crowds of visitors come to admire this town, which was popularized by the Victorian painter David Cox.

From Betws-y-Coed take the A470, following the eastern bank of the River Conwy north as it winds its way to the sea. After passing through the village of Tal-y-Cafn, look for **Bodnant Gardens** (NT) on your right. Garden lovers will enjoy almost a hundred acres of camellias, rhododendrons, magnolias, and laburnum, which provide incredible displays of spring color. Above are terraces, lawns, and formal rose and flower beds; below, in a wooded valley, a stream runs through the secluded, wild garden. (*Open mid-March–October.*)

The swell of **Conwy Bay** is flanked by high cliffs and the town of **Conwy** is unforgettable for its picturesque castle set on a promontory at the confluence of two rivers and for the town's wall—over ¾ mile in length with 22 towers and 3 original gateways. **Conwy Castle** was begun in the 13th century for Edward I and suffered the scars of the turbulent years of the Middle Ages and the Civil War. The defensive complex includes an exhibit on Edward I and his castles in Wales. On the top floor of the Chapel Tower is a scale model of how the castle and the town might have appeared in 1312. (*Open April–October.*)

Leaving the castle, cross the road to the quay to visit a tiny home that claims to be the smallest house in Britain, then turn onto the High Street and visit the oldest house in Wales, **Aberconwy House** (NT). (*Open April–October, closed Tuesdays.*)

Leave Conwy and follow the A55 as it hugs the coast in the direction of Caernarfon. Rather than going directly to Caernarfon, follow signs for Bangor (A5122) and call in at **Penrhyn Castle** (NT), a fabulous sham castle built as a grand home by a local slate magnate in the 19th century. This impressive house of intricate masonry and woodwork is filled with stupendous furniture. (*Open April–October, closed Tuesdays.*)

Cross over the Menai Straight to the **Isle of Anglesey** on the Menai suspension bridge, the first of its kind, built by that famous engineer Thomas Telford, then follow the road that hugs the coast to **Beaumaris** (see listing) with its closely huddled houses painted in pastel shades strung along the road. **Beaumaris Castle**, the last of the castles built by Edward I in his attempt to control Wales, is a squat, moated fortress with grassy grounds inside thick walls facing a harbor full of sailboats. (*Open all year.*)

Return to the Menai bridge and, if you are inclined to have your picture taken by the sign of the town with the longest name in the world, follow directions to **Llanfair**, the abbreviation (that fits on signposts) for Llanfairpwllgwyngyllgogerychwyndrobwyllllan-tysiliogogogoch. This translates as "St. Mary's Church by the white aspens over the whirlpool and St. Tysilio's Church by the red cave." The drab little town has little to recommend it but commercial opportunists have cleverly situated a large shopping complex directly next to the station.

The A5 (Bangor road) quickly returns you to the mainland via the Britannia road bridge where you pick up signs for **Caernarfon**. Edward I laid the foundations of **Caernarfon Castle** in 1283 after his armies had defeated the princes of North Wales. Many revolts against English rule took place in this imposing fortress and during the Civil War it was one of Cromwell's strongholds. The first English Prince of Wales was born here in 1284. The investitures of the Duke of Windsor in 1911 and of Prince Charles in 1969 as Prince of Wales both took place in this majestic setting. This is the most massive and best preserved of the fortifications in this itinerary. It takes several hours to clamber up the towers, peep through arrow slits in the massive walls, and visit the exhibitions on the Princes of Wales, Castles of Edward I, and the Museum of the Royal Welsh Fusiliers. (*Open April–October.*)

Caernarfon Castle

Leave the coast at Caernarfon with the beauty of Snowdonia ahead of you, following the A4086 Llanberis road. The **Snowdonia National Park** is a region of wild mountains which, while they cannot be compared in size to the Alps or the Rockies (Snowdon rises to 3,560 feet), are nevertheless dramatically beautiful with ravines and sheer cliffs whose sides plummet into glacier-cut valleys sparkling with wood-fringed lakes and cascading waterfalls.

The village of **Llanberis** is the starting point for the ascent of the highest mountain in Wales, **Mount Snowdon**. Easier than the rugged walking ascent is the two-hour round-trip journey on the **Snowdon Mountain Railway**, an adorable "toy" steam train that pushes its carriages up the mountainside on a rack-and-pinion railway. The little train winds you along the edges of precipices and up steep gradients to the mountain's summit. If the weather is fine (the train runs only in clear weather) and especially if it is July, August, or the weekend, arrive for your adventure early to secure a pass that entitles you to return at an appointed time. On the day we visited a 10:30 am arrival assured us of a place on the 4:30 pm return train. Remember to take warm clothing with you as it is always cold on the summit. (*Open April–October.*)

When you return from your mountain experience make your way to the other side of the lake to ride the **Llanberis Lake Railway** (rarely do you have to book in advance). The adorable little train that once served the slate quarries now puffs along 2 miles of track by the edge of the lake beneath the towering mountains. On fine days you have lovely views of Snowdon.

When you leave Llanberis the road climbs the pass and the scenery becomes ever more rocky and rugged: small wonder that Hillary and Hunt trained for the 1953 Everest ascent in this area. At the Pen-y-Gwryd hotel turn right on the A498 for Beddgelert. The landscape softens as you pass Lake Gwynant and, with the River Glaslyn as its guide, the road passes through a valley that is softer and more pastoral than those of Snowdonia's other lakes.

Crowding the riverbank where three valleys meet is the little village of **Beddgelert**, nestled in the foothills of Mount Snowdon. From Beddgelert, the road follows the tumbling River Glaslyn which settles into a lazy glide as it approaches **Porthmadog**, the terminus of the hard-working little **Ffestiniog Narrow-Gauge Railway**, which runs to and from nearby Ffestiniog. The train provides riders with a mobile viewpoint from which to enjoy the most spectacular scenery as it follows the coast and chugs up into rugged Snowdonia, at one point traveling almost in a circle to gain altitude, to terminate its journey at **Blaenau Ffestiniog**. Here, in summer, you can connect with a bus that takes you for a visit to the nearby slate caverns before taking you back to the station for your return journey to Porthmadog. This rugged little train for many years carried slate from the mines to the port of Porthmadog. (*Open April–October, 2½ hours return journey.*)

A short drive on the A487 brings you to Minffordd where you turn right to the extravagant fantasy village of **Portmeirion**, which looks like a little piece of Italy transported to Wales. It has a piazza, a campanile, and an eclectic mixture of cottages and buildings squeezed into a small space and surrounded by gardens full of subtropical plants and ornate pools. The village is a mass of color—the façades are terra cotta, bright pink, yellow, and cream, and the gardens full of brightly colored flowers and shrubs. Portmeirion was the realization of a dream for Sir Clough Williams-Ellis who bought this wooded hillside plot above the broad sandy river estuary and built the village to show that architecture could be fun and could enhance a beautiful site, not defile it. His architectural model was Portofino and, while there are many Italianate touches to this fantasy village, there are also lots of local recycled houses. Sir Clough rescued many old buildings and cottages from destruction (he termed Portmeirion "the home for fallen buildings"), transporting them here and erecting them on the site. Day visitors are charged an admission fee but if you really want to fully enjoy the fantasy (the setting for the BBC television series *The Prisoner*), spend the night at the hotel or in one of the rooms in the village and enjoy it after the visitors have left.

Leave the coast behind you and turn inland to Blaenau Ffestiniog where terraced houses huddle together beneath the massive, gray-slate mountain to form a village. Taking the A470 towards Betws-y-Coed, the road follows terrace upon terrace of somber gray slate up the mountainside to the **Llechwedd Slate Caverns**. Exhibits show the importance of slate mining but the most exciting part of a visit here is to travel underground into the deep mine and follow a walking tour through the caverns. (*Open all year.*)

Continuing north (A470), a 15-minute drive takes you over the pass to **Dolwyddelan Castle**, a 13th-century keep built by Prince Llewyn which was captured by Edward I and subsequently restored in the 19th century.

From Betws-y-Coed take the A5 to **Llangollen**, a town that has become the famous scene of the colorful extravaganza, the International Musical Eisteddfod, the contest for folk dancers, singers, orchestras, and instrumentalists. Llangollen's 14th-century stone bridge spanning the salmon-rich River Dee is one of Wales's Seven Wonders.

Leave Llangollen on the A542 and travel over the scenic Horseshoe Pass past the ruins of the Cistercian abbey, Valle Crucis, to **Ruthin**. Nestled in the fertile valley of Clwyd and closed in by a ring of wooded hills, Ruthin is an old, once-fortified market town whose castle is now a very commercialized hotel complete with medieval banquets.

From here a fast drive on the A494 returns you to England and motorways that quickly take you to all corners of the realm. But before leaving the area, visit the charming medieval city of **Chester** (see listing). The Romans settled here in 79 A.D. and made Chester a key stronghold. Much of the original Roman wall survives, although many towers and gates seen today were additions from the Middle Ages. Chester is a fascinating city with a 2-mile walk around its **battlements**—the best way to orient yourself. It's great fun to browse in **The Rows**, double-decker layers of shops—one layer of stores at street level and the other stacked on top.

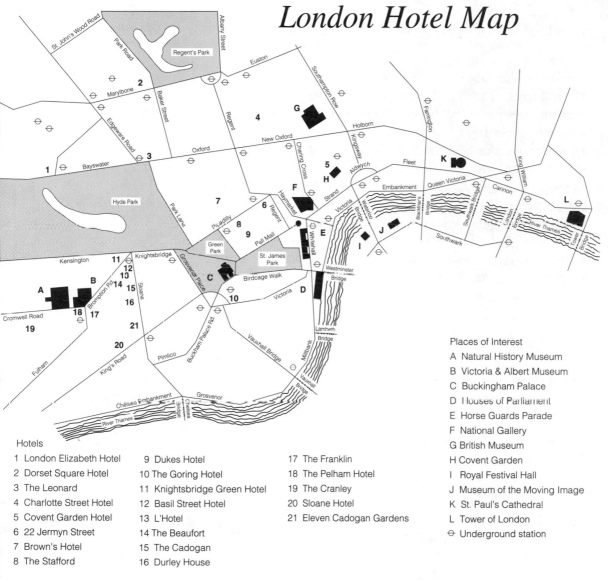

London Hotel Map

Hotels

1 London Elizabeth Hotel
2 Dorset Square Hotel
3 The Leonard
4 Charlotte Street Hotel
5 Covent Garden Hotel
6 22 Jermyn Street
7 Brown's Hotel
8 The Stafford
9 Dukes Hotel
10 The Goring Hotel
11 Knightsbridge Green Hotel
12 Basil Street Hotel
13 L'Hotel
14 The Beaufort
15 The Cadogan
16 Durley House
17 The Franklin
18 The Pelham Hotel
19 The Cranley
20 Sloane Hotel
21 Eleven Cadogan Gardens

Places of Interest

A Natural History Museum
B Victoria & Albert Museum
C Buckingham Palace
D Houses of Parliament
E Horse Guards Parade
F National Gallery
G British Museum
H Covent Garden
I Royal Festival Hall
J Museum of the Moving Image
K St. Paul's Cathedral
L Tower of London
⊖ Underground station

If you're looking for a charming, family-owned Edwardian hotel in the heart of Knightsbridge where you can even take your dog (by arrangement), head straight for The Basil Street. This hotel combines a friendly, home-away-from-home atmosphere with elegant, antique-filled surroundings. Particularly striking are the spacious foyer with its distinctive old light fixture and sweeping staircase, the lovely writing corridor with its unusual antiques and side cubby holes set with desks and chairs, and the handsome dining room with its pale-green walls, tables topped with starched linens, abundant greenery, and evening piano music. Guestrooms are all different in size, shape, and decor, generally with pastel color schemes and matching drapes and bedspreads. Some have lovely moldings, some have glass-fronted wardrobes, and some have marble bathrooms, but all have a sitting area with desk, satellite TV, and 24-hour room service. Four family rooms are available. During their visit, female guests (and, by invitation, their male guests) become honorary members of the on-site Parrot Club for women, a quiet haven for working or relaxing.

THE BASIL STREET HOTEL
Manager: Charles Legares
Basil Street
London SW3 1AH, England
Tel: (020) 7581 3311, Fax: (020) 7581 3693
Email: info@thebasil.com
80 rooms
Double: £190–£205*
*Breakfast & VAT not included
Credit cards: all major
Nearest underground: Knightsbridge
www.karenbrown.com/ews/thebasil.html

Nestled in a residential neighborhood, The Beaufort is an alluring example of a small luxury hotel that puts the comfort and convenience of guests first. Corporate guests love the email access, personal fax, and computer outlets while leisure travelers revel in breakfast in bed and the hotel's location just round the corner from Harrods. Decorated either in warm pastel shades or brighter, bolder colors, each air-conditioned guestroom has a CD player and VCR (there is a library of videos and CDs), brandy, shortbread, and chocolates—all included in the price, as are all drinks, afternoon cream tea, Continental breakfast, and free airport transfer (junior suites only) to or from the hotel. The comfortable, attractively decorated sitting room with its blue walls, *trompe l'oeil* columns and arches, and soft lighting has plump sofa and chairs, books, and an abundance of fresh flowers. Art lovers will enjoy the hotel's display of over 400 original watercolors

THE BEAUFORT
Owners: Sir Michael & Lady Wilmot
Manager: Liz Vallance
33 Beaufort Gardens
London SW3 1PP, England
Tel: (020) 7584 5252, Fax: (020) 7589 2834
Email: enquiries@thebeaufort.co.uk
28 rooms
Double: £180–£260*, Suite: from £295*
*VAT not included, Credit cards: all major
Nearest underground: Knightsbridge
www.karenbrown.com/ews/thebeaufort.html

The five-star, bustling Brown's Hotel is quintessentially English. An old-fashioned, even Victorian, rather stuffy elegance prevails, from the paneled drawing room with comfortable sofas, where guests enjoy the hotel's famous afternoon tea, to the guestrooms with their traditional decor. The individually decorated bedrooms are all double-glazed, superbly equipped, and immaculately maintained, and some of the suites are positively grand. It is no wonder that Brown's has so much character—it was founded by Byron's valet, James Brown, and was a favorite of Kipling. Brown's is a superb choice for those who want a hotel with a very British atmosphere in the heart of the theatre district. Since this hotel is so popular, the public rooms can be very busy.

BROWN'S HOTEL
Manager: Peter Richards
Albermarle Street
London W1X 4BP, England
Tel: (020) 7493 6020, Fax: (020) 7493 9381
118 rooms
Double: £304–£399*
*Breakfast (£18.50) & VAT not included
Credit cards: all major
Nearest underground: Green Park

Soon after it was finished in 1888, The Cadogan hotel became linked with two of the most famous people of the age—Lillie Langtry, the beautiful actress and mistress of Edward VII, and her admirer Oscar Wilde, the famous dramatist. Lillie's drawing and dining room are still to be seen in the hotel today. From the comfortable paneled drawing room where afternoon tea is served to the spacious studios and elegant suites (all soundproofed and most air-conditioned), the hotel exudes quality and the staff showers its guests with personal attention. Breakfast is served in the elegant restaurant on tables set with silver and fresh flowers. The Oscar Wilde Suite with its front corner turret is understandably popular for its historical interest as this is where the writer resided. The location is handy for museums, smart shops, Hyde Park, and restaurants.

THE CADOGAN
Manager: Milton Hussey
75 Sloane Street
London SX1X 9SG, England
Tel: (020) 7235 7141, Fax: (020) 7245 0994
Email: info@cadogan.com
65 rooms
Double: £210–£350*, Suite: £400*
*Breakfast (£16.50) & VAT not included
Credit cards: all major
Nearest undergrounds: Sloane Square & Knightsbridge
www.karenbrown.com/ews/thecadogan.html

The Kemps have done it again: presented London with a stunningly stylish and luxurious hotel that rapidly achieved popular success. The Charlotte Street Hotel, situated in the bustling neighborhood of North Soho, buzzes with activity, particularly in the busy brasserie, a visual feast with its open-plan kitchen and original murals depicting contemporary London life. Decor throughout has a modern, English flavor, with pastel colors, gorgeous fabrics, well-placed works of art, and striking flower arrangements. The drawing room, with its beige walls and carpet, pale-blue couches, and log-burning fireplace, is irresistibly comfortable and inviting. Bedrooms, like those in the sister Covent Garden Hotel, are superbly appointed with amenities like CD players, VCRs, fax/modem points, and cellular phones, and even have color TVs in their magnificent granite-and-oak bathrooms. Particularly appealing are the four loft suites (bedrooms upstairs, sitting room with sofa bed downstairs) with their soaring ceilings and windows. For even more luxury, opt to stay in a penthouse suite with private elevator and working fireplace. Superb!

CHARLOTTE STREET HOTEL
Owners: Kit & Tim Kemp
Manager: Carrie Wicks
15 Charlotte Street
London W1T 1RJ, England
Tel: (020) 7806 2000, Fax: (020) 7806 2001
52 rooms
Double: £195–£280*, Suite: £330–£510*
*Breakfast (£16.50), service charge (12.5%) & VAT
not included
Credit cards: all major
Nearest undergrounds: Goodge Street
& Tottenham Court Rd

In keeping with its location at the heart of London's theatre district, the Covent Garden Hotel is dramatic and exuberant in its decor, flamboyant yet tasteful, and unabashedly luxurious. The lobby welcomes you grandly with lavish flower arrangements and Oriental carpets, then the imposing stone staircase sweeps you up to the wood-paneled, red-themed drawing room which manages to look cozy despite its grand scale and quirky furniture. Bedrooms are generously sized—even single rooms have queen beds—and, while individually decorated, each has air conditioning, a hand-quilted bedspread and trademark tailor's mannequin in matching fabric, a large writing desk, a sumptuous granite and mahogany bathroom, and every modern amenity including CD player and cellular phone. Favorite rooms include 304 with its king four-poster bed, beautiful blue drapes, huge mirror, and fireplace; 205 with its coronet-draped king brass bed, massive oil painting, wing chairs, and lovely desk; and 417 with its high ceilings, exposed beams, and turret dining area. The hotel also features 24-hour room service, a gym, treatment room, private screening room, and popular brasserie.

COVENT GARDEN HOTEL
Owners: Kit & Tim Kemp
Manager: Helle Jensen
10 Monmouth Street
London WC2H 9HB, England
Tel: (020) 7806 1000, Fax: (020) 7806 1100
58 rooms
Double: £220–£280*, Suite: £325–£595*
*Breakfast (£16.50), service (12.5%) & VAT not included
Credit cards: all major
Nearest underground: Covent Garden

The Cranley is a delight—a Victorian townhouse hotel on a quiet street in South Kensington, handy for museums, shopping, and exhibition areas, run by an attentive, friendly, and enthusiastic team. Its public areas and 38 immaculate bedrooms are decorated with great taste and a superb eye for detail. The elegant drawing room is serene and inviting, with blue walls, long blue drapes, comfortable seating, antique pieces, and a lovely mirror over the fireplace. The spacious, air-conditioned guestrooms, three with four-posters, all have excellent beds with attractive white spreads, soothing decor, good lighting, working desks, ISDN lines, TV Internet access, and sparkling bathrooms stocked with plush bathrobes. Three bedrooms have views of London and the penthouse room enjoys its own terrace. Guests are spoiled with special treats such as a welcome drink, fruit basket in the bedroom, and afternoon tea, and baby-sitting service is available. Also available are ten nice suites/apartments (in line for renovation) with cooking facilities and dining areas, perfect for families.

THE CRANLEY
Manager: Karen Dukes
10–12 Bina Gardens
London SW5 0LA, England
Tel: (020) 7373 0123, Fax: (020) 7373 9497
Email: info@thecranley.com
38 rooms
Double: £180–£220*, Suite/Apt: £210–£250*
*Breakfast & VAT not included
Credit cards: all major
Nearest underground: Gloucester Road
www.karenbrown.com/ews/cranley.html

Dorset Square Hotel, a beautifully restored Regency townhouse, is located in the area of London made famous by Sherlock Holmes and just down the road from Madame Tussaud's. The traditional English decor uses lots of antiques, original oils, and unusual flower arrangements. The air-conditioned bedrooms have marble bathrooms and the more expensive rooms are lovely. If you stay in one of the hotel's smallest, least expensive rooms, you find yourself enjoying the fabulous ambiance of an elegant hotel at a price that is good value for money. The Potting Shed Restaurant, where you can hear live jazz, lives up to its name in its design, with terra-cotta pots piled up against the wall, pots of flowers on the tables, and a glass ceiling over half of the room. There's a very country feeling to this small hotel within easy reach of Bond Street, Regent's Park, the theaters, and the West End.

DORSET SQUARE HOTEL
Owners: Kit & Tim Kemp
Manager: Justin Childs
39–40 Dorset Square
London NW1 6QN, England
Tel: (020) 7723 7874, Fax: (020) 7724 3328
37 rooms, 1 suite
Double: from £140*, Suite: from £240*
*Breakfast (£11.75–£14), service (12.5%) & VAT not included
Credit cards: all major
Nearest undergrounds: Marylebone & Baker Street

Dukes is a very special little hotel—it remains one of our favorites. Conveniently located only steps from St. James's Street, Dukes is tucked into its own little gas-lit courtyard. Just off the lobby is a snug lounge and beyond is a paneled cocktail bar famous for its dry martini cocktails and selection of vintage cognacs where Gilberto, one of the most delightful barmen in London, holds court with a twinkle in his eye. The airy conservatory is an excellent place to enjoy light meals, coffee, and afternoon tea. The air-conditioned guestrooms are of the luxurious country-house genre, varying in size from spacious rooms through splendid suites with large bedrooms and impressive lounges to the Penthouse suite with its spectacular nighttime view across the rooftops to floodlit Big Ben and Westminster Abbey. A health club opened in June 1999.

DUKES HOTEL
Manager: Andrew Phillips
35, St. James's Place
London SW1A 1NY, England
Tel: (020) 7491 4840, Fax: (020) 7493 1264
89 rooms, 8 suites
Double: £225–£260*, Suite: £350–£550*
*VAT not included
Credit cards: all major
Nearest underground: Green Park

The suites at Durley House on Sloane Street are for those who want to have their own pied-à-terre in the heart of Knightsbridge. Kit and Tim Kemp (who also own the Dorset Square Hotel and the exquisite Pelham) have spared no expense in outfitting the suites in an attractive, traditional country-house style. Besides a bedroom and separate living room, all have a well-stocked kitchen. The large, luxurious suites, although expensive for two, would prove a good value for a family or couples traveling together. If requested, a waiter will bring you dinner and serve it to you in your apartment. Energetic guests have the use of a tennis court in the private gardens across the way. A short walk brings you to Sloane Street's sophisticated shops.

DURLEY HOUSE
Owners: Kit & Tim Kemp
Manager: Elizabeth Bates
115 Sloane Street
London SW1X 9PJ, England
Tel: (020) 7235 5537, Fax: (020) 7259 6977
11 suites
Double: £295–£550*
*Service (12.5%) & VAT not included
Credit cards: all major
Nearest underground: Sloane Square

There is no sign that this Victorian townhouse in a quiet part of Chelsea is a hotel. You ring the doorbell, step into the paneled hall, sign the visitors' book, and are enveloped by the refined atmosphere of days gone by. It is rather like a discreet private club: Victorian wing chairs, guests daintily sipping afternoon tea, whispered conversations, a chauffeured Mercedes at your bidding. There is no restaurant, though light meals and breakfast are available to you through room service. Larger bedrooms are very quiet as all but one are at the back of the hotel. The hotel also has a fully equipped gymnasium.

ELEVEN CADOGAN GARDENS
Manager: Mark Fresson
11 Cadogan Gardens
London SW3 2RJ, England
Tel: (020) 7730 7000, Fax: (020) 7730 5217
60 rooms
Double: £208–£270*, Suite: £295–£398*
*Breakfast (£13.50) & service (3%) not included,
VAT included
Credit cards: all major
Nearest underground: Sloane Square

The Franklin is three houses in a mansion terrace knocked into one, just off the bustle of Brompton Road, an intimate hotel of the home-away-from-home genre. An elegant, traditional drawing room opens up to a tranquil oasis of green garden, the communal backyard for the mansions that abut it. Breakfast can be taken either in the dining room or in the privacy of your bedroom and 24-hour room service is available. Rooms come in all shapes and sizes, the premier ones being the loveliest of rooms with exquisite décor. I would opt for a large room rather than a junior suite.

THE FRANKLIN
Manager: Karen Marchant
28 Egerton Gardens
London SW3 2DB, England
Tel: (020) 7584 5533, Fax: (020) 7584 5449
47 rooms
Double: £200–£350*, Suite: £260–£350*
*Breakfast (£10–£16) & VAT not included
Credit cards: all major
Nearest undergrounds: Knightsbridge & S. Kensington

On a quiet side street just round the corner from Buckingham Palace, The Goring prides itself on being one of London's premier luxury hotels. George Goring and his dedicated staff take great pride in offering guests a warm welcome and every Sunday Mr Goring invites guests to his cocktail party (6–7 pm). The standard bedrooms offer the highest level of comfort, with luxurious decor and beautiful marble bathrooms. All are air-conditioned and several overlook a peaceful garden (three have private balconies). Although elegant and polished, the decor displays a humorous theme. Comic strips from Mr Goring's personal memoirs are exhibited throughout and two large West-Country sheep sit either side of the drawing-room fireplace while the rest of the flock reside in several of the bedrooms.

THE GORING
Owner: George Goring
Manager: William Cowpe
Beeston Place
Grosvenor Gardens
London SW1W 0JW, England
Tel: (020) 7396 9000, Fax: (020) 7834 4393
74 rooms
Double: £240–£290*, Suite: £320–£375*
*Breakfast (£17.50) & VAT not included
Credit cards: all major
Nearest underground: Victoria

Henry Togna's grandfather opened 22 Jermyn Street in 1915 as residential chambers—that is, in-town accommodation for country squires. Now it's a gracious townhouse hotel on an upscale street in close proximity to West End theatres and Piccadilly. A long hallway leads you between a bespoke gentlemen's tailors and Bates, a wonderful old-fashioned gentlemen's hat shop, to the desk at the foot of the stairs (there are no public rooms) and from here you are escorted to your luxurious room or elegant suite. Rooms are beautifully decorated in lovely, rich-colored fabrics. A kitchen provides room service and bread for feeding the ducks in St. James's Park. From taking you jogging to advising you about everything London, the staff is extremely friendly and the location is perfect.

22 JERMYN STREET
Owner: Henry Togna
Manager: Laurie Smith
22 Jermyn Street
London SW1Y 6HL, England
Tel: (020) 7734 2353, Fax: (020) 7734 0750
Email: office@22jermyn.com
5 studios, 13 suites
Studio: £210*, Suite: £295–£335*
*Breakfast (£12.65) & VAT not included
Credit cards: all major
Nearest underground: Piccadilly Circus
www.karenbrown.com/ews/jermyn.html

Close to Harrods and Hyde Park and just a few yards from the Knightsbridge tube station, the Knightsbridge Green Hotel stands out as a hotel where the staff is wonderfully friendly, the location superb, the price reasonable, and ice always available. It is located in a tall, narrow building where an old-fashioned lift takes you from the street-level lobby to the six floors of bedrooms. Refurbishments are constantly ongoing and every bedroom is large and air-conditioned. Rooms are spacious and suites have a separate sitting room, some with a sofa bed. The decor is sunny, with pastel-washed walls and pretty fabrics and bathrooms are sparkling and modern. An English, Continental, or Express breakfast is served in the rooms. Complimentary coffee and tea are available on request. Guests have the use of a nearby health club with fully equipped gymnasium and swimming pool. This is a very popular hotel, so it is advisable to book well ahead.

KNIGHTSBRIDGE GREEN HOTEL
Owners: Marler family
Manager: Paul Fizia
159 Knightsbridge
London SW1X 7PD, England
Tel: (020) 7584 6274, Fax: (020) 7225 1635
Email: thekghotel@aol.com
28 rooms
Double: £145*, Suite: £170*
*Breakfast not included
Credit cards: all major
Nearest underground: Knightsbridge
www.karenbrown.com/ews/knightsbridgegreen.html

This little gem is the sister property of the adjacent Capital Hotel. A small brass plaque discreetly identifies its doorway and the desk in the entrance hall serves as the very informal reception. The lobby's beautifully stenciled walls are most attractive and you find lovely artwork throughout. L'Hotel is a sophisticated bed and breakfast decorated in a delightfully simple, French-country style with pine furniture. There are no public rooms—breakfast is served either in the restaurant, Le Metro, or in the guestrooms. Le Metro also has good-value lunches and dinners. Bedrooms are delightful and each offers some special appeal, whether it is a larger bath, more spacious bedroom, or its own fireplace. With enough notice, you may be able to reserve the top-floor suite or a fireplace room.

L'HOTEL
Owner: David Levin
28 Basil Street
London SW3 1AS, England
Tel: (020) 7589 6286, Fax: (020) 7823 7826
Email: reservations@lhotel.co.uk
12 rooms
Double: £145*, Suite: £165*
*VAT not included
Credit cards: all major
Nearest underground: Knightsbridge
www.karenbrown.com/ews/lhotel.html

The Leonard, occupying a historic handsome townhouse, sits on a quieter street behind Marble Arch and just steps from Portman Square. The reception area is very elegant, featuring a gorgeous flower arrangement on a lovely antique table. The 20 air-conditioned suites and 11 bedrooms are beautifully decorated with a combination of traditional furniture, both contemporary and antique, elegant fabrics, and distinctive objects d'art. Each has a marble en-suite bathroom, mini bar, satellite television, video player, telephone, and dedicated line for fax or modem. The hotel's four dramatic Grand Suites are particularly impressive. The café-bar offers breakfast and light meals throughout the day, and the professional "can-do" staff provide valet, concierge, and 24-hour room service. An exercise room and secretarial facilities are special bonuses.

THE LEONARD
Managing Director: Bijan Daneshmand
15 Seymour Street
London W1H 5AA, England
Tel: (020) 7935 2010, Fax: (020) 7935 6700
Email: the.leonard@dial.pipex.com
11 rooms, 20 suites
Double £220*, Suite: £280–£550*
*Breakfast (£18.50) & VAT not included
Credit cards: all major
Nearest underground: Marble Arch
www.karenbrown.com/ews/theleonard.html

Sitting on the edge of Hyde Park, the London Elizabeth Hotel has a wide variety of well-priced accommodations (Continental breakfast is included in the room rate), a relaxed atmosphere, and dedicated, hands-on owners. Formerly three Victorian private houses, the hotel retains many of the lovely original features such as wooden wall paneling and stained glass. Guestrooms come in all shapes and sizes, from spacious and high-ceilinged on the lower floors to small and snug with sloping floors on the top floor, once the servants' quarters. Second-floor rooms are extremely appealing—more like living rooms with beds than bedrooms—and those at the front enjoy their own balconies. The four-poster room is romantic with oak beams and brick fireplace, but my favorite spot is the light-filled, split-level, semicircular Conservatory Suite with its panoramic stained-glass windows and private terrace. The Hyde Park Suite is huge and lavishly appointed, while the Greville Janner Suite is quietly comfortable. Adding to the London Elizabeth's charm are two sweet gardens, one producing herbs for the restaurant and the other ablaze with roses—a tranquil retreat for a "country moment" in the center of town.

LONDON ELIZABETH HOTEL
Owners: Karen & Peter Newman
Lancaster Terrace
London W2 3PF, England
Tel: (020) 7402 6641, Fax: (020) 7224 8900
Email: reservations@londonelizabethhotel.co.uk
49 rooms
Double: £115–£160*, Suite: £140–£250*
*Continental breakfast & VAT included
Credit cards: all major
Nearest underground: Lancaster Gate
www.karenbrown.com/ews/elizabeth.html

You might well pass by The Pelham thinking this is a private club, for with its discreet exterior, only the flag and classy brass plaque signify that a hotel is within. Inside, no expense has been spared to create an inviting, traditional atmosphere—lavish bouquets of flowers, gorgeous antiques, and original oil paintings set the mood of a fetching English country house hotel. Public areas such as the lovely small, paneled lounge and attractive lower-ground restaurant and bar invite you to linger. Accommodations, which range from large suites to smaller rooms with twin, queen, or king beds, are equipped with every amenity including mobile phones, modem points, and VCRs. The very friendly staff really strives to make this a home away from home. The Kemps' cuisine and stylish decor attract a number of celebrities. Surrounding you are the interesting boutiques, museums, antique shops, and restaurants of South Kensington and Knightsbridge.

THE PELHAM HOTEL
Owners: Kit & Tim Kemp
Manager: Sharon Pinchbeck
15 Cromwell Place
London SW7 2LA, England
Tel: (020) 7589 8288, Fax: (020) 7584 8444
51 rooms
Double: £180–£250*, Suite: £275–£690*
*Breakfast (£15.50), service (12.5%) & VAT not included
Credit cards: all major
Nearest underground: South Kensington

One of the joys of staying in this luxurious boutique hotel is that you can enjoy an avant-garde, offbeat decor. The Sloane's distinct personality is apparent from the moment you enter the lobby with its antique luggage piled beneath an ancestral portrait and beside a Napoleonic sofa covered in fake leopard skin (for those who can't resist, know that absolutely everything is for sale). A tiny lift whisks you up to the bedrooms, each very differently decorated, generally with heavy tapestry fabrics, and furnished with lovely antiques. I loved the decadence of room 101 (a superior deluxe room) but preferred room 302, a two-level suite presided over by a grand canopied bed ornately draped in shades of lime-green and mauve. The hotel takes great pride in offering guests attentive service.

SLOANE HOTEL
Manager: Xavier Colin
29 Draycott Place
London SW3 2SH, England
Tel: (020) 7581 5757, Fax: (020) 7584 1348
Email: sloanehotel@btinternet.com
12 rooms
Double: £150–£195*, Suite: £240*
*Breakfast (£12) & VAT not included
Credit cards: all major
Nearest underground: Sloane Square
www.karenbrown.com/ews/sloane.html

The bustle of London seems far away from this quiet, refined hotel in historic St. James's, just a short walk from Piccadilly. Some of London's most exclusive real estate is tucked back in the privacy of this cul de sac. The Stafford carries the air of a private club for a privileged few. Ornate plaster ceilings grace the elegant lounge and excellent dining room. The amiable, private-club atmosphere is enhanced by a colorful little bar with attractive patio leading onto a cobbled courtyard. Deluxe bedrooms and The Guv'nor's Suite are found in the Carriage House, built in the 1700s. Like the guestrooms located within the hotel they are all decorated in a most luxurious manner and equipped with absolutely everything, including two phone lines and air conditioning.

THE STAFFORD
Manager: Terry Holmes
16–18 St. James's Place
London SW1A 1NJ, England
Tel: (020) 7493 0111, Fax: (020) 7493 7121
Email: info@thestaffordhotel.co.uk
67 rooms, 14 suites
Double: £290–£310*, Suite: £365–£735*
*Breakfast (£16.50) & VAT not included
Credit cards: all major
Nearest underground: Green Park
www.karenbrown.com/ews/thestafford.html

Hotels in England

Rothay Manor is an exceptionally enjoyable hotel with the feel of a refined, old-fashioned British resort hotel where everything is done with kindness and without fuss. In the afternoon an array of trim little sandwiches, decorated cakes, and biscuits tempts you to partake of tea. Bedrooms, decorated in a modern style, are comfortable and spotlessly kept—those at the front have balconies opening up to the garden and are preferable to those at the rear where a main road can disturb a quiet night's sleep during the summer when you are likely to have your windows open. A most attractive downstairs bedroom is available for those who use a wheelchair or have difficulty with stairs. The weather report is posted in the hallway so you can be prepared for the fickle Lake District weather. The Lake District's picturesque villages and stunning scenery are easily reached by car or explored on foot. Dove Cottage, Wordsworth's home, now a museum, is nearby. *Directions:* From Ambleside follow signs for Coniston (A593) and you will find the hotel in the middle of the one-way system on the outskirts of town.

ROTHAY MANOR
Owners: Nigel & Stephen Nixon
Rothay Bridge
Ambleside
Cumbria LA22 0EH, England
Tel: (015394) 33605, Fax: (015394) 33607
Email: hotel@rothaymanor.co.uk
15 rooms, 3 suites
Double: £125–£195, Suite: £175–£230
Closed Jan 3 to Feb 8
Credit cards: all major
Children welcome
www.karenbrown.com/ews/rothay.html

People enjoy themselves at Amerdale House—they relax, they unwind, shed tension, and slip into unconcerned relaxation. They spend their time walking the miles of paths that beckon walkers to this part of the world, meandering along the lanes exploring the Yorkshire Dales, or just pottering round the picturebook village and popping in for a drink and a chat at the pub. Nigel and Paula Crapper set this mood of utter relaxation. While Paula concentrates on seeing that guests are well taken care of, Nigel makes sure that they are well fed, offering every evening a set menu with choices in all but the fish course. This large Victorian house lends itself beautifully to accommodating guests and while the public rooms are spacious and airy, bedrooms tend to be on the snug side. It's an utterly quiet and peaceful spot—a perfect base for touring the Dales and visiting Fountains Abbey, Skipton Castle, and Harewood House. York is just 50 miles distant and Settle (the start of the Settle to Carlisle railway) is a spectacular 14-mile drive away. *Directions:* From Grassington (on the B6265 Ripon to Skipton road) take the B6160 towards Kettlewell and just after Kilnsey Crag turn left into Littondale. Amerdale House is on your left as you enter Arncliffe.

AMERDALE HOUSE HOTEL
Owners: Paula & Nigel Crapper
Arncliffe, Littondale, Skipton
North Yorkshire BD23 5QE, England
Tel: (01756) 770250, Fax: (01756) 770266
11 rooms
Double: £150*
*Includes dinner, bed & breakfast
Open mid-Mar to Oct
Credit cards: MC, VS
Children welcome

Just off the main A6 between the delightful market town of Bakewell and the Victorian spa town of Buxton is the pretty village of Ashford-in-the-Water. In the center of the village, next to the ancient Sheepwash bridge, Riverside House sits in a walled garden that borders the River Wye. The smartly appointed drawing room looks towards the river but the heart of the house is the comfortable golden-oak-paneled bar where a log fire burns brightly when needed. Here, before and after dinner, drinks are served. In the adjacent dining rooms dinner is from a set menu, which changes regularly. More casual fare is available in the conservatory. Bedrooms in the old house vary in size and are tastefully decorated, with the premier room being Kingfisher, a four-poster room with its large bay window offering lovely river views. Rooms in the "new" (albeit traditionally designed) wing are uniform in size, individually decorated, and have the advantage of immaculate modern bathrooms. Off the beaten tourist track, Derbyshire is an area of unsurpassed beauty. Long country walks in the Peak District National Park, visits to neighboring village pubs, and explorations of the stately Chatsworth estate, Haddon Hall, and Hardwick Hall are pursuits to be recommended. *Directions:* Ashford-in-the-Water is 2 miles northwest of Bakewell on the Buxton road (A6).

RIVERSIDE HOUSE
Manager: James Lamb
Ashford-in-the-Water
Near Bakewell
Derbyshire DE45 1QF, England
Tel: (01629) 814275, Fax: (01629) 812873
15 rooms
Double: £115–£155
Open all year
Credit cards: all major
Children over 8

Blagdon Manor is a spacious 17th-century farmhouse tucked away at the heart of the gently undulating northwest Devon countryside. Like our favorite romantic hideaways, it is very remote and sits in a landscape of fields and quiet country lanes. The manor was built as a large farmhouse in 1600, with an addition of a spacious Georgian drawing room contributing elegance. Liz and Steve run their little hotel almost single-handedly so that guests really feel they are staying in the countryside with friends. Steve prepares a three-course dinner (five or six choices per course), which is served at individual tables in the dining room. After dinner, guests often enjoy a game of billiards in the bar, or relax by the fire in the library lounge—rooms reached by going up the narrow winding staircase, past the bedrooms, and down again. Most of the country-cozy bedrooms are decorated in bright, sunny colors. Each is accompanied by an immaculate white bathroom. To the west lie Boscastle Harbor and the ruins of Tintagel Castle while to the south you find Llanhydrock, a not-to-be-missed stately home. *Directions:* Leave Launceston on the A388, Holsworthy road. Pass Chapman's Well and the first sign to Ashwater. Turn right at the second Ashwater sign (8 miles from Holsworthy) and first right, signposted Blagdon. Blagdon Manor is on the right.

BLAGDON MANOR
Owners: Liz & Steve Morey
Ashwater
Devon EX21 5DF, England
Tel: (01409) 211224, Fax: (01409) 211634
7 rooms
Double: £95
Open all year
Credit cards: all major
Children over 12

There can be no better fate for a rundown country estate than to fall into the hands of Historic House Hotels who have meticulously restored Hartwell House, which opened its doors as a luxurious country house hotel in 1989. The Great Hall with its ornate fireplace and decorative ceiling sets the scene for the grandeur of the place, yet this is no stuffy hotel—there is a comfortable air of informality. To the left is the oak-paneled bar which leads to the morning room and the library. The dining room is composed of several adjoining rooms that overlook the garden. The second-floor bedrooms, named after the members of the exiled King of France Louis XVIII's court who occupied them, are the largest and several have four-posters. Cozier, and less expensive, are the attic bedrooms, some of which open out onto a sheltered roof terrace where rabbits were reared and vegetables grown by the French émigrés. More bedrooms are found in the stable building adjacent to the conference center and Hartwell Spa with its spacious indoor swimming pool, gym, and beauty salons. A path leads into the walled garden, which houses two tennis courts. The surrounding parkland with its ruined church, pavilion, and lake is perfect for long country walks. Oxford is just 20 miles away and Heathrow airport is less than an hour's drive. *Directions*: Hartwell House is 2 miles from Aylesbury on the A418, Oxford road.

HARTWELL HOUSE
Manager: Jonathan Thompson
Aylesbury
Buckinghamshire HP17 8NL, England
Tel: (01296) 747444, Fax: (01296) 747450
Toll-free fax from USA: (800) 260-8338
46 rooms
Double: £225–£395*, Suite: £395–£700*
*Breakfast not included: £15.90
Open all year, Credit cards: all major
Children over 8
Relais & Châteaux Member

The Cavendish Hotel sits at the edge of the Chatsworth estate, which surrounds one of England's loveliest stately houses, the home of the Duke and Duchess of Devonshire. Eric Marsh, the owner, has restored and expanded what was originally an 18th-century fishing inn into a fine hotel. The Garden Room (perfect for lunch and informal dinners) frames a panoramic view of the River Derwent meandering through green fields across the estate; comfy sofas and chairs in the adjacent lounge invite you to linger and relax. The bar is a cozy gathering spot for drinks before dinner in the highly commended dining room (you can request a table in a corner of the kitchen if you are anxious to peek at what happens behind the scenes). Bedrooms in the oldest part of the hotel have a lovely feel to them: I particularly enjoyed the spaciousness and old-world ambiance of the superior rooms. An adjoining wing of bedrooms with a more contemporary style has been built to match the original building and called the Mitford Rooms after their designer, the Duchess of Devonshire, and her Mitford family. A pathway leads you on a beautiful walk through the Chatsworth estate to Chatsworth House. Explorations farther afield reveal unspoilt villages set in beautiful rolling countryside of stone-walled fields, green valleys, and spectacular dales. *Directions*: Exit the M1 motorway at junction 29 and follow signs for Chatsworth through Chesterfield to Baslow.

CAVENDISH HOTEL
Owner: Eric Marsh
Baslow
Derbyshire DE45 1SP, England
Tel: (01246) 582311, Fax: (01246) 582312
Email: info@cavendish-hotel.net
24 rooms
Double: £125–£145*, Suite: £195*
*Breakfast not included: £12.55
Open all year, Credit cards: all major
Children welcome
www.karenbrown.com/ews/cavendish.html

Fischer's at Baslow Hall is a dream place for a relaxed getaway, with splendid cooking, especially friendly service, and the nearby delights of the Peak District National Park. This superb house with its lead-paned windows set in stone frames, dark-oak paneling, and wide-plank wooden floors has the feeling of a Tudor manor, yet it was built only in 1907 as a home for the Reverend Jeremiah Stockdale. It continued as a home until 1989 when Susan and Max Fischer purchased it to house their successful restaurant Fischer's, relocated from nearby Bakewell, and also provide the most tasteful of accommodation. The house is furnished and decorated with imagination and flair, with a delightful use of soft yet quite vivid colors to create a feeling of warmth. Additional, lovely garden rooms surround an adjacent courtyard—four have views of the little walled garden while the fifth has a secluded private entry—perfect for hiding away. Max is a dedicated chef, offering traditional English dishes as well as more elaborate fare on his mouthwatering menus. Café Max is a simpler, less expensive dining alternative to the restaurant. The surrounding countryside offers plenty to keep you busy for a week or longer—Chatsworth House, Haddon Hall, and (farther away) Hardwick Hall; mellow stone villages, the spa town of Buxton, and glorious Peak District scenery. *Directions:* Exit the M1 motorway at junction 29 and follow signs for Chatsworth through Chesterfield to Baslow where you follow the A623, Manchester road. Baslow Hall is on the right.

FISCHER'S AT BASLOW HALL
Owners: Susan & Max Fischer
Calver Road, Baslow
Derbyshire DE45 1RR, England
Tel: (01246) 583259, Fax: (01246) 583818
11 rooms
Double: £100–£150*, Suite: £150*
*Continental breakfast
Closed Christmas, Credit cards: all major
Children over 10
www.karenbrown.com/ews/fischersatbaslowhall.html

From the moment you enter through the rustic porchway into the long, low, whitewashed Pheasant inn, you are captivated by its charms: a front parlor all decked in chintz with an old-fashioned, open fire; a dimly lit, Dickensian bar with tobacco-stained walls and ceiling, oak settles, and clusters of tables and chairs; a long, low-beamed dining room, its tables covered with crisp damask cloths; dramatic fresh and dried flower arrangements; a blazing fire in the hearth beneath a copper hood in the large, airy sitting room, the former farmhouse kitchen dating back over 400 years. It is reputed that the legendary John Peel used to be one of the 19th-century regulars in the bar. I attest to the deliciousness of their traditional Cumbrian afternoon tea. Each spacious and inviting bedroom has a large modern bathroom. I much prefer the bedrooms in the main house to those in the adjacent Garden Lodge. Behind the inn a garden, with benches lining its pathways, tumbles into the beechwoods, which belong (as does the inn) to Lord Inglewood's estate. The Pheasant sits on a quiet country lane just out of sight of Bassenthwaite Lake. This is a peaceful part of the Lake District with beautiful views round every corner. Sailing, boating, fishing, bird watching, and, of course, walking are available nearby. *Directions:* The Pheasant is signposted on the A66, at the head of Bassenthwaite Lake, between Keswick and Cockermouth.

THE PHEASANT
Manager: Matthew Wylie
Bassenthwaite Lake
Near Cockermouth
Cumbria CA15 9YE, England
Tel: (017687) 76234, Fax: (017687) 76002
Email: pheasant@easynet.co.uk
16 rooms
Double: £110–£140, Suite: £140–£180
Closed Christmas
Credit cards: MC, VS
Children over 8
www.karenbrown.com/ews/pheasant.html

Recently renovated and restored to its original Georgian style and with all the conveniences expected of a thoroughly modern townhouse hotel, Dukes enjoys a prominent position on Great Pulteney Street, one of Bath's more prestigious boulevards. As might be expected, the bedrooms and suites are named after dukes. Most are airy and spacious and have period plasterwork details and enormous sash windows looking out onto the bustle of the surrounding streets. Owners Sebastian and Philippa Hughes have combined forces with local Michelin-award-winning chef Martin Blunos to create Fitzroys, an intimate brasserie-style restaurant. Accompanied by a chic, green-paneled bar and walled patio, it provides a wonderful setting for lunch, pre-theater drinks, or a complete evening meal. As with all of the Hughes's hotels, Dukes, given adequate notice, accepts well-behaved dogs in the guestrooms. Five minutes' walk from the famous Pulteney Bridge, the hotel is superbly positioned to take advantage of Bath's multitude of sightseeing, shops, and Georgian architecture. *Directions:* Leave the M4 motorway at Junction 18 and head south on the A46. After approximately 9 miles, at the bottom of a long hill, follow signs onto the A4. On the outskirts of town turn left at a traffic light, signposted A36 Warminster (Bathwick Road). At the first roundabout take the second exit into Sydney Place and approximately 150 yards farther on take a half right turn into Great Pulteney Street. Dukes is on the left on the corner with Edwards Street.

DUKES HOTEL   New
Manager: Niall Edmondson
Great Pulteney Street
Bath, Somerset BA2 4DN, England
Tel: (01225) 787960, Fax: (01225) 787961
Email: info@dukesbath.co.uk
18 rooms
Double: £185–£200*, Suite: £235–£250*
*Continental breakfast
Open all year, Credit cards: all major
Children welcome
www.karenbrown.com/ews/dukesbath.html

If you want a fancy city hotel, then The Queensberry Hotel is not for you. However, if you want a small, very friendly, good-value-for-money hotel in the heart of Georgian Bath, on a quiet side street, then this is the place to stay. The ladies who run the front desk are very helpful and friendly and have lots of information on Bath, which you can peruse in the adjacent comfortable drawing room. Guestrooms that were at one time enormous drawing rooms with their tall and often decorative plaster ceilings command the highest tariff. I loved my attic room with its windows looking out across the rooftops though I appreciated having the lift as an alternative to the stairs. In fact, whether your room is below stairs or under the rafters, you will find it appealingly decorated and tastefully appointed. A Continental breakfast is served in your bedroom or a full breakfast in the basement restaurant, the Olive Tree. Decorated in a casual Mediterranean style, the restaurant presents food that merits rave reviews, so it's best to make dinner reservations. *Directions:* When you make your reservation, ask the hotel for the very specific directions on how to find The Queensberry, just a few minutes' walk from the Royal Crescent, to be sent to you. On arrival, double-park in front of the hotel while you unload your bags and receive advice on parking.

THE QUEENSBERRY HOTEL
Manager: Simon Galic
Russel Street
Bath
Somerset BA1 2QF, England
Tel: (01225) 447928, Fax: (01225) 446065
Email: queensberry@dial.pipex.com
29 rooms
Double: £120–£210*
*Continental breakfast included, full breakfast: £9.50
Closed Christmas, Credit cards: MC, VS
Children welcome
www.karenbrown.com/ews/queensberry.html

Two hundred years ago, when the gentry came to Bath to "take the waters," the Royal Crescent was the most prestigious address. Two townhouses in the center of this famous cobbled crescent have been restored and incorporated into an elegant hotel complex with the Dower House, the Bath House, the Garden Villa, and the Pavilion buildings, reached by way of the garden. Furnished with period furniture and works of art, the hotel re-creates the atmosphere of Georgian Bath, which was the social center of England for many years. The elegant drawing room sets the quiet, refined, formal atmosphere of the hotel. An additional drawing room and the gourmet restaurant, Pimpernels, are found in the Dower House. In the main house the sweeping central staircase or the book-lined "library" lift gives access to the stylish, high-ceilinged bedrooms and sumptuous suites, many with ornate plasterwork ceilings. Two totally elegant suites are the Sir Percy Blakeney and the exquisite Duke of York. A range of grand suites and rooms is also found across the garden. To one side of the garden is a small plunge pool where you can swim against a current; to the other is the Bath House, an adult spa that takes you through a sequence of bathing and cleansing—the ultimate in relaxation and pleasure. In the evening you can take a ride in a 1920s launch along the Avon Canal and in the early morning take off from the front lawn in a hot-air balloon. *Directions:* The Royal Crescent is prominently marked on any detailed map of Bath.

THE ROYAL CRESCENT HOTEL
Manager: Kevin Poulter
16 Royal Crescent
Bath
Somerset BA1 2LS, England
Tel: (01225) 823333, Fax: (01225) 339401
45 rooms
Double: £230–£330*, Suite: £440–£880*
*Breakfast not included: from £14.50
Open all year
Credit cards: all major
Children welcome

The Blue Bell Hotel began life in the 1600s as a coaching inn on the London to Edinburgh route, but now the A1 bypasses Belford, a peaceful little place with a couple of shops and The Blue Bell Hotel lining one side of the cobbled market square. Several years ago the Shirley family purchased the inn and they have done a superb job of refurbishing it, keeping its old-fashioned character and decorating throughout in a flowery, warm style. Behind the hotel lies a nicely jumbled garden with lots of nooks and crannies, the perfect place for tea on a warm summer afternoon. Enjoy a drink in the bar (or the more lively tavern next door) and dine in the restaurant or more simply decorated buttery or bar where you can choose from a selection of dishes. A comfortable residents' lounge is yours to relax in. Upstairs, the bedrooms range from smaller double-bedded rooms overlooking the square to the especially attractive room 15, the largest room with a view of the garden. Belford makes a perfect stopover to or from Edinburgh but stay a while and enjoy the many sights that the area has to offer: countless castles, lovely coastal scenery, and nearby Lindisfarne (Holy Island). *Note*: To obtain the special dinner, bed, and breakfast rate please state that you are a Karen Brown reader when making a reservation. *Directions:* From Newcastle take the A1 north for 40 miles, turn left for Belford, and The Blue Bell Hotel faces you when you reach the village square.

THE BLUE BELL HOTEL
Owners: Jean & Paul Shirley
Market Place
Belford
Northumberland NE70 7NE, England
Tel: (01668) 213543, Fax: (01668) 213787
17 rooms
Double: £72–£96
Open all year, Credit cards: all major
Children welcome

Arriving in Blanchland gives one a sense of achievement, for it is far from the beaten path, nestling in a little valley amidst moors and forests. With little cottages, a church, and the Lord Crewe Arms set round a cobbled square, it is a fascinating village which has changed little since it was bequeathed by the Crewe family, in 1721, to a trust that administers the village. Public rooms are intriguing: the abbey kitchen is now the reception-lounge with two elegant old sofas drawn round its fire; the adjacent room has a gigantic fireplace with a "priest's hole," where General Forster hid after his band of Royalist Jacobites was defeated by Cromwell in 1715; the bar with its barrel-vaulted ceiling was once an abbey storeroom. Stairs twist up and around to the bedrooms: Number 17 with large windows overlooking the garden, and 19 with its four-poster bed set under the eaves are the most spacious. Across the cobbled square an additional ten bedrooms occupy The Angel, a former rival temperance hotel. September is the biggest bedroom with a large attic window looking across the cobbled square. The Lord Crewe Arms is an ideal base for explorations of Hadrian's Wall and visiting Beamish Museum. *Directions:* From Newcastle take the A69 to Hexham and turn left in the center of town for the 10-mile drive to Blanchland.

LORD CREWE ARMS
Owners: Alex Todd, & Lindsey Sands
* Peter Gincell & Ian Press*
Blanchland
Near Durham
County Durham DH8 9SP, England
Tel: (01434) 675251, Fax: (01434) 675337
Email: lord@crewearms.freeserve.co.uk
18 rooms
Double: £110
Open all year, Credit cards: all major
Children welcome
www.karenbrown.com/ews/lordcrewe.html

The Devonshire, previously a fishing inn, is now a traditional country house hotel resplendent with swimming pool and health spa. A wing of what were originally contemporary rooms has received a country-house-style refurbishment, though our favorite rooms are the 11 in the original fishing inn (the hotel refers to these as themed rooms). Mitford is feminine, Crace has an elegant four-poster, and Chatsworth with its fireplace is especially spacious. The Duke and Duchess of Devonshire's family portraits add a richness to the Long Lounge with its many groupings of comfortable chairs. Dinner in the Burlington restaurant is a formal affair: request a table in the pretty conservatory. For a move from country house to modern you might want to frequent the adjacent brasserie and bar, reached by a covered flagstone passageway. Just across the garden the barns have undergone a skillful conversion to a spa with indoor swimming pool, gym, and beauty salons. Fast roads lead to York and Harrogate. Upper Wharfedale, one of the most scenic Yorkshire Dales, begins at your back door, the ruins of Bolton Abbey are across the fields, and a short drive brings you to Haworth and the Brontë sisters' parsonage. *Directions:* The hotel is on the B6160, 250 yards north of its roundabout junction off the A59, Skipton to Harrogate road.

THE DEVONSHIRE ARMS
Owners: Duke & Duchess of Devonshire
Managing Director: Jeremy Rata
Bolton Abbey
Near Skipton
North Yorkshire BD23 6AJ, England
Tel: (01756) 710441, Fax: (01756) 710564
Email: sales@thedevonshirearms.co.uk
41 rooms
Double: £180–£235, Suite: £350
Open all year
Credit cards: all major
Children welcome
www.karenbrown.com/ews/devonshirearms.html

Woolley Grange, a gracious, 17th-century manor just outside Bradford-on-Avon, is the only listing in this guide that actively encourages families—they have a very relaxed attitude towards children, and a resident dog completes the picture. The old coach house has been converted to a nursery (there is also a huge games room for older children) where children can spend an hour or a day. Little ones can have lunch and tea in the nursery and be tucked up in bed or watch a video in the library while parents enjoy the most excellent of dinners in the lovely dining room—the essence of a stay at Woolley Grange is eating the most delicious food. The bedrooms are scattered throughout the rambling house and the large cottage across the courtyard. Many have old fireplaces, most have creaking old floorboards, and all have sturdy antiques and old brass or Victorian beds topped with goose-down duvets. There is a large heated swimming pool in the grounds and bikes are available for guests' use. The area is packed with interesting things to do and places to go: historic Bath and Wells, inviting Bradford-on-Avon and Lacock, Longleat House and Safari Park, and Stourhead House and Gardens. *Directions:* Woolley Grange is 8 miles from Bath at Woolley Green, off the B3109 north of Bradford-on-Avon.

WOOLLEY GRANGE
Manager: Clare Hammond
Woolley Green
Bradford-on-Avon
Wiltshire BA15 1TX, England
Tel: (01225) 864705, Fax: (01225) 864059
Email: info@woolleygrange.com
23 rooms
Double: £110–£215, Suite: £180–£255
Open all year, Credit cards: all major
Children welcome
www.karenbrown.com/ews/woolley.html

Farlam Hall is a superb place to hide away for a relaxed holiday and be thoroughly spoiled, enjoying the pampering attentions of this family-run hotel. Mum, dad, son, daughter, and spouses make up the friendly team of one of only a handful of British hotels admitted to the French Relais & Châteaux group. You enter directly into the reception lounge, which is full of sofas and chairs—a perfect spot for afternoon tea. The quality of everything, from the abundant antique furniture to the sumptuous food, is a delight. The same quality and good taste continue in the bedrooms, which vary greatly in shape and size. My favorite larger rooms are the Garden Room, a grand, high-ceilinged room with an enormous four-poster bed, and the Guest Room, a spacious corner room whose large bathroom sports a Jacuzzi tub and separate shower. While Farlam Hall is a perfect place to break your journey if you are traveling between England and Scotland, it would be a shame to spend only one night in this charming hotel. Nearby sightseeing includes Carlisle and Hadrian's Wall. Day trips can be made to the Lake District and the Scottish border towns. *Directions:* Leave the M6 motorway at junction 43 and take the A69 towards Newcastle for 12 miles to the A689 signposted Alston. The hotel is on your left after 2 miles (not in the village of Farlam).

FARLAM HALL
Owners: Joan, Lynne, Barry & Alan Quinion
  Helen & Alastair Stevenson
Brampton, Cumbria CA8 2NG, England
Tel: (016977) 46234, Fax: (016977) 46683
Email: farlamhall@dial.pipex.com
12 rooms
Double: £230–£270*
*Includes dinner, bed & breakfast
Closed Dec 23 to 31, Credit cards: MC, VS
Children over 5
Relais & Châteaux Member
www.karenbrown.com/ews/farlam.html

Gently rolling hills where sheep graze peacefully and shaded valleys with meandering streams surround the picturesque village of Broad Campden where The Malt House hugs the quiet main street and opens up to the rear to a beautiful garden. Years ago barley was made into malt here for brewing beer. Now a picturesque country house, it provides a perfect central location for exploring other Cotswold villages. It is very much a family operation with Nick and Jean at the front of the house and son Julian as the talented chef. Julian offers three choices for each of the three dinner courses served in the inviting dining room where an open fire blazes on chilly evenings. Of the two lounges the little sitting room with its comfortable chairs arranged round the massive inglenook fireplace and mullioned windows offering glimpses of the magnificent garden is a favorite place to relax. The bedroom decor ranges from cottage-cozy to contemporary, and all the immaculate bathrooms have old-fashioned tubs. Five bedrooms, including an 18th-century four-poster room, are in the house, while an inviting ground-floor suite and two bedrooms are in the stable block. Lovely Cotswold villages to explore include Chipping Campden, Bourton-on-the-Water, Upper and Lower Slaughter, Stow-on-the-Wold, Bibury, and Broadway. Garden lovers will enjoy Kiftsgate, Hidcote Manor, and Batsford. *Directions:* On entering Chipping Campden, take the first right: you know you are in Broad Campden when you see the Bakers Arms. The Malt House is opposite the wall topped by a tall topiary hedge.

THE MALT HOUSE
Owners: Jean, Julian & Nick Brown
Broad Campden, Chipping Campden
Gloucestershire GL55 6UU, England
Tel: (01386) 840295, Fax: (01386) 841334
Email: nick@the-malt-house.freeserve.co.uk
8 rooms, Double: £94.50–£117
Closed Christmas, Credit cards: all major
Children welcome
www.karenbrown.com/ews/themalthouse.html

Separated from the main road through Broadway by a grassy green, The Broadway Hotel dates back to Elizabethan times though it has had various additions over the years. The heart of the hotel is a tall, galleried sitting room whose white-plasterwork beamed walls rise to a raftered ceiling. The adjacent Jockey Bar with its horseracing memorabilia is popular with locals and full of old-world pub atmosphere. Tables in the restaurant are set in a room open to the bannistered upstairs hallway or tucked cozily under beams in a room dressed with old copper. Bedrooms stretch back in two wings with one wing accessed off an open stair that winds up from the dining room. All the bedrooms are decorated in country-house style using modern fabrics and antiques. We enjoyed a lovely, quiet room located at the end of the hallway and overlooking the back lawn. The feeling was very traditional, with dark woods complemented by handsome plaid fabrics. Broadway is one of the most bustling Cotswold villages, along with Chipping Campden, Stow-on-the-Wold, and Moreton in Marsh. While in the area do not overlook the quieter villages such as nearby Snowshill where Snowshill Manor, a lovely Tudor home, is open to the public. *Directions:* Broadway is off the A44 between Evesham and Stow-on-the-Wold. The Broadway Hotel is located on the High Street with a car park to the rear.

THE BROADWAY HOTEL
Manager Simon Foster
The Green
Broadway
Worcestershire WR12 7AA, England
Tel: (01386) 852401, Fax: (01386) 853879
19 rooms
Double: £115–£165
Open all year
Credit cards: all major
Children welcome

Set in the popular Cotswold village of Broadway, The Lygon Arms has been an inn since the 16th century. Its numerous little nooks include "the Gin Corner," the original snug with its old log fire; the Inglenook lounge, the inn's ancient kitchen, its huge fireplace hung with blackened spits and hooks; and the domed-ceiling drawing room, all chintz and elegance. The main wing with its creaking floors, heavy beams, and charming rooms furnished with grand antique pieces has a range of different rooms from the least expensive with bathrooms down the hall to the most expensive: the Great Chamber whose ceiling soars to a thicket of beams and the Charles I suite whose oak paneling has a secret staircase. A wing of turn-of-the-century rooms leads to the 1960s Garden Wing with numerous contemporary-style rooms. Old adjoining properties have been taken over: a charming thatched cottage in the garden now houses four of the most luxurious bedrooms; the 18th-century Great Hall with its minstrels' gallery is now the Lygon's restaurant; and across the courtyard is the Lygon Arms spa where residents can enjoy a game of billiards, use the weight room, or swim in the luxurious heated pool. In an adjacent house is Oliver's brasserie. Broadway is the most appealing of the mellow Cotswold stone villages, its main street lined with antique shops and picture galleries. *Directions:* Broadway is off the A44 between Evesham and Stow-on-the-Wold. The Lygon Arms is located on the High Street, with a car park to the rear.

THE LYGON ARMS
Manager: Barry Hancox
Broadway
Worcestershire WR12 7DU, England
Tel: (01386) 852255, Fax: (01386) 858611
Email: info@the-lygon-arms.co.uk
65 rooms
Double: £175–£255*, Suite: £275–£395*
*Breakfast not included: £16.50
Open all year, Credit cards: all major
Children welcome
www.karenbrown.com/ews/lygonarms.html

Two miles from the hustle and bustle of Broadway is the pretty, small village of Buckland where adjacent to the village church sits Buckland Manor surrounded by acres of gorgeous gardens. Wisteria hugs the walls, blowzy roses fill the flowerbeds, and a rushing stream tumbles beside the woodland walk. The exterior sets the tone for an interior where everything is decorated to perfection. Add masses of flowers and enviable antiques and you have the perfect country house hotel. Relax and enjoy a drink before the huge fireplace in the richly paneled lounge, curl up with a book in the sunny morning room, and relish the sense of occasion in the refined dining room. Bedrooms are elegant and every attention has been paid to every luxurious detail—some have wood-burning fireplaces and four-poster beds. From the moment Terry, the hall porter, greets you at the door you will be enveloped in the atmosphere of hushed gentility that pervades this gracious Cotswold manor. Warm weather enables you to enjoy the swimming pool, tennis court, and croquet lawn. Surrounding Buckland are other Cotswold villages with such appealing names as Chipping Campden, Upper and Lower Slaughter, Stow-on-the-Wold, and Upper and Lower Swell. Stratford-upon-Avon, Worcester, Bath, and Oxford are all within an hour's driving distance. Garden lovers will enjoy Kiftsgate, Hidcote Manor, and Batsford. *Directions:* Buckland is 1½ miles from Broadway on the B4632.

BUCKLAND MANOR
Owners: Daphne & Roy Vaughan
Manager: Nigel Power
Buckland, near Broadway
Worcestershire WR12 7LY, England
Tel: (01386) 852626, Fax: (01386) 853557
Email: enquire@bucklandmanor.com
13 rooms, Double: £220–£355, Suite: £325–£355
Open all year, Credit cards: all major
Children over 12
Relais & Châteaux Member
www.karenbrown.com/ews/bucklandmanor.html

Burford House, a charming half-timbered building on the corner of Burford's main street, is owned by Jane and Simon Henty who have lavished much attention on the hotel's interior. Just off the inviting entry with its old wood floors is an enchanting room with tables set for afternoon tea while on the other side is a cozy sitting room whose soft-cushioned chairs sit before an open log fire. The soft-yellow walls of the morning room are especially attractive in the early hours and doors open onto the pretty back courtyard and garden. Burford House has seven guestrooms, all named for local villages and all with en-suite bathrooms (five of the seven rooms have separate walk-in showers in addition to a tub). Swinbrook is a spacious, pretty, garden-level room located in the wing off the courtyard, referred to as the "coach house" (although it is actually part of the main building). At the top of the stairs in the main house and overlooking the bustle of the main street is Sherbourne with its four-poster bed and an enormous bathroom complete with dramatic claw-foot tub. Jane and Simon take great pride in the comfort and enjoyment of their guests and all the rooms enjoy considerate touches such as fresh flowers and reading materials. This small hotel is their home and one is definitely made to feel welcome and cared for. *Directions:* Burford is midway between Oxford and Cheltenham (A40). Burford House is on the main street.

BURFORD HOUSE
Owners: Jane & Simon Henty
99 High Street
Burford
Oxfordshire OX18 4QA, England
Tel: (01993) 823151, Fax: (01993) 823240
Email: stay@burfordhouse.co.uk
7 rooms, Double: £95–£125
Open all year, Credit cards: all major
Children welcome
www.karenbrown.com/ews/burfordhouse.html

The clomp of hooves as horses pulled carriages down the main street of Burford has long disappeared, but the inns that provided lodging and food to weary travelers remain and if you are in search of a simple, quaint hostelry, you can do no better than to base yourself at The Lamb for the duration of your Cotswold stay. A tall, upholstered settle sits before the fireplace on the flagstone floor of the main room, the hall table displays gleaming brass jelly-molds, and an air of times long past pervades the place, particularly in winter when the air is heavy with the scent of woodsmoke and a flickering fire burns in the grate. Little staircases and corridors zigzag you up and down to the little bedrooms, all en suite and simply decorated in a charming, cottagey style. In the dining room choose from the short à-la-carte menu or enjoy the set three-course dinner, which offers three choices for starters and main courses. The homey little bar with its stone-flagged floor and wooden settles has an indefinable mixture of character and atmosphere. Burford's main street is bordered by numerous hostelries and antique, gift, and tea shops. There are mellow Cotswold villages to explore and Blenheim Palace and Oxford are less than an hour's drive away. *Directions:* Burford is midway between Oxford and Cheltenham (A40). The Lamb Inn is on Sheep Street, just off the village center.

THE LAMB INN
Owners: Caroline & Richard De Wolf
Manager: Paul Swain
Sheep Street
Burford
Oxfordshire OX18 4LR, England
Tel: (01993) 823155, Fax: (01993) 822228
15 rooms
Double: £115–£125
Closed Christmas & Boxing Day
Credit cards: MC, VS
Children welcome

The Fell Hotel (as it was known) has long been serving visitors to this lovely part of the Yorkshire Dales and acquired the "Devonshire" in its title in 1998 when it was purchased by the Duke and Duchess of Devonshire to be a sister hotel to the Devonshire Arms, a country house hotel just down the road. Consequently, I expected a traditional interior for this sturdy Yorkshire hotel looking over the River Wharfe to the village of Burnsall, but the interior could not be further from traditional—it is dashingly modern. With the decor offering a broad palette of vivid colors, any rainy-day gloom is instantly dispelled. Relax in the boldly decorated bar and enjoy lunch or an evening meal in the bistro or the conservatory. Selections are made from the menu or from daily specials posted on the board. Bedrooms are found on two floors (no elevator) and range from the crisp Linton room, all decked out in black and white, to oh-so-sunny Cracoe, all in bright yellow hues. Walking is *de rigueur* in this part of the world and several scenic footpaths are on your doorstep. Just down the road are the magnificent ruins of Bolton Abbey, while just up the road is the bustling village of Grassington, which leads you up Wharfedale to the heart of the Yorkshire Dales. Harrogate is close at hand while York is an hour's drive away. *Directions:* From the A59 (Skipton to Harrogate road) take the B6160 past Bolton Abbey and north to Burnsall. As you see the village below you to your right, you find the hotel on your left.

THE DEVONSHIRE FELL
Owners: Duke & Duchess of Devonshire
Managing Director: Jeremy Rata
Burnsall, Skipton
North Yorkshire ND23 6BT, England
Tel: (01756) 729000, Fax: (01756) 729009
E-mail: sales@thedevonshirearms.co.uk
12 rooms
Double: £90–£130
Open all year, Credit cards: all major
Children welcome
www.karenbrown.com/ews/devonshirefell.html

Carlisle makes an excellent place to break the journey when driving between England and Scotland. Your host, Philip Parker, an ardent enthusiast of Carlisle and the surrounding area, encourages guests to use Number Thirty One as a base for visiting the city and exploring the northern Lake District and Hadrian's Wall. One of Philip's great passions is cooking and the dinner he prepares for guests depends on what is fresh in the market that day. Philip and Judith often join guests for a chat after dinner. Upstairs, the three bedrooms are equipped to a very high standard, with TV, trouser press, tea tray, and hairdryer, and furnished in a style complementing this large Victorian terrace home. I admired the spaciousness of the Blue Room with its sparkling Mediterranean bathroom and king-sized bed and enjoyed the sunny decor of the smaller Green Room with its large golden dragon stenciled on the black headboard. The equally attractive Yellow Room has a half-tester bed that can be king-sized or twin and faces the front of the house. A ten-minute stroll finds you in the heart of Carlisle with its majestic cathedral, grand castle, and Tullie House museum, which portrays Carlisle's place in the turbulent history of the Borders. *Directions:* Leave the M6 at junction 43 and follow Carlisle City Centre signs through five sets of traffic lights (the fifth is pedestrian). Howard Place is the next turning on the right (before you reach the one-way system). Number 31 is at the end of the street on the left.

NUMBER THIRTY ONE
Owners: Judith & Philip Parker
31 Howard Place
Carlisle, Cumbria CA1 1HR, England
Tel & fax: (01228) 597080
Email: bestpep@aol.com
3 rooms, Double: £80–£95
Open Mar to Nov
Credit cards: all major
Children over 16
www.karenbrown.com/ews/numberthirtyone.html

Paul and Kay Henderson have achieved their goal of providing one of the finest small hotels and restaurants in England. Guests have come to expect the best and this is what they receive. Prices are high but so are the standards of luxury and the attention to detail. There are only 16 lovely bedrooms: 14 in the beautiful, Tudor-style home and a 2-bedroom suite in a quaint, thatched cottage overlooking the croquet lawns. The largest bedrooms are on the second floor and those at the front of the house offer lovely views across the valley. The public rooms are paneled in oak with open log fires burning throughout the year. Chef Michael Caines professionally designs the evening meal, considering the fresh produce available each day from local farmers, the hotel's own garden, and the catch from local fishermen. Paul is particularly proud of his extensive wine list, one of the finest in Britain. Chagford is a delightful country town on the edge of Dartmoor. The wild beauty of Dartmoor, with its sheltered villages and towns beneath the looming moor, has a magic all its own—country rambles and cream teas are *de rigueur* when visiting this area. *Directions:* From Chagford Square turn right (at Lloyds Bank) into Mill Street. After 150 yards fork right and go downhill to Factory Crossroad. Go straight across into Holy Street and follow the lane for 1½ miles to the end.

GIDLEIGH PARK
Owners: Kay & Paul Henderson
Manager: Catherine Endacott
Chagford, Devon TQ13 8HH, England
Tel: (01647) 432367, Fax: (01647) 432574
Email: gidleighpark@gidleigh.co.uk
14 rooms, 1 cottage
Double: £400–£500*, Suite: £430–£500*
Cottage: £400–£460*
*Includes dinner, bed & breakfast
Open all year, Credit cards: MC, VS
Children welcome
Relais & Châteaux Member
www.karenbrown.com/ews/gidleigh.html

Hotel Kandinsky is probably the last thing you would expect to find in the heart of Regency Cheltenham. A wildly eclectic mix of old and new, business and casual, and decked out with European and Oriental carpets, furniture, and *objets d'art*, this hotel is an experience for the young and young at heart. The expansive entrance with its Indonesian marionettes, lion's-head trophy on the wall, comfortable seating area, and background Muzak gives a hint of what lies beyond. Stylish, spacious, and comfortable bedrooms are equipped with all the latest electronics, from data ports to entertainment systems—even electronic eyes that allow you to scan various areas of the hotel. The bar and adjoining Victorian conservatory are places to enjoy a pre-dinner drink and reflect on the tranquillity of the neighboring Cotswolds. Café Paradiso offers a simple but elegant menu including pizzas, grilled meats, fish, and game accompanied by organic salads and vegetables. A visit to the lipstick-red private dining room, presided over by an impressive painting of an Indian rajah, is a must. Downstairs, U-bahn, in basic black, offers exotic cocktails, food, and dancing in a cosmopolitan nightclub atmosphere. Don't miss the bathrooms! *Directions:* Leave the M5 motorway at Junction 11 and take the A40 into Cheltenham, following signs for the town center. After about 3 miles you pass a Texaco gas station on your right. At the next roundabout take the second exit and Hotel Kandinsky is 200 yards ahead on the sharp right bend.

HOTEL KANDINSKY   New
Manager: Lorraine Jarvie
Bayshill Road, Montpelier
Cheltenham, Gloucestershire GL50 3AS, England
Tel: (01242) 527788, Fax: (01242) 226412
Email: info@hotelkandinsky.com
48 rooms
Double: £90–£115*, Suite: £160*
*Breakfast not included
Open all year, Credit cards: all major
Children welcome
www.karenbrown.com/ews/kandinsky.html

Cheltenham was a fashionable destination during the Regency period and today the classical squares and terraces built in delightful garden settings are the town's pride. A fine Regency villa on the edge of Pittville Park has been beautifully restored and opened as a most attractive hotel by Darryl Gregory. Guests share the comfortable library-sitting room with Emily the cat and enjoy drinks and after-dinner coffee in the high-ceilinged drawing room-cum-bar. While there are several restaurants within walking distance, you can do no better than to dine in the hotel, choosing your meal from the seasonal menu or enjoying the meal of the day. The elegant, smartly decorated bedrooms are named after historic figures associated with the house. I especially enjoyed the Duke of Gloucester room, richly decorated in shades of dark red, and Mead with its sunny yellow decor. Billed as the capital of the Cotswolds, Cheltenham offers excellent shopping and lots of specialist antique shops. Horseracing takes place at Cheltenham during the autumn and winter months. A ten-minute drive finds you in the midst of the honey-colored stone Cotswold villages. *Directions:* Arriving in Cheltenham, follow signs for city center onto the one-way system, then follow signposts for Evesham. The Hotel on the Park is on the left, just as you reach Pittville Park (right) after passing a row of Regency town houses.

HOTEL ON THE PARK
Owner: Darryl Gregory
Evesham Road
Cheltenham
Gloucestershire GL52 2AH, England
Tel: (01242) 518898, Fax: (01242) 511526
Email: stay@hotelonthepark.co.uk
12 rooms
Double: £102.50–£122.50*, Suite: £132.50–£162.50*
*Breakfast not included: £9
Open all year, Credit cards: all major
Children over 8
www.karenbrown.com/ews/hotelonthepark.html

Teresa White, who hails from Edinburgh, prides herself on offering a warm Scottish welcome to her up-market bed-and-breakfast hotel located a brisk 20-minute walk from the heart of medieval Chester. When she bought the Redland in the 1980s, it was very different from the flower-decked, frothily Victorian establishment you find today. Teresa has kept all the lovely woodwork and ornate plasterwork, adding modern bathrooms, central heating, vast quantities of sturdy Victorian furniture, four suits of armor, and masses of Victorian bric-a-brac. Guests help themselves to drinks at the honesty bar and relax in the sumptuous drawing room, which includes among its array of furniture high-backed armchairs that almost surround you. Traditional Scottish porridge is a must when you order breakfast in the dining room where little tables are covered with starched Victorian tablecloths. For dinner Teresa is happy to advise on where to eat in town. Pay the few extra pounds and request one of the "best" rooms, for not only are they more spacious, but you will be treated to a lovely old bed (with modern mattress, of course) and decor where everything from the draperies to the china is color-coordinated. Walking round Chester's Roman walls is a good way to orient yourself to the city. It's fun to browse in The Rows, double-decker layers of shops. *Directions:* Redland Hotel is located on the A5104, 1 mile from the city center.

REDLAND HOTEL
Owner: Teresa White
64 Hough Green
Chester CH4 8JY, England
Tel: (01244) 671024, Fax: (01244) 681309
Email: teresawhite@redlandhotel.fsnet.co.uk
12 rooms
Double: £65–£85, Suite: £75–£85
Open all year, Credit cards: none
Children welcome
www.karenbrown.com/ews/redlandhotel.html

Setting this country house hotel apart are the outstanding facilities offered by its luxurious indoor pool, saunas, steam rooms, solariums, and gym. Coincidentally, it is one of only a handful of hotels where I found families with young children in residence. This old Cotswold manor has two lounges (one all cozy with heavy beams and a welcoming fireplace and the other smart and formal) and a restaurant that extends into several cozy, low-ceilinged rooms. The majority of bedrooms are in adjacent converted farm buildings that have been cleverly connected to the main house by long corridors. I especially enjoyed Corbett, a most attractive room in the original house, and Stratford, a superior room in the one-time farm buildings. Children are welcomed into the dining room at breakfast but in the evening it is preferred that they are served an early supper and tucked into bed so that dinner is an adult occasion. Within 2 miles of Charingworth are Hidcote and Kiftsgate Gardens and Chipping Campden, an adorable 14th-century wool village peppered with heavily thatched cottages. Hidcote Manor Gardens is a series of alluring gardens each bounded by sculpted hedges with linked paths and terraces. Next door, another outstanding garden, Kiftsgate Court, has exquisite displays of roses. *Directions:* From Chipping Campden take the B4035 towards Shipston on Stour and Charingworth Manor is on the left-hand side after 3 miles.

CHARINGWORTH MANOR
Manager: Walter Fallon
Chipping Campden
Gloucestershire GL55 6NS, England
Tel: (01386) 593555, Fax: (01386) 593353
Email: charingworthmanor@englishrosehotels.com
26 rooms
Double: £150–£250, Suite: £275
Open all year
Credit cards: all major
Children welcome
www.karenbrown.com/ews/charingworth.html

Amongst the Cotswolds' picturesque villages you'll discover the town of Chipping Campden, as rich in history as it is in exquisite architecture. In the early-17th-century marketplace stands the Cotswold House Hotel where Irishman Ian Taylor and his American-born wife, Christa, set the highest of standards. Step into the impressive hallway with its stone-paved floor from which a grand staircase spirals up the ornate, *trompe l'oeil* stairwell. Opening up from the hallway are the handsome, high-ceilinged sitting rooms, decked out in traditional country-house finery. Bedrooms display a charming individuality though all have big beds with crisp linen sheets and offer a choice of pillows to ensure a wonderful night's rest. For dinner, choose either the elegant Garden Restaurant where ceiling-high French windows frame views of the garden or the more informal street-front Hicks Brasserie-Bar. The hotel is ideally placed for visits to Shakespeare's Stratford-upon-Avon, Regency Cheltenham, Warwick Castle, and many historic houses and gardens. Add to this the hotel's personal touches—tour guides, picnics, day membership at local golf clubs—and you have a perfect recipe for an enjoyable stay. *Directions:* From Broadway take the A44 towards Moreton in Marsh and turn left for Chipping Campden. At the T-junction turn right into the High Street, and Cotswold House Hotel is on your left in the main square. There is parking for residents behind the hotel.

COTSWOLD HOUSE HOTEL
Owners: Christa & Ian Taylor
The Square, Chipping Campden
Gloucestershire GL55 6AN, England
Tel: (01386) 840330, Fax: (01386) 840310
Email: reception@cotswold-house.com
15 rooms
Double: £140–£195
Open all year, Credit cards: all major
Children over 3
www.karenbrown.com/ews/cotswoldhousehotel.html

Built in the 1930s as a re-creation of a medieval manor that once stood on the site, Bailiffscourt is today a lovely country hotel, an "authentic fake" set in spacious grounds. The snug, golden-stoned buildings really are authentic in that they are constructed from medieval stone, with woodwork and windows obtained from derelict cottages, mansions, and farmhouses. Thick stone walls, small mullioned windows, beamed ceilings, dark paneling, large open fireplaces, courtyards, peacocks, and pieces of medieval furniture all combine to give an "old-world" atmosphere. The interconnecting lounges have warm colors, tapestries, and log fires. Flagstoned halls, reminiscent of castle passageways, lead to the large bedrooms, 15 of which have four-poster beds while 11 have working fireplaces. Bathrooms are large, with wonderful 1930s fixtures, and modern plumbing is a welcome 21st-century addition. Baylies, a decadent suite, has a bathroom with side-by-side "his and hers" baths. Guestrooms are also found in several outlying buildings. The grounds contain tennis courts and a large swimming pool in a parklike setting. Just minutes from the sea, Bailiffscourt is an ideal base for exploring the south coast, being close to Arundel's magnificent castle, the Pavilion at Brighton, Chichester's celebrated theatre, and glorious Goodwood. *Directions:* Climping is between Littlehampton and Bognor Regis just off the A259.

BAILIFFSCOURT
Manager: Axel Bambach
Climping
Near Littlehampton
West Sussex BN17 5RW, England
Tel: (01903) 723511, Fax: (01903) 723107
Email: bailiffscourt@hshotels.co.uk
31 rooms
Double: £150–£270, Suite: £290–£320
Open all year, Credit cards: all major
Children over 8
www.karenbrown.com/ews/bailiffscourt.html

In the middle of the pretty redbrick village of Cuckfield you find Ockenden Manor, in part Tudor, with Victorian and contemporary additions. Viewing the manor from the garden, you appreciate that this combination of building styles is very pleasing. The spacious sitting room overlooks the garden and the adjacent dining room, with its dark-oak paneling and low, decorative-plasterwork ceiling, is most attractive. A maze of winding corridors and stairs leads to the atmospheric rooms in the older wing with their paneled walls, uneven floors, and plethora of four-poster beds (mostly queen-sized). I particularly enjoyed the Charles room with its large stone fireplace, Elizabeth for its third-floor isolation atop a narrow staircase, and Master, a spacious, paneled twin-bedded room with an adorable little parlor overlooking the garden. Avoid the possibility of getting lost in the maze of corridors and opt for easier-to-locate rooms in the Garden Wing with its new rooms made to look old. Less than a half-hour drive finds you in Brighton where seaside honky-tonk contrasts with the vivid spectacle of the onion domes of the Royal Pavilion, the Prince Regent's extravaganza of a home. Enjoy browsing in Brighton's Lanes where old fishermen's cottages are now antique and gift shops. *Directions:* From Gatwick airport take the M23/A23 to the B2115 signposted Cuckfield. In Cuckfield village, turn right into Ockenden Lane—the manor is at the end.

OCKENDEN MANOR
Manager: Kerry Turner
Ockenden Lane, Cuckfield
West Sussex RH17 5LD, England
Tel: (01444) 416111, Fax: (01444) 415549
Email: ockenden@hshotels.co.uk
22 rooms
Double: £140–£210, Suite: £250–£280
Open all year, Credit cards: all major
Children welcome
www.karenbrown.com/ews/ockenden.html

Gravetye is a truly handsome Elizabethan manor house set in the most glorious of gardens. It is one of the very best country house hotels and remains steadfastly one of our favorites. You catch the spirit of the place as soon as you walk into the oak-paneled hall with its big fireplace and comfortable armchairs enticing relaxation. The lovely sitting room with its enormous stone fireplace has the same atmosphere of age-old comfort. Bedrooms are elegantly yet comfortably furnished with soft-toned fabrics, which contrast warmly with intricately carved wood paneling. Firescreens hide televisions and interesting books are close at hand. You will love the acres of gardens flourishing just as former owner William Robinson, who pioneered the natural look in English gardens, would have wished them to. His beloved kitchen garden has been restored and chef Mark Raffan (who has been awarded a Michelin star) knows well what to do with its produce. Other glorious English gardens within easy driving distance include Sissinghurst and Sheffield Park with its splendid examples of rare trees. Just down the road is Standen, one of the finest Arts and Crafts houses, with furnishings by Morris and Benson. It's a very handy place to stay for both Glyndebourne and Gatwick airport. *Directions:* Exit the M23 at junction 10 onto the A264, signposted East Grinstead. After 2 miles, at the roundabout, take the B2028 (Haywards Heath and Brighton) and after Turners Hill watch for the hotel's sign.

GRAVETYE MANOR
Owner: Peter Herbert, Manager: Andrew Russell
Near East Grinstead
West Sussex RH19 4LJ, England
Tel: (01342) 810567, Fax: (01342) 810080
Email: info@gravetyemanor.co.uk
18 rooms, Double: £200–£260*, Suite: £310–£330*
*Breakfast not included: £16
Open all year, Credit cards: MC, VS
Babes in arms & children over 7
Relais & Châteaux Member
www.karenbrown.com/ews/gravetye.html

Nestling up to the little village of Evershot deep in Thomas Hardy country, Summer Lodge was built by the Earl of Ilchester in 1789. Thomas Hardy (who was an architect before he became a writer) designed the Lodge's first addition, the elegant high-ceilinged drawing room. In more recent times Margaret and Nigel Corbett added their own changes with the conversion of the stables into luxurious bedrooms and the building of a swimming pool and tennis court. The result is a house of contrasts where you walk from cozy-cottage sitting room (complete with resident cat) to gracious, high-ceilinged drawing room with floor-to-ceiling windows. It's a similar situation with the bedrooms, which vary from cottage-cozy to the expansive spaciousness of room 1 (I particularly enjoyed rooms 17 and 18 with their private patios bordering the swimming pool). If you want complete privacy, opt for a room in the old cottage that fronts the village street. Whatever room you choose, you will enjoy the mellow tranquillity of this hotel with its exquisite restaurant and delightful decor enhanced by beautiful flower arrangements. *Directions:* From Dorchester take the A37 towards Yeovil for 10 miles and turn left for Evershot. When you arrive at the village, turn left into Summer Lane and the hotel is on your right after 100 yards.

SUMMER LODGE
Owners: Margaret & Nigel Corbett
Manager: Thierry Lepinoy
Evershot
Dorset DT2 0JR, England
Tel: (01935) 83424, Fax: (01935) 83005
Email: reception@summerlodgehotel.com
17 rooms
Double: £125–£245, Suite: £285
Open all year
Credit cards: all major
Children welcome
www.karenbrown.com/ews/summer.html

This dignified old house was built in 1840 by a local lad, Sir Charles Hanson, who, having made a fortune in Canada, returned home to construct an impressive mansion. Fortunately, it has come into the hands of the Luxury Family Hotels group (Woolley Grange was their first venture) who have lovingly restored, decorated, and furnished the place. Directly you walk in the front door you catch the spirit of the house with its spacious, airy rooms, sturdy antiques, huge windows, and comfortable, inviting settees and armchairs—all of this without one iota of hauteur. Dine *al fresco* in the informal Palm Court terrace where soup, sandwiches, burgers, and fries are on the menu or enjoy classic country-house fare in the plush, oak-paneled restaurant. The only room I was able to see was a premier suite with a small bedroom, large sitting room, and bathroom overlooking the estuary. The largest bedrooms are the eight in the adjacent coach house. There's a lot to keep you busy: splashing in the pool and playing badminton, Nintendo, table tennis, table soccer, and pool. For the under-sevens the "Bears Den" is staffed by nannies. It's a wonderful place whether or not you have children—a perfect base for exploring Cornwall with its rugged coastline and plethora of gardens. *Directions:* One mile after Lostwithiel (going south on the A390) turn left onto the B3269 to Fowey. Follow the main road into the village, bearing right on Hanson Drive. Pass the car park on your right and Fowey Hall is the next entry to the right.

FOWEY HALL
Manager: Hazel Brocklebank
Hanson Drive
Fowey
Cornwall PL23 1ET, England
Tel: (01726) 833866, Fax: (01726) 834100
Email: info@foweyhall.com
25 rooms
Double: £150–£275, Suite: £200–£275
Open all year, Credit cards: all major
Children welcome
www.karenbrown.com/ews/fowey.html

Fowey is one of Cornwall's most picturesque villages. Former fishermen's cottages and narrow streets step down the steep hillside to the river estuary where boats bob in the sheltered harbor. Sitting beside the water, The Marina Hotel was built in 1815 as a handsome townhouse. On a 2000 visit I found the new owners, the Westwell family, in residence and eager for the season to be over to give all the bedrooms and bathrooms a complete face-lift. It would be a shame to stay here and not have a bedroom with a view, the best views being from rooms with French windows opening onto private balconies. At the top of the house two lovely rooms capture the same outlook through little curved windows. If you want to be right beside the water, opt for the Fo'c's'le Suite, a wooden cabin on the lower patio with a nautical pine interior. While the bedroom and sitting room face the patio, French windows open to a private waterside terrace. Every table in the Waterside Restaurant looks out over the harbor and the menu includes lots of fish choices. Guests often come to see the places where Fowey's most illustrious former resident, Daphne du Maurier, set her most famous novels. *Directions:* One mile after Lostwithiel (going south on the A390) turn left onto the B3269 to Fowey. Continue down into the narrow lanes of the village and turn right on the Esplanade. Park outside the hotel to unload and get parking directions.

THE MARINA HOTEL
Owner: Stephen Westwell
Manager: James Coggan
17 Esplanade, Fowey
Cornwall PL23 1HY, England
Tel: (01726) 833315, Fax: (01726) 832779
Email: marina@dial.pipex.com
11 rooms
Double: £80–£150, Suite: £130–£150
Open Mar to mid-Dec, Credit cards: all major
Children over 9
www.karenbrown.com/ews/marina.html

At the mouth of the River Helford you find Tregildry Hotel set on a bluff high above the sea overlooking the river estuary and in the distance the broad reaches of Falmouth Bay—a magnificent seascape. Perhaps a former owner's desire to cram as much building as possible into this lovely spot accounts for Tregildry's higgledy-piggledy exterior. However, under the direction of Huw and Lynne Phillips Tregildry has become a harmonious whole. The spacious drawing room, decorated in soft pastels, leads to a cozy nook with low sofas drawn round the fire. Next door the dining room has an almost Caribbean flavor with high-back cane chairs. The bedrooms have been decorated with light rattan furniture contrasting with Provençal-type draperies and bedspreads, giving a crisp, airy feel to the rooms. Huw is in charge of the kitchen while Lynne is the convivial hostess, making sure that guests are well taken care of. A path leads down the hillside to join the coastal walking trail. *Directions:* From Helston take the A3083 (Lizard road) for 3 miles, turn left on the B3293 signposted St. Keverne, and from here follow signposts carefully for Helford (you do not go there), then Manaccan, and finally Gillan. Tregildry is signposted from Gillan.

TREGILDRY HOTEL
Owners: Lynne & Huw Phillips
Gillan, Manaccan, Helston
Cornwall TR12 6HG, England
Tel: (01326) 231378, Fax: (01326) 231561
Email: trgildry@globalnet.co.uk
10 rooms
Double: £130–£170*
*Includes dinner, bed & breakfast
Open Mar to Oct
Credit cards: MC, VS
Children over 8
www.karenbrown.com/ews/tregildry.html

The heart and soul of a successful country house hotel are its owners and at Stock Hill House Nita and Peter Hauser fill the bill perfectly, with the ebullient Nita presiding over the front of house and Peter being the chef. Prior to opening, Nita and Peter spent several years restoring and furnishing this Victorian home. The result is a pleasing, eclectic decor and the mood is that of a luxurious private residence where you can stroll through the acres of garden to work up an appetite. At dinner vegetables from the garden and local Dorset produce are the order of the day, but remember to save room for one of Austrian-born Peter's decadent desserts. Bedrooms are delightful, and while I was particularly drawn to the opportunity to repose in an elegant, extra-large, ornate wrought-iron bed, which once belonged to a Spanish princess, I settled on an equally lovely room with a non-historic bed and a large bathroom. This lovely hotel is the perfect place for you to treat yourself to an extra-special getaway. If you are tempted to leave the grounds, you'll find the location ideal for visiting Sherbourne Abbey, Stourhead Gardens, Wells Cathedral, Glastonbury with its King Arthur connections, and the Saxon town of Shaftesbury. *Directions:* Leave the M3 at junction 8 and take the A303 towards Exeter for 54 miles, turning onto the B3081 for Gillingham and Shaftesbury. Stock Hill House is on your right after 3 miles.

STOCK HILL HOUSE
Owners: Nita & Peter Hauser
Gillingham
Dorset SP8 5NR, England
Tel: (01747) 823626, Fax: (01747) 825628
Email: reception@stockhill.co.uk
9 rooms
Double: £250–£300*
*Includes dinner, bed & breakfast
Open all year, Credit cards: MC, VS
Children over 7
Relais & Châteaux Member
www.karenbrown.com/ews/stockhill.html

High on the hillside above the popular Lake District village of Grasmere, isolated by 3 acres of secluded gardens, sits Michael's Nook, a grand Victorian house now run as a superlative country house hotel by Elizabeth and Reg Gifford. You enter into a large wood-paneled, antique-filled entrance hall which leads to the drawing room with its large windows framing gorgeous green views of the garden, soft damask sofas, Oriental carpets, and on either side of the grand fireplace massive flower arrangements. Guests gather in the homely, old-world-hostelry-style bar before dinner. The heart of Michael's Nook is the restaurant whose deep-red walls and gleamingly polished tables set with silver and crystal form an elegant backdrop for dinner. Chef Michael Wignall's Michelin-star cooking is a major attraction. Bedrooms come in all shapes and sizes (and all price ranges) from the least expensive, small but pretty room to the grandest suite, which has a sitting room upstairs, a spiral staircase leading down to the bedroom, and French doors opening onto a garden terrace. Personal favorites are the twin, Woodpecker, and the four-poster room, Chaffinch. Just down the lane is Dove Cottage, where poet William Wordsworth lived from 1799 to 1808. Also nearby is Beatrix Potter's home at Sawrey. *Directions:* Take the A591 to Grasmere: do not go into the village but turn uphill off the A591 beside the Swan Hotel.

MICHAEL'S NOOK
Owners: Elizabeth & Reg Gifford
Grasmere, near Ambleside
Cumbria LA22 9RP, England
Tel: (015394) 35496, Fax: (015394) 35645
Email: m-nook@wordsworth-grasmere.co.uk
14 rooms
Double: £192–£370*, Suite: £370–£410*
*Includes dinner, bed & breakfast
Open all year, Credit cards: all major
Children by arrangement
www.karenbrown.com/ews/michaelsnook.html

This cozy little hotel tucked in a garden off the Ambleside to Grasmere road has (like so many places hereabouts) associations with poet William Wordsworth who lived just down the road at Rydal Mount—his descendants lived in it until the 1930s. Now it is owned by Susan and Peter Dixon who, while giving guests their personal attention, give the same attention to detail that you find at much fancier establishments. Peter exercises his culinary talents in the delightful five-course dinners, which are freshly prepared and served in the cottage-style dining room. The small adjacent lounge guarantees conviviality amongst the guests. Room 1, an attractive twin-bedded room with a ribbon-and-bow-motif running through the bedspread fabric, has a tiny bathroom and small grassy patio. Room 7, found atop a spiral staircase, offers a spacious bathroom and can be king-bedded or twin. Room 6, decorated in shades of blue, also enjoys a larger bathroom and private patio. Two additional bedrooms are close by in Brockstone Cottage. Guests can fish on nearby Rydal Water and have free use of a local leisure club. Lakeland scenery is glorious whether you come in spring when the famous daffodils bloom, in summer with the crowds, or in autumn when the bracken and leaves turn golden-brown. You can stroll to Rydal Mount and Dove Cottage, Wordsworth's famous homes. *Directions:* White Moss House is on the A591 between Ambleside and Grasmere.

WHITE MOSS HOUSE
Owners: Susan & Peter Dixon
Rydal Water
Grasmere
Cumbria LA22 9SE, England
Tel: (015394) 35295, Fax: (015394) 35516
Email: sue@whitemoss.com
9 rooms
Double: £80–£130
Open Mar to Dec, Credit cards: MC, VS
Children over 8, Restaurant closed Sun evening
www.karenbrown.com/ews/whitemoss.html

Near the center of England lies Oakham, the proud capital of England's smallest county, Rutland. Close by is Rutland Water where you drive onto a spit of land stretching out into the middle of the lake. At its end is the quiet village of Hambleton and a jewel of a hotel, Hambleton Hall. The staff is caring, anxious above all else to please. The motto over the front door echoes the relaxed, happy atmosphere: "Fay Ce Que Voudras" or "Do As You Please"—I cannot imagine anyone leaving Hambleton Hall discontented. The garden tumbles towards the vast expanse of water with rolling hills as a backdrop and behind a wall is a sheltered, heated pool. The interior is decorated with great flair and complemented by enormous flower arrangements. The drawing room with its large inviting windows provides glorious water views. In fine weather enjoy lunch and tea on the terrace. Delicious smells will tempt you to the award-winning restaurant. The bedrooms are adorable, the decorations varying from soft English pastels to the vibrant rich colors of India. Tim Hart produces a witty booklet, "Things to do around Hambleton Hall," which covers shopping in Oakham and Stamford, visits to the country houses of Burghley and Belton, and trips to Cambridge and Lincoln. *Directions:* From the A1 take the A606 (Oakham road) through Empingham and Whitwell and turn left for Hambleton.

HAMBLETON HALL
Owners: Stefa & Tim Hart
Hambleton, near Oakham
Rutland LE15 8TH, England
Tel: (01572) 756991, Fax: (01572) 724721
17 rooms
Double: £210–£345*, Suite: £515*
*Continental breakfast included, full breakfast: £12
Open all year
Credit cards: all major
Children welcome
Relais & Châteaux Member

On the banks of the River Avon sits The Mill at Harvington, converted from the bakery served by the original mill downstream. This is an unpretentious, very welcoming hotel run with great enthusiasm by Jane and Simon Greenhalgh and Sue and Richard Yeomans. Several small rooms have been combined into a sitting room where heavy bakehouse oven doors decorate the fireplace mantle, small Victorian-style parlor chairs in shades of burgundy and jade are arranged into little conversation groups, and French windows open to a broad expanse of lawn sloping down to the river. Smaller rooms named after different types of bread are found in the old mill while a newer wing houses larger, more luxurious rooms. All are prettily decorated in very soft shades of pink, blue, and peach. If you stay for two nights, ask for the well-priced dinner, bed, and breakfast rate. From Harvington a half-hour drive brings you to the china factories at Worcester, the magnificent castle at Warwick, Shakespearean Stratford, and Cotswold villages such as Chipping Campden and Broadway. *Directions:* Take B4088 north out of Evesham towards Norton. At the Norton roundabout, turn right towards Bidford, ignoring signs to Harvington. Turn right after 1 mile down Anchor Lane where The Mill is clearly signed.

THE MILL AT HARVINGTON
Owners: Jane & Simon Greenhalgh
  Sue & Richard Yeomans
Anchor Lane
Harvington, Evesham
Worcestershire WR11 5NR, England
Tel & fax: (01386) 870688
21 rooms
Double: £88–£129
Closed Christmas
Credit cards: all major
Children over 10
www.karenbrown.com/ews/harvington.html

Hathersage is a typically picturesque Derbyshire village situated in the lovely Hope Valley. It is a place that has impressed many visitors over the years, the most famous being Charlotte Brontë who was said to be so taken with it that she based parts of her novel *Jane Eyre* on it. The George sits imposingly at one end of the main street that runs through the village. Parts of the hotel date back to the 14th century when it was an alehouse, but it wasn't until the 1770s that The George became an inn. The lounge is a light and airy room, well furnished with lots of comfy sofas and decorated in blues and terra-cottas, which give it warmth, while amusement is offered by the whirligig sculpture which periodically performs its antics. The bar, in the corner, makes this an ideal place to relax and enjoy a pre-dinner drink. The color schemes are carried through to the restaurant, which has an intimate, bistro-like feel. Upstairs, the bedrooms have the same light and airy feel as the lounge. I really liked room 3, which is pretty and spacious with a four-poster bed and a very unusual round stained-glass window depicting St. George. The hotel is set amidst glorious walking country and the reception staff are happy to lend you maps and offer advice. Hathersage is well placed for visiting the Peak District National Park, Chatsworth House, Haddon Hall, and Castleton's caverns. *Directions:* Exit the M1 at junction 29 towards Baslow then take the A623 to the B6001 through Grindleford to Hathersage. At the junction with the main road the George faces you.

THE GEORGE
Owner: Eric Marsh, Manager: Peter Marsh
Hathersage
Derbyshire S32 1BB, England
Tel: (01433) 650436, Fax: (01433) 650099
Email: info@georgehotel.net
19 rooms
Double: £99.50–£119.50
Open all year, Credit cards: all major
Children welcome
www.karenbrown.com/ews/thegeorge.html

Helmsley, a collection of gray-stone houses grouped round a traditional market square, lies at the edge of the glorious North York Moors, an area of wild and magnificent scenery where webs of little roads cross vast stretches of heather-covered moorlands joining hamlets and villages nestling in snug green valleys. Bordering the market square, a traditional old Yorkshire coaching inn has served travelers for well for over 150 years in this beautiful town. Old adjoining properties have been taken over—a Georgian house and a black-and-white Tudor rectory. A large new wing of rooms has been built next to the lovely back garden where chairs are set on the lawns amongst beds of scented flowers. But The Black Swan is little changed: its higgledy-piggledy maze of little low-beamed rooms gives it a snug feeling, and its traditional furniture, lounges with old-fashioned chintzy chairs, and attentive staff all add to its charms. Eating and drinking is a great joy at The Black Swan. The chef knows how to satisfy Yorkshire tastes and appetites with traditional roasts, fillets, and chops. Fresh fish and vegetarian dishes are always on the menu. The most popular places to visit are Rievaulx Abbey, York, Castle Howard, Robin Hood's Bay, Whitby, and the folk museum at Hutton-le-Hole. *Directions:* Helmsley is on the A170 midway between Thirsk and Pickering.

THE BLACK SWAN
Manager: Gavin Dron
Helmsley
North Yorkshire Y06 5BJ, England
Tel: (01439) 770466, Fax: (01439) 770174
45 rooms
Double: £145–£160
Open all year
Credit cards: all major
Children welcome

Hintlesham Hall is a serene country house hotel that you will soon come to love. The grand Georgian façade is well matched inside, with the grand salon sumptuously decorated in soft pastels highlighting its lofty ceiling. More intimate in their proportions are the pine-paneled dining room and the book-lined library lounge with its Regency-red walls and soft-green sofas. There is an array of bedrooms varying in size from opulent, two-story affairs, through grand, traditional four-poster rooms to small, snug bedrooms. The warm, pine-paneled bar with its comfortable sofas and chairs grouped round a large fireplace and the large book-lined library with its magnificent old billiard table are particularly inviting. Bedrooms have lovely fabrics, sparkling modern bathrooms with a profusion of toiletries, and views over miles of peaceful countryside. There is a state-of-the-art fitness and health center and just a few yards from the hotel is a magnificent 18-hole golf course, which is very popular with guests. A 45-minute drive will find you in Cambridge, while closer at hand you can visit Flatford Mill, the area where Constable painted several of his most famous paintings, and the medieval wool towns Lavenham, Kersey, and Long Melford with their majestic churches and timber-framed buildings. *Directions:* Just before reaching Ipswich on the A12 take the A1071 (signposted Hintlesham and Hadleigh)—Hintlesham Hall is on your right after 3 miles.

HINTLESHAM HALL
Manager: Tim Sunderland
Hintlesham, near Ipswich
Suffolk IP8 3NS, England
Tel: (01473) 652268, Fax: (01473) 652463
33 rooms
Double: £120–£235*, Suite: £250–£375*
*Breakfast not included: £7.50
Open all year
Credit cards: all major
Children welcome

Langshott Manor is a beautiful Elizabethan house with 3 acres of gorgeous gardens and ponds, which, with just 15 bedrooms in the main house and adjacent stable wings, still retains the intimate feeling of a home. The interior more than exceeds the promise of the historic exterior: at every turn you admire low-ceilinged, beamed rooms, polished oak paneling, and stained-glass windows with motifs of flowers in bloom and birds in flight. The Mulberry Restaurant is an especially spacious room overlooking a small lake and lovely gardens. Bedrooms are an absolute delight. I especially enjoyed Leeds with its four-poster bedroom and whimsical four-poster bathroom and Lewes, a most spacious room whose windows frame the rose garden. Two smaller bedrooms (Hever and Wakehurst) are found on the ground floor. Equally lovely rooms are found across the gardens in the former stables, now a luxurious mews offering spacious, bright rooms with king-sized beds and comfortable seating areas. The manor is just 2½ miles from Gatwick airport (not on the flight path) and offers complimentary transfer to the airport on departure. Churchill's home, Chartwell, the Royal Horticultural Society Gardens at Wisley, and Brighton are amongst the most popular visitor attractions. *Directions:* From Gatwick take the A23 north towards Redhill for 2½ miles to the large roundabout with a garage in the middle and bordered by the Chequers pub. Take the Ladbroke Road exit from the roundabout and follow the lane to the hotel on the right.

LANGSHOTT MANOR
Owners: Deborah & Peter Hinchcliffe
Manager: Kenneth Sharp
Horley, Surrey RH6 9LN, England
Tel: (01293) 786680, Fax: (01293) 783905
E-mail: admin@langshottmanor.com
15 rooms
Double: £175–£250, Suite: £275
Open all year, Credit cards: all major
Children over 10
www.karenbrown.com/ews/langshott.html

No need to request a room with a view at Nonsuch House, for every room offers a spectacular panorama of the sheltered harbor of Dartmouth with its castle, houses tumbling down the wooded hillside to the river, and yachts tugging at their moorings. The view won the hearts of Patricia, Geoffrey, and Christopher Noble (a parents-and-son trio) who decided to reduce the workload involved in running an upscale country house hotel (Langshott Manor) and concentrate on the aspect of the hospitality business that gives them most satisfaction—looking after their guests. After a day of sightseeing, enjoy a set, three-course dinner in the conservatory and watch the activity in the harbor below. Bedrooms, which come with a choice of queen, king, or twin beds, are absolutely delightful and each is accompanied by an immaculate modern bathroom. A fun day trip involves taking a ferry and steam train into Paignton. On Tuesdays in summer you can take the ferry to Totnes and stroll around the market admiring the townsfolk in their colorful Elizabethan costumes. *Directions:* Two miles before Brixham on the A3022 take the A379. After 2 miles fork left onto the B3205 for Kingswear, go onto the one-way system through the woods, and take the first left up Higher Contour Road. Go down Ridley Hill and Nonsuch House is on the seaward side at the hairpin bend. Parking is on the street.

NONSUCH HOUSE
Owners: Patricia, Geoffrey & Kit Noble
Church Hill
Kingswear, Dartmouth
Devon TQ6 0BX, England
Tel: (01803) 752829, Fax: (01803) 752357
Email: enquiries@nonsuch-house.co.uk
5 rooms
Double: £80
Open all year, Credit cards: none
Children over 10
www.karenbrown.com/ews/nonsuch.html

At the Sign of the Angel is a black-and-white timbered inn at the heart of the well-preserved National Trust village of Lacock. This 15th-century wool merchant's house is easy to spot as it contrasts strikingly with its neighboring stone buildings. The main dining room is a mixture of antique tables clustering around a large fire. A smaller, adjacent dining room is perfect for private parties. Dinner is always by candlelight and centers around a traditional English roast main course (with a fish or vegetarian alternative) and choices being given for starters and desserts. Heavy old beams, low ceilings, and crooked walls add to the rustic elegance of the inn. The bedrooms are small and cozy with low doors, uneven creaking floors, and ancient timbers. If you have difficulty with narrow stairs and uneven floors, you may prefer the ground-floor double-bedded room. Nestled among the bedrooms on the first floor is a comfortable, inviting residents' lounge. Four additional delightful country-style bedrooms are found in the cottage at the bottom of the garden. Be sure to leave time to visit the Fox Talbot Museum of early photographs and Lacock Abbey. Lacock is just 12 miles from Bath. *Directions:* If you are arriving from London, exit the M4 at junction 17 and take the A350 Melksham road south to Lacock.

AT THE SIGN OF THE ANGEL
Owner: George Hardy
Church Street
Lacock
Near Chippenham
Wiltshire SN15 2LB, England
Tel: (01249) 730230, Fax: (01249) 730527
Email: angel@lacock.co.uk
10 rooms
Double: £99–£137.50
Closed last week of Dec, Credit cards: all major
Children welcome
www.karenbrown.com/ews/signoftheangel.html

The village of Lastingham is unhurried and peaceful, an oasis of green surrounded by the rugged, untamed beauty of the North York Moors National Park. Lastingham Grange preserves a 1950s style—everything is in apple-pie order, with such things as flowery wallpapers, patterned carpets, and candlewick bedspreads giving an old-fashioned air. I love the long lounge crowded with intimate groupings of sofas and chairs where in the morning the smell of furniture polish mixes with fresh-brewed coffee as you enjoy your morning coffee and homemade biscuits. The charm of the house extends outside where a broad terrace leads to the rose garden and acres of less formal gardens, which give way to fields and the distant moor. Guests of all ages and their dogs are welcome—there are listening devices for babies and a large adventure playground tucked beyond the formal garden where older children can romp and play. The village church dates back to 1078 when a group of monks built a crypt to house the sacred remains of St. Cedd, which now remains a church beneath a church. Thirty miles distant lies medieval York and, closer at hand, narrow roads lead you to the coast with its fishing villages and long sandy beaches. *Directions:* Take the A170 from Thirsk towards Pickering. Just after Kirbymoorside turn left to Hutton-le-Hole where you turn right and cross the moor to Lastingham. The hotel is on your left in the village.

LASTINGHAM GRANGE
Owners: Jane & Dennis Wood
Lastingham
York Y062 6TH, England
Tel: (01751) 417345, Fax: (01751) 417358
Email: reservations@lastinghamgrange.com
12 rooms
Double: £168–£210
Closed Dec to Feb
Credit cards: MC, VS
Children welcome
www.karenbrown.com/ews/lastingham.html

Lavenham with its lovely timbered buildings, ancient guildhall, and spectacular church is the most attractive village in Suffolk. The Great House on the corner of the market square, a 15th-century building with an imposing 18th-century façade, houses a French restaurant-with-rooms run by Martine and Regis Crepy. Dinner is served in the oak-beamed dining room with candlelight and soft music and is particularly good value for money from Monday to Friday when a fixed-price menu is offered. On Saturday you dine from the à-la-carte menu. The restaurant is closed on Sundays and Mondays. In summer you can dine *al fresco* in the flower-filled courtyard. The large bedrooms all have a lounge or a sitting area and bathroom. Architecturally the rooms are divinely old-world, with sloping plank floors, creaking floorboards, little windows, and a plethora of beams. Enjoy the village in the peace and quiet of the evening after the throng of daytime summer visitors has departed. Next door, Little Hall is furnished in turn-of-the-century style and is open as a museum. Farther afield are other historic villages such as Kersey and Long Melford, and Constable's Flatford Mill. *Directions*: Lavenham is on the A1141 between Bury St. Edmunds and Hadleigh.

THE GREAT HOUSE
Owners: Martine & Regis Crepy
Market Place
Lavenham
Suffolk CO10 9QZ, England
Tel: (01787) 247431, Fax: (01787) 248007
Email: greathouse@clara.co.uk
5 rooms
Double £90–£140, dinner £19.95 (not Sun or Mon)
Closed Jan
Credit cards: all major
Children welcome
www.karenbrown.com/ews/greathouse.html

Lavenham is the epitome of an old-world English village with many half-timbered houses, and a 16th-century cross and Guildhall, an impressive structure built in the 1520s, which now contains a museum tracing 700 years of wool trade. The Swan is now a sophisticated hotel but was once several houses—the town's ancient Wool Hall and humbler weavers' dwellings. The hotel is the flagship of the Forte Heritage group who have tastefully joined these lovely old buildings round a courtyard garden, preserving ancient beams and whitewashed plaster and timbered walls. The delightful galleried entrance leads you to quaint, beamed lounges that beckon you to partake of a traditional afternoon tea. The hub of the hotel is its snug bar whose floor is made of bricks brought to Lavenham after being used as ships' ballast and which is full of World War II memorabilia from the time it was the local for American airmen. Narrow corridors and steep staircases wind you to 51 beamed bedrooms tucked into nooks and crannies. The larger, quieter rooms with views are termed "feature rooms." The restaurant offers a set three-course dinner with lots of choices. As a dining alternative consider the Great House, a country-French restaurant on the Market Square. A few miles from here are other delightful Suffolk villages: Kersey, Long Melford, and Constable's Flatford Mill. *Directions*: Lavenham is on the A1141 between Bury St. Edmunds and Hadleigh.

THE SWAN
Manager: Francis Guildea
High Street
Lavenham
Suffolk CO10 9QA, England
Tel: (0870) 4008116, Fax: (01787) 248286
51 rooms
Double: £145–£165*, Suite: £175–£195*
* Breakfast (£14.95) & service (12.5%) not included
Open all year
Credit cards: all major
Children welcome

As you walk directly into the oak-paneled hall, you catch the spirit of this lovely house with its enormous stone fireplace, ornate, stone mullioned windows, and plump sofas enticing you to sit and relax. The adjacent paneled dining room has the same comfortable, inviting atmosphere. The dark-oak paneling, the carvings, and the ornate plasterwork ceilings are the grand embellishments added by Lewtrenchard Manor's most famous owner, the Reverend Sabine Baring Gould, who composed many well-known hymns. The lovely bedrooms are all different, named after the melodies of the Reverend's tunes—Melton and Prince Rupert are four-poster rooms. Sue and James run the house themselves and guests appreciate the homelike atmosphere. You do not see many hotelkeepers making tea for guests, serving drinks in the bar, and chatting in front of the fire with guests as Sue does. You cannot beat this hotel for friendliness and hospitality. Within a short drive are Castle Drogo, a fanciful Lutyens house, Lydford Gorge, an outstanding beauty spot, Dartington Glass, wild Dartmoor, and the north and south coasts of Devon. *Directions:* From Exeter (the M5) take the A30 for Okehampton and Bodmin and after 25 miles take the A386 slip road off the highway. Immediately turn right and left onto the old A30 for Bridestowe and Lewdown. After 6 miles of single carriageway (just after Jethro's) turn left at the sign marked "Lewtrenchard ¾ mile."

LEWTRENCHARD MANOR
Owners: Sue & James Murray
Lewdown
Near Okehampton
Devon EX20 4PN, England
Tel: (01566) 783256, Fax: (01566) 783332
Email: s&j@lewtrenchard.co.uk
9 rooms
Double: £125–£170, Suite: £180
Open all year, Credit cards: all major
Children over 8
www.karenbrown.com/ews/lewtrenchardmanor.html

The Arundell Arms is a traditional fishing inn that provides its guests the opportunity to fish for salmon, trout, and sea trout in miles of river and a 3-acre lake. Owner Anne Voss-Bark, an expert fisherwoman ably assisted by head bailiff Roy Buckingham and instructor David Pilkington, offers a variety of residential fishing courses. Fisherfolk gather in the morning in the hotel garden's 250-year-old cock pit (a long-since retired cock-fighting arena), now the rod-and-tackle room. In the evening the catch of the day is displayed on a silver platter on the hall table. The traditional fishing inn has been extended over the years to encompass the village assembly rooms—now the elegant, tall-ceilinged dining room where you enjoy the most delectable of dinners—and the courthouse and jail—now the adjacent village pub. Cozy bedrooms, all but two of which face the garden, are found in a converted stable block and the main house. Non-fisherfolk can enjoy walking, riding, golf, and, of course, traditional cream teas of scones, clotted cream, and jam. Sightseers head for Dartmoor and the north Cornish coast with the ruins of Tintagel Castle and the ancient fishing villages of Boscastle and Port Isaac. *Directions:* Exit the M5 at Exeter and take the A30 (signposted Bodmin) for approximately 40 miles to the Lifton Village exit. Once off the dual carriageway turn right for Lifton and the hotel is on your left in less than a mile.

ARUNDELL ARMS
Owner: Anne Voss-Bark
Manager: Sally Hill
Lifton
Devon PL16 0AA, England
Tel: (01566) 784666, Fax: (01566) 784494
Email: reservations@arundellarms.com
22 rooms
Double: £120, Suite: £150
Closed Christmas, Credit cards: all major
Children welcome
www.karenbrown.com/ews/arundell.html

Lower Slaughter Manor sits beside the church tucked behind a high stone wall in the heart of one of England's prettiest villages. The style of the house is grand and the furnishings are elegant, but the friendly, down-to-earth hospitality saves the hotel from being too formal. One of the most attractive rooms is the blue-and-pink-paneled drawing room with its magnificent ornate plasterwork ceiling and attractive decor. Upstairs the window seat in the galleried landing overlooks the garden and a 15th-century dovecote. The bedrooms are large and attractively decorated with quality fabrics. Splurge and request Antoinette, with its ornate 19th-century four-poster bed and views across the front lawn. I preferred the rooms in the house to the luxurious suites in the adjacent coach house. Extras include sherry, toffees, biscuits, and bathrobes, which are handy for crossing the cellars to the indoor heated swimming pool and sauna. Amongst the more popular (crowded) nearby Cotswold villages are Bourton-on-the-Water, Stow-on-the-Wold, Chipping Campden, and Broadway. On the quieter side, consider the hamlets of Lower and Upper Swell, Stanton, Stanway, and Snowshill. *Directions:* From the A429 on the outskirts of Bourton-on-the-Water a small signpost indicates "The Slaughters." Follow the lane and the manor is on your right.

LOWER SLAUGHTER MANOR
Owners: Daphne & Roy Vaughan
Manager: Sean Davies
Lower Slaughter
Gloucestershire GL54 2HP, England
Tel: (01451) 820456, Fax: (01451) 822150
16 rooms
Double: £175–£350, Suite: £350–£400
Open all year
Credit cards: all major
Children over 12

The gently flowing River Eye meanders past the mellow golden-stone cottages of Lower Slaughter, an idyllically pretty, much-photographed Cotswold village. With acres of lawn stretching down to the river, the Washbourne Court Hotel is made up of a row of 17th-century cottages cleverly combined and extended to form an inviting country house hotel of great charm. Flagstone floors topped with Oriental rugs, low, beamed ceilings, and huge fireplaces are the order of the day in the series of cozy lounges that lead one to the other. The spacious, more contemporary dining room is the setting for long, elegant dinners, like those served in its gracious sister hotel, Lower Slaughter Manor. Cottage suites with their own sitting rooms occupy two separate building in the grounds, but I much preferred the bedrooms in the main house. Rose is an outstandingly pretty room in the oldest party of the building while April, June, Sarah, Polly, and Amy are other very attractive bedrooms. Popular places to visit include bustling Bourton-on-the-Water and Stow-on-the-Wold. Shakespeare's Stratford-upon-Avon, Warwick Castle, Blenheim Palace, and Georgian Bath are all within an hour's drive. *Directions:* From the A429 on the outskirts of Bourton-on-the-Water a small signpost indicates "The Slaughters." Follow the lane and the Washbourne Court is on your left.

WASHBOURNE COURT HOTEL
Owners: Daphne & Roy Vaughan
Manager: Adam Smith
Lower Slaughter
Gloucestershire GL54 2HJ, England
Tel: (01451) 822143, Fax: (01451) 821045
Email: washbournecourt@.msn.com
17 rooms, 11 suites
Double: £155–£225, Suite: £185–£225
Open all year
Credit cards: all major
Children over 12
www.karenbrown.com/ews/washbourne.html

The Blackett family have been prominent citizens around these parts since 1673 when Sir William Blackett was knighted for his support of the king during the Civil War. The hall has grown over the years, with most of what you see having been built in the 1830s in the grand Gothic style. When Sir Hugh inherited the estate it had fallen on hard financial times, so he set about the task of keeping the ship afloat by building a golf course and converting the family seat into a country house hotel. There is also a splendid wedding and conference facility in the magnificent Great Hall with its own private entrance. For hotel guests there is an elegant drawing room with the adjacent Library restaurant, though the heart of the place is the sunny conservatory, which also serves as the hotel's bar and gathering spot for golfers. Bedrooms range from cozy and low-ceilinged at the back of the house to enormous and high-ceilinged overlooking the golf course. Several have beds made by Sir Hugh. Behind the hall is the picturesque estate-village of Maften and just down the road is Hadrian's Wall, 70 miles of wall, lookout towers, and barracks built by the Romans almost 1900 years ago to defend the frontier of their empire. The beautiful Northumbrian coast with all its castles is about a 30-mile drive away. *Directions:* From the A1, take the A69 towards Carlisle and Hexham. Exit at Heddon-in-the-Wall and pick up the B6318, just before the Three Tuns pub, heading west towards Chollerford for 7 miles. The turning to Maften Hall is on the right.

MAFTEN HALL   **New**
Owners: Sir Hugh & Lady Blackett
Maften, Northumberland NE20 0RH, England
Tel: (01661) 886500, Fax: (01661) 886055
Email: info@maftenhall.com
31 rooms
Double: £120–£160, Suite: £190–£225
Open all year, Credit cards: all major
Children welcome
www.karenbrown.com/ews/maften.html

Malmesbury is a remarkably unspoiled small town, well placed for jaunts to Bath, Oxford, and the Cotswolds. At its heart are the wisteria-clad Old Bell, the grassy churchyard, and the parish church (formed from the nave of a 12th-century abbey). The Old Bell began life as a guesthouse for the abbey and a recent remodel uncovered a fireplace from 1220—just one of the endearing old-world features of the place. Yet this hotel is not slavishly old-world: there's a cyberspace room, Nintendos are available, and a coach house wing of modern bedrooms is simply decorated with a Japanese theme. Bedrooms in the main building, some with claw-foot tubs for two, are larger than those in the coach house and are decorated with antiques and specially commissioned paintings. The stylish Edwardian dining room is hung with smiling portraits of Edwardian beauties and serves modern British food. Lighter fare is served amongst the beams and nooks of the informal Great Hall. It's a child-friendly place where lots of rooms can accommodate an extra bed or crib and there's a day nursery for children under seven. Popular tourist venues include Cirencester, the stone circles at Avebury and Stonehenge, the quaint stone villages of Lacock and Castle Combe, and golf on the Earl of Shelbourne's estate at Bowood. *Directions:* Exit the M4 at junction 17 and take the A429 for 5 miles to Malmesbury. Follow the road through the town center and you will find The Old Bell on your right next to the abbey.

THE OLD BELL
Manager: Richard Neal
Abbey Row
Malmesbury
Wiltshire SN16 0AG, England
Tel: (01666) 822344, Fax: (01666) 825145
31 rooms
Double: £95–£150, Suite: £165–£180
Open all year
Credit cards: all major
Children welcome

Perched high on a hill above Matlock with the ruins of Riber Castle as its only close neighbor, Riber Hall, which dates from the 15th century, is the most attractive of manor houses. A crackling log fire blazes in the enormous, ornate, dark-wood fireplace in the cozy lounge where guests gather for drinks before dinner. English classical and French provincial cuisine are the order of the day in the elegant dining rooms where the polished tables are set with fine china, gleaming silver, and sparkling crystal. Three bedrooms are found in the hall and the remainder across the courtyard in a converted stable block. A great attraction of the bedrooms is that many of them have antique Jacobean and Elizabethan four-poster beds—be sure to request a queen-sized bed. Room 10 is an especially spacious room with a lovely view of the garden. The tranquil setting can be appreciated in the old walled garden and orchard while energetic guests enjoy pitting their skills against the tennis-ball machine on the tennis court. Nearby are the jewels of Derbyshire—rolling green dales and lovely stone villages, medieval Haddon Hall, and the Chatsworth estate. *Directions:* Exit the M1 at junction 28 (Chesterfield) and take the A38 and the A615 (Matlock road) to Tansley where you turn left at the petrol station, up Alders Lane to Riber Hall.

RIBER HALL
Owners: Gill & Alex Biggin
Riber
Matlock
Derbyshire DE4 5JU, England
Tel: (01629) 582795, Fax: (01629) 580475
Email: info@riber-hall.co.uk
14 rooms
Double: £127–£170*
*Breakfast not included: £8
Open all year, Credit cards: all major
Children over 10
www.karenbrown.com/ews/riber.html

This peaceful little corner of Norfolk boasts miles of flat sandy and shingle beaches backed by salt marshes lined with quaint villages of gray-flint houses trimmed with red brick. One of these villages is Morston with its pub, 13th-century church, and Morston Hall. Fortunately for visitors, Galton (Chef of the Year for 2001) and Tracy Blackiston forsook the Miller Howe in the Lake District to open Morston Hall as a small country house hotel. Being seduced by Galton's exquisite dinners is a large part of your stay here—fortunately, there are plenty of opportunities for exercise, so you can afford to repeat the divine experience. Bedrooms are extremely large, beautifully decorated, and accompanied by sparkling new bathrooms. Birdwatchers will find nearby marshes a paradise. Guests often take a boat from Morston's little quay to visit the seal sanctuary at Blakeney Point. Nearby Holkham Hall, an imposing Palladian mansion, contains grand paintings and items of bygone days. Blickling Hall is elegantly furnished. *Directions:* Morston Hall is situated on the A149 King's Lynn to Cromer road between Wells-next-the-Sea and Cley-next-the-Sea.

MORSTON HALL
Owners: Tracy & Galton Blackiston
Morston
Near Holt
Norfolk NR25 7AA, England
Tel: (01263) 741041, Fax: (01263) 740419
Email: reception@morstonhall.com
6 rooms
Double: £200–£220* Suite: £200–£240*
*Includes dinner, bed & breakfast
Closed Jan
Credit cards: all major
Children welcome
www.karenbrown.com/ews/morstonhall.html

A 45-minute drive from Heathrow airport can find you dipping your toes in the River Thames and soaking up the pastoral scenery around Moulsford—the perfect place to relax after a transatlantic flight. This quiet stretch of the river was immortalized in *The Wind in The Willows*, provided the setting for *The History of Mr Polly*, and was home to Jerome K. Jerome who chronicled his friends' antics in *Three Men in a Boat*. But here you find so much more than a pretty setting with literary connections—The Beetle & Wedge hotel with its delightfully comfortable bedrooms guarantees that you will be well fed and well taken care of by proprietors Kate and Richard Smith. For dining you can choose to eat in the elegant wall-to-wall-windowed dining room or in the lively and informal Boathouse perched on the riverbank with tables that spill out onto a riverside terrace. The latter specializes in dishes cooked on a charcoal grill. All guestrooms have large beds and an airy decor, with pastel walls highlighted with stenciling. Be sure to request a room with a river view. Take a refreshing walk by the Thames to Goring, visit nearby Henley and Marlow, or explore farther afield with excursions to Oxford, Salisbury, Bath, and Winchester. *Directions:* From junction 12 of the M4 take the A4 south. At the second roundabout head towards Wallingford, through Pangbourne and Streatley to Moulsford, where you turn right on Ferry Lane to the river.

THE BEETLE & WEDGE
Owners: Kate & Richard Smith
Ferry Lane
Moulsford on Thames
Oxfordshire OX10 9JF, England
Tel: (01491) 651381, Fax: (01491) 651376
10 rooms
Double: £150–£165
Open all year, Credit cards: all major
Children welcome
www.karenbrown.com/ews/beetle.html

Chewton Glen was voted "best country house in the world" by *Gourmet* readers in April 2000. It's an image that Martin and Brigitte Skan have carefully nurtured and their efforts have been rewarded by considerable success—we had difficulty getting a room midweek in the summer. The secret of their success is not just the luxuriousness of the entire place—though it is indeed decadently luxurious, with lovely suites and bedrooms decked out with all the mod cons—but their understanding that luxury extends to offering absolutely outstanding, genuine service. To experience this level of service is one of the true pleasures in life. In between Nirvana-like meals you relax completely—perhaps with a little croquet on the lawn, a splash in the pool, or tea on the terrace. You can exert yourself in the health club complex with its magnificent indoor pool, gym, indoor and outdoor tennis; indulge yourself in various beauty treatments; disport yourself on the nine-hole golf course; or walk through the grounds and along the glen to the beach. If you feel the urge to go sightseeing, the New Forest where wild deer and ponies roam is nearby, and Stonehenge, Salisbury, and Winchester cathedrals are within an hour's drive. *Directions:* From the A35 follow signposts for Highcliffe (not New Milton), go through Walkford, then turn left down Chewton Farm Road—the hotel is on your right.

CHEWTON GLEN
Owners: Brigitte & Martin Skan
New Milton
Hampshire BH25 6QS, England
Tel: (01425) 275341, Fax: (01425) 272310
Email: reservations@chewtonglen.com
60 rooms, 1 suite
Double: £300–£425*, Suite: £530–£755*
*Breakfast not included: £22
Open all year, Credit cards: all major
Children over 7
Relais & Châteaux Member
www.karenbrown.com/ews/chewtonglen.html

The peaceful, steep-sided Newlands Valley, which stretches from Buttermere towards Derwent Water, is the location of 19th-century Swinside Lodge Hotel. Kevin Kniveton grew up spending holidays and weekends in the Lake District and has always wanted to live here so when he and wife Susan decided to move there was no debate as to where. They chose Newlands for its utter peacefulness. Decorated throughout in warm, soft, pastel tones, the entire house has a fresh and welcoming ambiance that shines through even on the dreariest of days. Lilac is a particularly attractive large bedroom whose bay window comfortably accommodates two armchairs and whose zip-link beds can be either twins or one king bed. Susan and Kevin prefer that guests dine in, but are happy for guests to eat in on some nights and out on others, so do ask if you want to leave your dinner plans flexible. In this part of the world fell (hill) walking is very popular and one of the delights of staying here is that walks begin almost on your doorstep. A favorite walk takes you up the Catbells Fell to Grange where you take a motor launch across Derwent Water to the dock five minutes from the hotel. *Directions:* Leave the M6 at junction 40 and follow the A66 past Keswick towards Cockermouth. Turn left through Portinscale towards Grange. You will find Swinside Lodge Hotel on your right after 2 miles (ignore all signposts for Swinside and Newlands.)

SWINSIDE LODGE HOTEL
Owners: Susan & Kevin Kniveton
Newlands, near Keswick
Cumbria CA12 5UE, England
Tel & fax: (017687) 72948
Email: info@swinside-lodge.co.uk
7 rooms
*Double: £144–£182**
**Includes dinner, bed & breakfast*
Open all year, Credit cards: MC, VS
Children over 10
www.karenbrown.com/ews/swinside.html

The Old Bank Hotel offers 42 guestrooms housed within an attractive four-story building dating from 1780, which was formerly—you guessed it—a bank. The hotel enjoys a prestigious location in the heart of Oxford, neighboring some of the oldest colleges and perfectly situated for exploring the city on foot. Quod, the stylish bar and grill located on the ground floor, serves meals from breakfast onwards. With 160 seats, open to non-resident as well as resident guests, the restaurant is contemporarily designed with stone floors, wooden tables, and an oval zinc-topped bar. The cooking has an Italian influence and in summer guests can enjoy dining on the terrace. Guestrooms are found on the upper levels and down the two back wings that band the south-facing courtyard. Especially luxurious, the two top-floor suites, afford "sleeping amongst the spires" and views over college rooftops. Guestroom interiors, the work of a French designer, are beautiful, all having the same theme of understated elegance and sumptuous marble bathrooms. *Directions:* Centrally located on the High Street at the heart of old Oxford. Parking is to the rear of the hotel off Merton Street.

THE OLD BANK HOTEL
Owner: Jeremy Mogford
92–94 High Street
Oxford OX1 4BN, England
Tel: (01865) 799599, Fax: (01865) 799598
Email: info@oldbank-hotel.co.uk
42 rooms
Double: £155–£300*
*Breakfast not included: £8–£11
Closed Christmas
Credit cards: all major
Children welcome
www.karenbrown.com/ews/oldbank.html

Between Keble and Somerville colleges you find the Old Parsonage Hotel, a mellow, golden-stone building dating back to 1660 draped with wisteria. In 1989 it was purchased by Jeremy Mogford and completely remodeled to become an upmarket small hotel. In years past the Old Parsonage grew like Topsy with a higgledy-piggledy collection of rooms and corridors added to the rear. Jeremy has done his best to give the rambling warren a cohesive feel. For the main sitting room several small rooms have been combined into one, giving a sense of space while still keeping some walls to provide cozy seating nooks for coffee, lunches, afternoon teas, and bar suppers. The delightful bedrooms are priced by size, with the less expensive ones tending to be on the compact side with just enough room for the bed, a couple of chairs, TV, and phone. Bathrooms are small and beautifully appointed with marble. The most attractive of the newer rooms are those that overlook the little garden. The largest rooms, and certainly our favorites, are the four rooms in the original house. Reached by going through a pretty little sitting room and up a narrow flight of stairs, these have slanting doors, uneven floors, and little windows peeking out through the wisteria. The location is perfect: park your car at the hotel and walk to everything in Oxford. *Directions:* The Old Parsonage is situated just beyond St. Giles Church on the A4260, Banbury Road.

OLD PARSONAGE HOTEL
Owner: Jeremy Mogford
Manager: Philip Mason-Gordon
1 Banbury Road
Oxford OX2 6NN, England
Tel: (01865) 310210, Fax: (01865) 311262
Email: info@oldparsonage-hotel.co.uk
30 rooms
Double: £155–£190, Suite: £200
Closed Dec 24 to 28
Credit cards: all major
Children welcome
www.karenbrown.com/ews/oldparsonoxford.html

In the oldest part of Penzance, on a narrow street overlooking the harbor, is The Abbey Hotel. With their penchant for house restoration and her love of antiques, Michael and Jean Cox purchased and restored the hotel, turning it into the gem it is today. Soft colors and lovely fabrics throughout provide a background for the old pine furniture, country antiques, and interesting old knickknacks. The ambiance is informal: on arrival you are given a key to the front door and there are no bedroom door keys. The second floor contains the three choice bedrooms. Room 1 is especially attractive, with its large patchwork-quilt-covered bed, fireplace, comfy chairs, and huge, pine-paneled bathroom with large antique tub. Room 3 has a delightful sitting nook and a bathroom hidden behind a bookcase door. Room 4 has twin beds covered with hand-embroidered covers and inviting window seats providing views of the harbor and its dry dock: a shower and WC are tucked into a large closet. A two-bedroom apartment offers the most spacious accommodation. Penzance is a lively town with a mishmash of architectural styles. Nearby are St. Michael's Mount, Mousehole, and Land's End (very commercialized). *Directions:* On entering Penzance stay on the seafront road. Just before the bridge (across the harbor) turn right and immediately left up the slipway—The Abbey Hotel is at the top of the hill.

THE ABBEY HOTEL
Owners: Jean & Michael Cox
Penzance
Cornwall TR18 4AR, England
Tel: (01736) 366906, Fax: (01736) 351163
Email: glyn@abbeyhotel.fsnet.co.uk
7 rooms
Double: £105–£160, Suite: £170–£220
Closed Christmas
Credit cards: all major
Children over 7
www.karenbrown.com/ews/theabbey.html

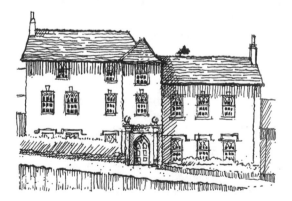

This lovely Edwardian house sits high above the pretty village of Porlock and was designed as a home where almost every room has views of the distant sea across the roofs and chimneys of the village. When Anne and Tim purchased The Oaks several years ago, it had already been converted to a hotel and while they have worked wonders in the decoration and bathroom departments, they have not been allowed to do anything about the fire-safety partitions surrounding the stairway. Downstairs, guests have a snug hallway parlor with chairs drawn round a log fire and an airy sitting room with flowered sofas and pink velvet chairs arranged into conversational groupings. The dining room has been extended and picture windows added so that, no matter where you sit, you have sea views across the fields or village views across the rooftops. Upstairs, the bedrooms enjoy identical interesting views. Though some are a bit larger than others, all rooms are priced alike and offer the same high standards, and each retains its own individual character. Stroll around the village with its attractive houses and shops and drive the short distance to the harbor of Porlock Weir. Just inland is Lorna Doone Country—the church at Oare was the scene of her wedding. *Directions:* From Dunster, as you enter Porlock down the hill on the one-way system, turn left into the hotel just as the road becomes two-way.

THE OAKS HOTEL
Owners: Anne & Tim Riley
Porlock
Somerset TA24 8ES, England
Tel: (01643) 862265, Fax: (01643) 863131
Email: info@oakshotel.co.uk
9 rooms
Double: £100
Open mid-Mar to Oct
Credit cards: all major
Children over 8
www.karenbrown.com/ews/theoaks.html

The Yorke Arms nestles beside the village green in Ramsgill, a handful of houses and farms and a tiny church. This hotel is a "foodie haven" in Nidderdale, one of Yorkshire's quietest and most attractive dales. Frances Atkins and her brigade perform culinary magic, offering food that enjoys modern flourishes but is firmly focused on fine local produce. Husband Bill calmly runs the front of the house. There's plenty of old-world charm: flagstone floors, traditional bars, and a comfortable dining room with high-backed Windsor chairs, an old dresser gleaming with pewter, and a blazing log fire. Bedrooms are very comfortable but by no means grand. Several rooms have received a complete update, so ask for one of these when making a reservation. I particularly liked Grouse and Pheasant, both spacious accommodations in the oldest part of the inn. For the roomiest quarters, opt for Gouthwaite, Ramsgill, or Longside with its grand four-poster bed. You can take beautiful walks from the hotel, which vary in length from strolls by the local reservoir to daylong hikes over the moorlands. The ruins of nearby Fountains Abbey are an awesome sight and medieval York and the 18th-century spa town of Harrogate are popular day trips. *Directions:* From Ripon take the B6285 to Pateley Bridge where you cross the river and turn right for Ramsgill. The Yorke Arms is beside the village green.

THE YORKE ARMS
Owners: Frances & Bill Atkins
Ramsgill by Harrogate
Yorkshire HG3 5RL, England
Tel: (01423) 755243, Fax: (01423) 755330
Email: enquiries@yorke-arms.co.uk
13 rooms
Double: £180–£220*, Suite: £220–£350*
*Includes dinner, bed & breakfast
Open all year, Credit cards: all major
Children over 10
www.karenbrown.com/ews/yorkearms.html

The Burgoyne family were people of substance hereabouts for they secured the premier building site in this picturesque Swaledale village and built an impressive home that dwarfs the surrounding buildings. Gone are the days when one family could justify such a large home and now it's a welcoming hotel run by Derek Hickson and Peter Carwardine. Derek makes guests feel thoroughly at home while Peter makes certain that they live up to their motto, "Tis substantial happiness to eat." Peter prepares a fixed-price, four-course meal every evening with plenty of choices for each course. The handsome lounge is warmed by a log fire in winter and full of inviting books on the area. There's abundant scope for walking and driving in this rugged area using Reeth as your base, though you'll be hard pressed to find a lovelier dales view than the one from your bedroom window of stone-walled fields rising to vast moorlands (one bedroom faces the back of the house). Redmire, being more spacious, is the premier room, while Marrick is a most luxurious four-poster suite. Robes and slippers are provided for the occupants of Keld, Grinton, and Thwaite who have to slip across the hall to their bathrooms. Richmond with its medieval castle and the Bowes Museum, near Barnard Castle, with its fine collection of French furniture and porcelain, are added attractions. *Directions:* From Richmond take the A6108 towards Leyburn for 5 miles to the B6270 for the 5-mile drive to Reeth. The Burgoyne Hotel is on the village green.

THE BURGOYNE HOTEL
Owners: Derek Hickson & Peter Carwardine
Reeth
Yorkshire DL11 6SN, England
Tel & fax: (01748) 884292
Email: enquiries@theburgoyne.co.uk
8 rooms
Double: £90–£110, Suite: £150
Open Feb 14 to Jan 2
Credit cards: MC, VS, Children over 10
www.karenbrown.com/ews/burgoyne.html

The St. Enodoc Hotel occupies an exquisite location on one of England's most scenic coastlines overlooking the broad Camel estuary. Combine this with a refreshing, stylishly chic, Mediterranean interior and you have a real winner. Enjoy the peace and quiet of the comfortable sitting room or take advantage of the well-stocked library featuring books on Cornwall and books by Cornish authors. Soak in the panoramic water view from the smart, split-level bar and restaurant specializing in New World cuisine, or stroll down the lane and take the little ferry across to the ancient fishing port of Padstow with its array of shops and restaurants. Bedrooms, decorated in shades of dark raspberry or blue, are a real treat. There is a choice of king-, queen-, or twin-bedded rooms, several with a large window seat with superb views that can be converted to a small child's bed, though families often opt for having bunk beds set up in the living room or using the sofa bed. With its heated outdoor pool, billiard room, gym, and adjacent golf course, the St. Enodoc is an ideal holiday hotel. The nearby little fishing village of Port Isaac with its craft and antique shops is charming, but also drive to Carbis Bay and take the little train to St. Ives for a visit to the Tate Gallery or meander up the coast to Tintagel of King Arthur fame. *Directions:* At the Wadebridge roundabout follow signs for Wadebridge, then at the next roundabout turn right for the 4-mile drive to Rock.

ST. ENODOC HOTEL
Owners: Marler family
Manager: Mark Gregory
Rock, near Wadebridge
Cornwall PL27 6LA, England
Tel: (01208) 863394, Fax: (01208) 863970
Email: enodoc@aol.com
15 rooms, 4 family suites
Double: £165*, Suite: £220*
*Breakfast not included: £6.50, Service charge: 10%
Closed mid-Dec to mid-Feb (except New Year)
Credit cards: all major, Children welcome
www.karenbrown.com/ews/stenodoc.html

Romaldkirk epitomizes a traditional north-of-England village with honey-colored stone cottages set spaciously round the large village green where the old pump and even older stocks (for punishing wrongdoers) still stand. The surprisingly sophisticated Rose and Crown pub bordering the village green has a pretty sitting room (where guests can escape the hubbub of the bar) and a paneled dining room serving four-course dinners. However, like all great pubs, the Rose and Crown also has an excellent traditional bar where beams are decorated with horse brasses and locals gather for a pint in the evenings. Delectable bar meals are served here or in the adjacent Crown Room. Up the narrow stairs you find five attractive bedrooms (room 10 is a lovely large double-bedded room overlooking the village green) and two suites, which are especially suitable for families as the sofas in the sitting rooms make into beds for children. Five additional, more modern bedrooms are in the courtyard behind the hotel. Walking is a popular pastime hereabouts and a few minutes' drive brings you into empty Pennine countryside. Barnard Castle is a lively local market town where the Bowes Museum merits an all-day visit. A 40-minute drive finds you at Beamish Museum, a turn-of-the-century mining town hosted by costumed staff. *Directions:* Romaldkirk is 6 miles northwest of Barnard Castle on the B6277 in the direction of Middleton in Teesdale.

THE ROSE & CROWN
Owners: Alison & Christopher Davy
Romaldkirk, Barnard Castle
County Durham DL12 9EB, England
Tel: (01833) 650213, Fax: (01833) 650828
Email: hotel@rose-and-crown.co.uk
12 rooms
Double: £86, Suite: £100
Closed Christmas
Credit cards: MC, VS
Children welcome
www.karenbrown.com/ews/roseandcrown.html

Stone House, the manor house for Rushlake Green, has belonged to the Dunn family for over 500 years. Built in 1432 with an addition in 1778, this glorious house, set on a 1,000-acre estate, is filled with wonderful antique furniture and old English china, which is complemented by chintzes and family memorabilia. There is a croquet lawn and an antique, full-size billiard table. Bedrooms vary in size from small and cozy to large and spacious. Almost all have old beams and are furnished with care and provided with practically everything you might need from TV to hot-water bottles, sewing kits, books, and tempting biscuits. Two rooms are gorgeous, with four-poster beds with equally lovely bathrooms—one of the bathrooms is decorated with antique samplers. A sumptuous dinner and breakfast are served in the oak-paneled dining room, and Continental breakfast is available in your bedroom. The 18th-century walled garden, old-fashioned rose garden, and lime walk are yours to enjoy. Other glorious gardens include Sissinghurst, Great Dixter, Scotney Castle, and Sheffield Park. Close by is the Glyndebourne Opera House (May to September). Nearby, Churchill's home, Chartwell, and Rudyard Kipling's home, Batemans, are very popular. *Directions:* From Heathfield take the B2096 towards Battle and then the fourth turning on the right to Rushlake Green. Turn left in the village (with the green on your right) and Stone House is on the far left-hand corner of the crossroads.

STONE HOUSE
Owners: Jane & Peter Dunn
Rushlake Green, near Heathfield
East Sussex TN21 9QJ, England
Tel: (01435) 830553, Fax: (01435) 830726
7 rooms
Double: £99.95–£195, Suite: £195
Closed Dec 23 to Jan 6
Credit cards: MC, VS
Children over 9
www.karenbrown.com/ews/stonehouse.html

I was actually thankful for the rainstorm that drove me inside to the shelter and warmth of The Greenway's beautiful drawing room and lounges. (Having noticed the inviting drawing room on arrival, I found any excuse to retire to it very welcome.) A peaceful afternoon reading before a crackling log fire happily took the place of an abandoned walk in the hillsides. What bliss to listen to the gentle rainfall! An equally delightful evening was spent in the conservatory dining room overlooking the lily pond and, in the far distance, the Cotswold Hills: lit by dancing candles, it set the mood for an intimate, delicious dinner. Upstairs, the luxurious, handsomely furnished bedrooms overlook the surrounding countryside. Another block of equally luxurious bedrooms is located beside the house in a converted 19th-century coach house. Situated on the edge of the Cotswolds and not far from the Welsh Marches, The Greenway is an ideal spot for exploration. If you are a devoted sightseer, I might almost recommend you bypass The Greenway, as it is so hard to leave and might upset your scheduled itinerary. The lovely Regency spa town of Cheltenham is just a few minutes' drive away. *Directions:* The Greenway is nestled under the Cotswold Hills, protected from the somewhat suburban location by acres of parkland and gardens. The hotel is 2 miles south of Cheltenham on the A46, Cheltenham to Stroud road.

THE GREENWAY
Manager: Andrew Mackay
Shurdington, near Cheltenham
Gloucestershire GL51 5UG, England
Tel: (01242) 862352, Fax: (01242) 862780
19 rooms
Double: £165–£215, Suite: £230–£275
Open all year
Credit cards: all major
Children over 7

The delightfully pretty little fishing village of St. Mawes, with its narrow, steep streets and boat-filled harbor strung along the River Fal, sports quite a Mediterranean look. The town's sheltered position makes it a warm hideaway even in winter and there is no more splendid place to hide away than in the elegant Hotel Tresanton. Terracing up steep steps, this spectacularly located, scrumptious hotel is dashingly modern, with a nautical, Mediterranean flair. Its minimalist decor—mainly in white and soft, neutral tones with royal-blue accents—is a perfect balance between classic and modern. Bedrooms all have magnificent sea views and two are spacious family suites for up to five people. Naturally, the restaurant specializes in seafood. Enjoy the hotel's extensive library or choose a film to watch in the hotel's cinema. A delightful walk takes you past the castle, following the coastal path to the exquisite 14th-century church at St. Just in Roseland. You can hire many different boats including the hotel's 48-ft classic yacht. Sightseers have lots of scope, from St. Michael's Mount to the Tate Gallery at St. Ives, while garden lovers are spoilt for choice: Trelissick, Glendurgan, Trebah, and the Lost Gardens of Heligan (now found and not to be missed). The Eden Project is absolutely fascinating. *Directions:* From St. Austell take the B3287 for 16 miles to St. Mawes where you follow the road along the front of the harbor, coming to the Tresanton on your right. Park in front, go up to reception, and the staff will unload your bags and park your car.

HOTEL TRESANTON
Manager: John Rogers
St. Mawes
Cornwall TR2 5DR, England
Tel: (01326) 270055, Fax: (01326) 270053
Email: info@tresanton.com
26 rooms
Double: £195–£265, Suite: £365
Closed Jan 4 to Feb 9
Credit cards: all major
Children welcome
www.karenbrown.com/ews/tresanton.html

The gallows sign outside The George stood as a warning to highwaymen not to rob coaches departing from the Stamford inn. The waiting room for London coaches is now an oak-paneled private dining room, while the adjacent York waiting room serves as a friendly bar. History positively oozes from this place and the staff is always happy to enliven your stay with tales of resident ghosts and secret passages. Do not be put off by the hotel's austere façade being directly on the busy Great Northern road (now bypassed) because most bedrooms face a peaceful inner courtyard and you are not aware of the road once you are inside the hotel. Horses once clip-clopped across the cobbled courtyard where overflowing tubs of flowers paint a pretty picture and tables and chairs are set beneath umbrellas for traditional afternoon tea. Most the bedrooms face this pretty courtyard and I particularly enjoyed the historic ambiance of room 29 (a standard double) with its dark-oak paneling—apparently Princess Anne has slept here—and room 49 decked out in maroon and blue and overlooking a quiet garden. Traditional roast dinners are the hallmark of the dining room—be sure to save room for an old-fashioned pud—while lighter, more casual fare is served in the indoor Garden Lounge. A short walk brings you to Stamford's antique shops and Burghley House is just down the road. *Directions:* From Peterborough take the A1 north for 14 miles to the first roundabout where you take the B1081 to Stamford. The George is on the left by the traffic lights.

THE GEORGE OF STAMFORD
Manager: Chris Pitman
71 St. Martins
Stamford
Lincolnshire PE9 2LB, England
Tel: (01780) 750750, Fax: (01780) 750701
47 rooms
Double: £105–£220, Suite: £145–£150
Open all year
Credit cards: all major
Children welcome

The Royalist's boldly simple claim to be "the oldest inn in England" (circa 947 A.D.) has been verified by carbon dating and accepted by the *Guinness Book of Records*. Evidence suggests that the building actually began its life as part of a Saxon community as early as 514 A.D. Its history is wreathed in myths and truths supported by leper holes, sealed tunnels, dry wells, bear pits, and the inevitable ghosts. All in all, it's a fascinating destination in its own right, but the number of reasons to visit The Royalist has grown as a result of changes wrought by its current owners, former London restaurateurs Georgina and Alan Thompson. Eight luxuriously appointed bedrooms, all with modern en-suite bathrooms, have been artfully and sympathetically engineered into the irregular spaces of the old structure. Meals are served in the appropriately named 947 A.D. restaurant, with pre-dinner drinks and post-dinner coffee in the comfortable residents' lounge in front of the log fire. For a less formal atmosphere you can meet the locals in the adjoining Eagle and Child pub, which shares not only a common wall but also the kitchen, providing typical bar meals of the same high standard. Here you can dine *al fresco* in the small landscaped garden or beneath the protection of the conservatory in inclement weather. This is a perfect location for exploring the Cotswolds. *Directions:* From the A429 at Stow-on-the-Wold turn left into Sheep Street (the Unicorn Pub is on the corner) and drive 200 yards into the center of the village. The Royalist is set back on the left-hand side.

THE ROYALIST   New
Owners: Georgina & Alan Thompson
Digbeth Street
Stow-on-the-Wold
Gloucestershire GL54 1BN, England
Tel: (01451) 830670, Fax: (01451) 870048
8 rooms
Double: £130–£170*, Suite: £170 *
*Continental breakfast
Open all year, Credit cards: MC, VS
Children welcome

Just a few minutes' walk from town, this square, three-story building with rich salmon-colored façade and white trim stands out amongst the many row houses offering bed and breakfast accommodation. Although we discovered the delightful, family-run Caterham House Hotel not long ago, it has existed under the same proprietorship for 25 years and the register boasts a majority of loyal returning guests. With the owners being originally from France, this hotel has a charming, subtly French influence both in its decor and ambiance. Soft tones of yellow and mauve dominate the color scheme and creative touches such as attractive stenciling, interesting art, and a beautiful quilt hung as a headboard make each room refreshing and unique. Off the entry there is a welcoming sitting room with full bar and outside terrace for guests to enjoy. To accommodate the ten guestrooms in the main building, Dominique and Olive cleverly took down the shared wall of two adjoining buildings, so when you climb the interior stairs it seems almost an illusion as an apparently mirrored staircase rises up to meet the other. A renovated neighboring cottage houses two additional rooms. Although there is no restaurant, Dominique tailors breakfast to whatever guests want, be it traditional English with eggs and sausage or French with croissants and coffee. *Directions:* Turn left at the American Fountain coming from the town center, and right coming from the train station, into Rother Street. The Caterham House Hotel is on the left just past the police station.

CATERHAM HOUSE HOTEL
Owners: Olive & Dominique Maury
58/59 Rother Street
Stratford-upon-Avon
Warwickshire CV37 6LT, England
Tel: (01789) 267309, Fax: (01789) 414836
12 rooms
Double: £80–£90
Open all year
Credit cards: MC, VS
Children welcome
www.karenbrown.com/ews/caterham.html

Plumber Manor has been a country home of the Prideaux Brune family since the early 17th century. Portraits hanging in the upstairs gallery hint at the grandeur of the family's past. (There is also a portrait of Charles I, which he personally presented to his mistress, a member of the family.) Billed as a "restaurant with bedrooms," Plumber Manor is under the personal supervision of the family. Richard and Alison Prideaux Brune look after guests; Brian Prideaux Brune, the chef, conscientiously provides a high standard of cuisine and wine. Six comfortable, spacious bedrooms are in the main house and just across the garden ten rooms surround a courtyard. Our favorites are 14, 15, 16, and 17— spacious, two-level rooms with luxurious modern bathrooms. Ten miles away lies Milton Abbas, a picture-perfect village of thatched cottages built in 1770 by the Earl of Dorchester who had the old village razed because it interfered with his view. Another pretty village is Cerne Abbas with thatched and Tudor cottages, 7 miles north of Dorchester (Hardy's Casterbridge). Within reach are Salisbury, Longleat, and the many attractions in and around Bath. *Directions*: In Sturminster Newton turn left from the A352 onto the road leading to the village of Hazelbury Bryan. Plumber Manor is 1¼ miles beyond on the left.

PLUMBER MANOR
Owners: Prideaux Brune family
Hazelbury Bryan
Near Sturminster Newton
Dorset DT10 2AF, England
Tel: (01258) 472507, Fax: (01258) 473370
Email: book@plumbermanor.com
16 rooms
Double: £100–£155
Closed Feb, Credit cards: all major
Children welcome
www.karenbrown.com/ews/plumber.html

Midway between the outstandingly pretty Cornish fishing villages of Looe and Polperro, Talland Bay Hotel sits in a quiet cove offering unobstructed views of headlands and the sea. Parts of this lovely Cornish manor date back to the 16th century and Annie and Barry Rosier were immediately drawn to it as it reminded them of Brittany where Annie grew up. The bar-lounge and fine paneled dining room are comfortably informal and overlook the gardens. The bedrooms are very comfortable and a great many have sparkling new bathrooms. I especially enjoyed room 9 with its large balcony and rooms 12 (set under the eaves up lots of stairs), 28, and 29 with their spectacular sea views. If you are looking for spaciousness and room for the children, opt for room 27 whose French windows open up to the garden or if you want total privacy, consider one of the four little cottages in the grounds (without sea view). The swimming pool on the back patio is heated during the summer months and a putting course is set up on the lawn. Gardens terrace down towards the headland where the coastal path takes you to either Polperro or Looe, avoiding the tourist-congested roads. The idyllically pretty seaside villages of Fowey, Looe, and Polperro are great attractions as are the National Trust houses of Cotehele and Lanhydrock. *Directions:* From Plymouth take the A38 towards Truro then turn left on the A387 towards Looe and Polperro. At the T-junction turn towards Polperro and turn first left for Talland.

TALLAND BAY HOTEL
Owners: Annie & Barry Rosier
Talland-by-Looe
Cornwall PL13 2JB, England
Tel: (01503) 272667, Fax: (01503) 272940
Email: tallandbay@aol.com
20 rooms
Double: £134–£198*, Suite: £164–£188*
*Includes dinner, bed & breakfast
Closed Jan, Credit cards: all major
Children welcome
www.karenbrown.com/ews/talland.html

Dale Head Hall occupies a stunning, isolated position on the shores of Thirlmere, one of Cumbria's quietest, most pastoral lakes, and provides the perfect base for exploring the entire Lake District. Bedrooms at the front of the hotel offer gorgeous lake views while the delightful rooms at the back in the old part of the house are low-ceilinged with old latch doors and beams. One of the back bedrooms has a small cradle room snug above the inglenook fireplace. Two lake-view rooms on the ground floor are handy for those who have a problem with stairs. I particularly like the ground-floor twin with its private lake-facing patio and own entrance patio with chairs. Superior rooms are rented only on a dinner, bed, and breakfast basis. Much of the lovely oak furniture found throughout the hotel is the handiwork of personable Alan Lowe who joins his wife Shirley, daughter Caroline, and son-in-law Hans in making certain that guests are well taken care of and well fed. Walks from the hotel range from a stroll around the lake to challenging hikes up the nearby fells. For a week's stay, Dale Head Hall has several delightful apartments in the adjacent stables. *Directions:* Leave the M6 at junction 40 and take the A66 towards Keswick then the B5322 signposted Windermere to join the A591, which you take in the direction of Windermere for half a mile. The entrance to Dale Head Hall is on your right.

DALE HEAD HALL
Owners: Shirley & Alan Lowe
* Caroline & Hans Bonkenburg*
Lake Thirlmere, Keswick
Cumbria CA12 4TN, England
Tel: (017687) 72478, Fax: (017687) 71070
Email: onthelakeside@dale-head-hall.co.uk
12 rooms, 7 apartments
Double £70–£110
Superior room: £180–£190*
*Includes dinner, bed & breakfast
Open Feb to Dec, Credit cards: all major
Children welcome
www.karenbrown.com/ews/daleheadhall.html

Tucked away at the edge of the small town of Thornbury is Thornbury Castle and from the moment you see it you will be enchanted. Construction began in 1510 at the order of the 3rd Duke of Buckingham, but ceased when he was beheaded in 1521 at the Tower of London. The current owners continue the upkeep of this partially restored castle, leaving other areas as a romantic ruin. Dinner in the baronial dining rooms is a leisurely affair. Softly carpeted hallways lead to the bedrooms—this is no longer a castle of drafty stone passages. The guestrooms are elegantly decorated as befits their castle surroundings, several with four-poster beds, all with lovely bathrooms. The large octagonal tower room has a four-poster bed and its own turret staircase. Nearby Slimbridge Wildfowl and Wetlands Centre was founded by Sir Peter Scott (son of the explorer) in 1946. Just south of Slimbridge is Berkeley and Berkeley Castle where Edward II was murdered in the dungeon in 1327. Also in the grounds is the Jenner museum, a tribute to Edward Jenner, discoverer of the smallpox vaccination. *Directions:* At the junction of the M4 and M5 motorways take the A38 north to Thornbury. At the bottom of the hill in the High Street fork left down Castle Street and the entrance to the castle is on the left of the parish church. Follow brown historic signs.

THORNBURY CASTLE
Manager: Brian Jarvis
Thornbury, near Bristol
South Gloucestershire B535 1HH, England
Tel: (01454) 281182, Fax: (01454) 416188
E-mail: thornburycastle@compuserve.com
24 rooms
Double: £130–£270*, Suite: £270–£350*
*Breakfast not included: £8.95
Closed early Jan
Credit cards: all major
Children over 16
www.karenbrown.com/ews/thornbury.html

Claiming the honor of being King Arthur's legendary birthplace, the ruins of Tintagel
Castle cling to a wild headland exposed to the coastal winds. It's a place of myths that
attracts visitors who come to soak up its past and enjoy its rugged scenery. While the
village of Tintagel is a touristy spot, just a mile away lies the quiet hamlet of Trenale, a
cluster of cottages, and the delightful Trebrea Lodge. Behind the impressive, tall
Georgian façade lies a much older building of cozy, comfortable rooms. Upstairs, the
drawing room is full of splendid antiques but you will probably find yourself downstairs
toasting your toes by the fire enveloped by a large armchair, enjoying drinks and coffee
after a delicious dinner in the paneled dining room with its views across stone-walled
fields to the distant sea. We particularly liked our room (4) furnished, as are all the
rooms, with lovely antiques and enjoying a large bathroom. Guests help themselves from
a tempting array of hot breakfast dishes on the buffet. Walkers enjoy spectacular clifftop
paths along rugged headlands that lead to hidden beaches and sheltered inlets such as
picture-perfect Boscastle harbor. To the north lies Clovelly with its whitewashed
cottages tumbling down cobblestone lanes to the harbor below. *Directions:* From
Tintagel take the road towards Boscastle. At the edge of Tintagel turn right at the
contemporary church, right at the top of the lane, and Trebrea is on your left.

TREBREA LODGE
Owners: John Charlick & Sean Devlin
Trenale, Tintagel
Cornwall PL34 0HR, England
Tel: (01840) 770410, Fax: (01840) 770092
Email: trebrea-lodge@supernet.com
7 rooms
Double £86–£98
Open mid-Feb to mid-Dec
Credit cards: all major
Children over 12
www.karenbrown.com/ews/trebrealodge.html

Victorians flocked to Tunbridge Wells—in fact, the young Princess Victoria always stayed here when she came to town. The Hotel du Vin's interior has changed considerably since those days, now presenting a light, airy, and uncluttered look. Like its sister hotel in Winchester, the hotel's theme is wine—the wine list is extensive and very well priced as is the accompanying bistro menu packed with tempting selections of top-quality food. Bedrooms are stylishly simple in their decor yet equipped with all the modern conveniences. They are generally high-ceilinged rooms, very smartly decorated in a tailored style with superb beds made up with Egyptian cotton linens. Each bedroom is accompanied by a sleek modern bathroom with oversized tub, power shower, and fluffy towels. Splurge and request a larger room with a view of the park. A short walk finds you in the heart of the town with its elegant Regency parades and houses designed by Decimus Burton. The Regency meeting place, The Pantiles, a terraced walk with shops behind a colonnade, is especially memorable. You can also use Tunbridge Wells as your base for visiting the gardens at Scotney Castle and Sissinghurst and exploring the delightful Hever and Bodian castles, the village of Chiddingstone with its 16th-century buildings, and the lovely town of Cranbrook with its white-board houses and shops. *Directions:* From the railway station in Tunbridge Wells go up the hill and at the first set of traffic lights turn right onto Crescent Road. The hotel is on your right after 150 yards.

HOTEL DU VIN
Manager: Matthew Callard
Crescent Road
Tunbridge Wells, Kent TN1 2LY, England
Tel: (01892) 526455, Fax (01892) 512044
Email: info@tunbridgewells.hotelduvin.co.uk
32 rooms
Double: £95–£155*
*Breakfast not included: £9.50–£12.50
Open all year, Credit cards: all major
Children welcome
www.karenbrown.com/ews/vintunbridge.html

Touching the water's edge, the Sharrow Bay Hotel has one of the most glorious views in England—a panorama of Ullswater mirroring the surrounding mountains. Francis Coulson and Brian Sack bought the hotel in 1948 armed with a vision of a country house hotel and for many years Sharrow Bay has been the yardstick by which other luxury country house hotels are measured. From the warmth of welcome from Brian, Nigel, and their staff to the divine, five-course dinner where portions are large and you have to pace yourself to complete your meal, a visit to Sharrow Bay Hotel is a wonderful experience. Bedrooms are furnished with antiques and come with absolutely everything. Ten lovely bedrooms are in the main house. Across the garden you find six decadent rooms, three of which are suites on two levels, enjoying panoramic views of the lake and fells. Just down the road is Bank House where guests enjoy a chauffeur-driven car to and from dinner, breakfast in the beamed refectory dining room, large bedrooms, and stunning views of the lake from this hillside location. Idyllic Lake District scenery is on your doorstep, tempting you to go no farther than the terrace patio. Close by are plenty of good walks, fishing, and boating. *Directions:* Exit the M6 at junction 40 onto the A66 towards Keswick. At the roundabout take the A592 towards Lake Ullswater. Turn left at the lake then go through Pooley Bridge where you turn right at the church, following signs for Howtown to Sharrow Bay.

SHARROW BAY HOTEL
Owner: Brian Sack, Director: Nigel Lightburn
Ullswater, near Penrith
Cumbria CA10 2LZ, England
Tel: (017684) 86301, Fax: (017684) 86349
Email: enquiries@sharrow-bay.com
26 rooms, Double: £300–£392*, Suite: £410–£420*
*Includes dinner, bed & breakfast
Closed Dec, Jan & Feb, Credit cards: MC, VS
Children over 13
Relais & Châteaux Member
www.karenbrown.com/ews/sharrowbay.html

Upper Slaughter, just up the hill from its sister village, Lower Slaughter, is a quiet, tranquil collection of idyllic cottages surrounded by bucolic Cotswold countryside. In the center of the village lies the former home of the Witts family, "lords of the manor" hereabouts for over 200 years—a massive portrait of the Reverend Witts sitting regally on his stallion graces the drawing room. Facing lush, rolling countryside, the main house with its well-proportioned, high-ceilinged rooms oozes country-house charm and peacefulness—three of the five largest bedrooms have four-posters. Cleverly blended into this large home is a curving wing of rooms built to appear like other farm buildings that overlook the narrow lane. Smaller than the grander rooms of the main house, these rooms are smartly outfitted and have well-equipped bathrooms. A walk leads through the fields to the old mill at Lower Slaughter. It is a perfect location for forays through the Cotswolds: nearby Lower and Upper Swell are very picturesque; Broadway and Bourton-on-the-Water are best visited early in the morning to avoid the crowds. The Cotswold Farm Park with its rare farm animals is nearby. *Directions:* From the A429 on the outskirts of Bourton-on-the-Water a small signpost indicates "The Slaughters." Follow the lane through Lower to Upper Slaughter.

LORDS OF THE MANOR HOTEL
Manager: Iain Shelton
Upper Slaughter
Cheltenham
Gloucestershire GL54 2JD, England
Tel: (01451) 820243, Fax: (01451) 820696
Email: lordsofthemanor@btinternet.com
27 rooms
Double: £149–£299*, Suite: £249–£299*
*Service charge: 12.5%
Open all year, Credit cards: all major
Children welcome
www.karenbrown.com/ews/lordsofthemanor.html

Standing on the River Frome on the edge of the lovely town of Wareham, this 16th-century building was once the priory of Lady St. Mary, a Benedictine monastery, and is now a particularly lovely hotel. The entrance, through a little walled courtyard, sets the tone for this most delightful hotel. Decorated in soft colors, the dining room is most inviting. Lovely furniture and a grand piano highlight the beamed living room whose French windows lead under the wisteria-laden trellis to a broad expanse of lawn, which slopes down to the lazily flowing river—a perfect place to enjoy lunch on a warm summer day. Up the narrow staircase, guests write their requests for early-morning tea and newspapers on a blackboard. A narrow maze of corridors and stairs winds amongst the rooms, which are on the small side but very smartly outfitted. If you are looking for the most deluxe of quarters, request one of the suites in the riverside boathouse. The gardens are a delight, full of roses in the summer, with a series of small, sheltered walled gardens. Wareham is an interesting mix of architectural styles encircled by earth banks built by the Saxons. Lawrence of Arabia's home is open to the public at nearby Clouds Hill. There are many wonderful places to visit, such as Lulworth Cove, Corfe Castle, Poole Harbor, Wool, Bindon Abbey, and Durlston Head. *Directions:* Wareham is on the A351 between Poole and Swanage.

THE PRIORY
Manager: Jeremy Merchant
Church Green
Wareham
Dorset BH20 4ND, England
Tel: (01929) 551666, Fax: (01929) 554519
19 rooms
Double: £130–£250, Boathouse suite: £275–£285
Open all year
Credit cards: all major
Children over 8

I was very pleased to find a hotel in this lovely part of Northumberland. The Waren House Hotel was more or less derelict when Anita and Peter Laverack bought it in 1988, but over the years they have undertaken a complete renovation and refurbishment program, taking care to retain all the lovely old architectural features of this traditional, Georgian country house. The chandelier-lit entrance hall is home to a grand piano and many dolls from Anita's extensive collection. The ornately decorated drawing room is furnished with deep sofas and the library with traditional leather. By contrast, the large dining room, decorated in soft peach, is much more restful on the eye, with family portraits and pictures adorning the walls. Bedrooms are decorated in different styles: Maria is very French while the Gray suite is all gray silk. Edwardian is a most spacious suite with a large bedroom and sitting room divided by a bathroom with curved tub. This is a particularly attractive part of Northumberland: Bamburgh Castle commands a rocky outcrop high above the dunes with the stone cottages of the village in its shadow. A short drive brings you to Holy Island, historically known as Lindisfarne. The island is surrounded by water only at high tide, so careful attention must be paid to tide tables. *Directions:* Forty-five miles north of Newcastle on the A1, turn right to Waren Mill and the hotel is on your right at the far end of the village.

WAREN HOUSE HOTEL
Owners: Anita & Peter Laverack
Waren Mill, Belford
Northumberland NE70 7EE, England
Tel: (01668) 214581, Fax: (01668) 214484
Email: enquiries@warenhousehotel.co.uk
10 rooms
Double: £120–£140, Suite: £160–£190
Open all year
Credit cards: all major
Children over 14
www.karenbrown.com/ews/waren.html

Tucked behind a rambling timbered façade with mullioned windows and steeply pitched roof, Wesley House is a delightful "restaurant with rooms," offering fabulous fare to appreciative travelers and faithful locals. From the entry with its comfortable seating you can look through to the staggered levels of the attractive restaurant whose enticing menu makes for difficult choices. An early dinner is available for guests attending the Shakespeare Theatre. Climb the stairs of this inn whose oldest part dates to 1435 to five snug guestrooms, each named for a local meadow. The smallest, charmingly named Mumble Meadow, has a double bed and the room is attractively decorated in fabrics of cream and reds. Embury, the oldest room and housed in what was once the fireplace, has twin beds and a sloping floor. At back, Sandy Hollow has a twin and double bed while Almsbury, like the restaurant below, enjoys a private terrace and views across to Sudeley Castle. Setchley is also identified as the emergency fire escape, so residents of this room would be the first ones out! Except for those staying a single Saturday night, Matthew does not expect overnight guests to eat dinner at the inn but I would definitely recommend it. Wesley House provides a reasonable and convenient base from which to explore the neighboring Cotswold villages. *Directions:* Winchcombe is on the B4632 between Cheltenham and Broadway. Wesley House is easy to find on the main street at the corner of Castle Street.

WESLEY HOUSE
Owner: Matthew Brown
High Street
Winchcombe
Gloucestershire GL54 5LJ, England
Tel: (01242) 602366, Fax: (01242) 609046
Email: enquiries@wesleyhouse.co.uk
5 rooms
Double: £75–£85
Open all year, Credit cards: all major
Children welcome
www.karenbrown.com/ews/wesley.html

Just steps away from Winchester cathedral sits the most attractive Hotel du Vin and Bistro in an elegant townhouse designed by Christopher Wren (of St. Paul's fame). The hotel's theme is wine, with each bedroom named for its sponsoring winery that provided the photos and memorabilia decorating the walls. The rooms' overall decor is very similar—smart striped curtains, a duvet-topped queen- or king-sized bed (there is one king four-poster), television, and bathroom with oversized tub and Victorian shower with power head. I particularly enjoyed the most expensive and very large Courvoisier room with its ornate plasterwork ceiling, large window framing the garden, and two-part bathroom. Beringer's view of the car park was more than compensated for by its spaciousness and attractive photos of the famous winery. Trompe l'oeil plasterwork is an interesting feature of the spacious drawing room. Continental breakfast is available in the privacy of your room. The bistro is central to the operation and its menu is fun and varied. *Directions:* Turn off the M3 at Junction 11 to Winchester and follow signposts for the city center. The Hotel du Vin is on the left with lots of parking to the rear.

HOTEL DU VIN
Manager: Lesley Skelt
14 Southgate Street, Winchester
Hampshire SO23 9EF, England
Tel: (01962) 841414, Fax: (01962) 842458
Email: info@winchester.hotelduvin.co.uk
23 rooms
Double: £99–£145*, Suite: £185*
*Breakfast not included: £9–£12
Open all year
Credit cards: all major
Children welcome
www.karenbrown.com/ews/hotelduvin.html

Just beside the cathedral in a maze of little streets in the oldest part of Winchester, you can find comfortable accommodation at The Wykeham Arms and, across the road, under the same ownership, at The Saint George. The 250-year-old Wykeham Arms is an extraordinarily convivial and welcoming inn, with log fires, candles, over 600 pictures on the walls, 1,500 tankards hanging from beams, walls, and windows, and masses of Winchester College memorabilia. In the pub food ranges from elaborate to tasty, traditional fare, while a more sophisticated menu is offered at quieter tables in the Bishop's Bar or the Watchmaker's Room. Refurbishment of bedrooms upstairs, each with a different theme, will be complete by mid-2002. I loved Hamilton, a twin with red walls above white paneling, dozens of pictures of royalty and all things military, and huge bathroom with brick fireplace. The Saint George was converted from two tiny row houses and has the quaint attraction of a post office and shop just off the parlor. Up the narrow staircase there are four large, immaculate bedrooms, with absolutely everything from a sumptuous bathroom to a fax or modem port, and a snug single. Offering most space is the Old College Bakehouse, a little cottage in the garden, with a large sitting room and bathroom downstairs, bedroom upstairs, and tall arched, leaded windows opening up to rooftop views. *Directions:* Winchester is between junctions 9 and 10 on the M3. The hotel is located near the cathedral—Peter will send you a map so that you can navigate through the pedestrian zone to the pub's car park.

THE WYKEHAM ARMS & THE SAINT GEORGE
Managers: Kate & Peter Miller
75 Kingsgate Street
Winchester, Hampshire SO23 9PD, England
Tel: (01962) 853834, Fax: (01962) 854411
Email: doreen@wykehamarms.fsnet.co.uk
12 rooms
Double: £130
Closed Christmas Day, Credit cards: all major
Children over 14
www.karenbrown.com/ews/wykehamarms.html

Family holidays for John Cunliffe meant coming to stay with grandma at Gilpin Lodge, so when he saw the former family home for sale in the '80s he and his wife forsook their restaurant with rooms in Bath and purchased the place, moving to the Lake District and bringing their longtime manager, Richard Marriott, with them. Wings of bedrooms have been added and a brigade runs the kitchen but John and Christine still keep the integrity of a family home. Choose from spacious lounges and sitting nooks, and dine in one of the three cozy restaurants. Bedrooms come in all shapes and sizes, from grand two-level suites with luxury bathrooms to smaller rooms, which are just as delightful. All are beautifully decorated and appointed, as one would expect from a top-of-the-line country house hotel. It's a peaceful spot overlooking rolling, sheep-dotted hills. A stone's throw away is Windermere golf course and just down the road is the bustle of Windermere with ferries plying the lake against a backdrop of majestic fells. A ferry takes you across the lake to Near Sawrey and Beatrix Potter's home, Hill Top Farm. Wordsworth fans head for Rydal House and Dove Cottage, while walkers head for the hills. Gilpin Lodge can arrange for a private car and driver to escort you on your sightseeing. *Directions:* Exit the M6 at junction 36, taking the A591 around Kendal towards Windermere. At the large roundabout, turn onto the B5284 through Crook village to Gilpin Lodge on your right.

GILPIN LODGE
Owners: Christine & John Cunliffe
Manager: Richard Marriott
Crook Road, near Windermere
Cumbria LA23 3NE, England
Tel: (015394) 88818, Fax: (015394) 88058
Email: hotel@gilpin-lodge.co.uk
14 rooms
Double: £90–£210
Open all year, Credit cards: all major
Children over 7
www.karenbrown.com/ews/gilpin.html

Windermere is one of the most popular and most crowded Lake District towns, but Holbeck Ghyll is set far from the traffic-clogged streets high above Lake Windermere in a rhododendron-filled garden overlooking the lake and the peaks of the Langdale fells— idyllic scenery that has made the Lake District such a magnet for visitors. Mellow, golden-oak paneling in the entrance hall extends up the staircase of Holbeck Ghyll and heavy beams create a nook large enough for chairs round a cozy winter fire. In summer guests prefer the sitting room whose window seat offers a magnificent view of the lake and the distant mountains. Dinner is delicious: there are lots of choices for each course and vegetarian dishes are available. Bedrooms come in all shapes and sizes, the premier rooms, of course, being those that offer lake views. Room 7, in the tower, has its own private, narrow staircase and is worth the climb for its view from the four-poster bed. Room 11, tucked under the eaves, has a sitting alcove that enjoys the same spectacular view. However the most breathtaking views are those offered by the six deluxe, luxuriously appointed Lodge rooms. Pamper yourself with a beauty treatment in the health spa. Within a 20-minute drive are Dove Cottage, Rydal Mount, and the villages of Hawkshead and Grasmere. *Directions:* From Windermere take the A591 (Ambleside road) for 3 miles, turn right on Holbeck Lane, and the hotel is on your left after half a mile.

HOLBECK GHYLL
Owners: Patricia & David Nicholson
Holbeck Lane, Windermere
Cumbria LA23 1LU, England
Tel: (015394) 32375, Fax: (015394) 34743
Email: stay@holbeckghyll.com
20 rooms
Double: £170–£300*, Suite: £210–£300*
*Includes dinner, bed & breakfast
Open all year, Credit cards: all major
Children welcome
www.karenbrown.com/ews/holbeckghyll.html

Four 17th-century townhouses at the very heart of this delightful Cotswold town have been cleverly interwoven to create this charming hotel. This accounts for the maze of little staircases going seemingly every which way up and around to the bedrooms, all of which are different: several have high ceilings and all are decorated in soft, muted colors in a most appealing, country-house style. Nightingale, Jay, Swan, and Robin are particularly attractive rooms. Equally delightful rooms (Barn Owl and Partridge) are found in an adjacent cottage. The recently refurbished dining room is enhanced by dramatic, large flower arrangements. There is a large drawing room upstairs. A central log fireplace burns a cheery blaze in the bar with its wood-paneled floor and peach-washed walls. An especially cozy nook is the tiny flagstone-floored room with its country-style chairs. French windows open up to a small garden where tables, benches, and colorful hanging baskets are encircled by a high stone wall—a lovely spot to enjoy lunch in the summer. The small town of Woodstock is at its best after the crowds have left. Walk through the grounds to visit Blenheim Palace. Oxford is 8 miles away and Stratford-upon-Avon 32 miles. Cotswold villages are on your doorstep. *Directions:* Market Street is off Oxford Street, the A44 Oxford to Stratford road.

THE FEATHERS
Manager: Peter Bate
Market Street, Woodstock
Oxfordshire OX20 1SX, England
Tel: (01993) 812291, Fax: (01993) 813158
Email: enquiries@feathers.co.uk
21 rooms
Double: £135–£185*, Suite: £240–£290*
*Includes Continental breakfast & service charge (12.5%)
Open all year
Credit cards: all major
Children welcome
www.karenbrown.com/ews/thefeathers.html

York, where Romans walked, Vikings ruled, and Normans conquered, is a fascinating city, its historical center encircled by a massive stone wall. The Grange, a lovely townhouse hotel, lies just beyond the city walls and ten minutes' walk from the Minster (cathedral), making it an ideal spot for exploring this wonderful city. The morning room, which leads directly off the stone-flagged lobby, has a rich, traditional feel with its Turkish carpet and Victorian portrait hung over the fireplace. The Ivy Restaurant's decor was chosen to enhance the gilt-framed oil paintings of St. Ledger winners on loan from the York Racehorse Museum. A seafood dinner, which is very good value for money, is available in the adjacent Seafood Bar, while the basement brasserie offers simpler, lighter fare. Each of the bedrooms—some with canopied four-poster or half-tester beds—has different decor: several are very dramatic. I was impressed by the amount of space in the standard double rooms. Though the standard king-bedded rooms had bigger beds, I found them tight on room space. York takes several days to explore: attractions include the Minster, the Jorvik Viking museum, the Treasurer's House, the medieval streets of The Shambles, the castle and its adjacent museum, walks along the walls, and a boat ride on the River Ouse. *Directions:* The Grange is located along Bootham, which is the A19, York to Thirsk road.

THE GRANGE
Manager: Shara Ross
1 Clifton
York Y030 6AA, England
Tel: (01904) 644744, Fax: (01904) 612453
Email: info@grangehotel.co.uk
30 rooms
Double: £125–£185, Suite: £215
Open all year
Credit cards: all major
Children welcome
www.karenbrown.com/ews/thegrange.html

Middlethorpe Hall is an imposing, red-brick William-and-Mary country house built in 1699 for Thomas Barlow, a successful cutler who wished to distance himself from his industrial success and establish himself as a country gentleman. It has been skillfully restored by Historic House Hotels and is now a very grand hotel, but without one iota of stuffiness. The two refined dining rooms have large windows overlooking the grounds. After enjoying elegant, country-house fare you retire to the enormous, graceful drawing room for coffee, chocolates, and liqueurs round the fire watched over by the massive portraits of long-departed gentry. Up the magnificent carved-oak staircase, bedrooms enjoy high ceilings, tall windows (those at the back with views across the grounds), and Edwardian-style bathrooms. Additional, very attractively decorated bedrooms are in the stable block across the courtyard. The spa contains a pool, steam room, sauna, fitness room, and three beauty-treatment rooms. York (a ten-minute drive away) will keep you busy for at least two days—add Castle Howard, explorations of the dales, moorlands, and the coast, and you can justify a week in this most superlative of country house hotels. *Directions:* The hotel is situated just outside the village of Bishopthorpe, next to York racecourse. Leave the A64 (which forms the southern part of the York Outer Ring Road) at the A1036, in the direction of York city center (signposted York West) and follow the hotel's map.

MIDDLETHORPE HALL
Manager: Stuart McPherson
Bishopthorpe Road
York 023 2GB, England
Tel: (01904) 641241, Fax: (01904) 620176
30 rooms
Double: £160–£250*, Suite: £220–£325*
*Breakfast not included: £14.50
Open all year, Credit cards: all major
Children over 8
Relais & Châteaux Member

Hotels in Scotland

Fifteen miles of winding, single-track road lead you through land and sea lochs in some of Scotland's wildest scenery to Achiltibuie, a few cottages straggling along the road overlooking a broad expanse of bay and the Summer Isles, grassy little islands whose name extends to include the five tiny communities on the peninsula of which Achiltibuie is one. Just beyond the post office you find the Summer Isles Hotel run by Mark and Geraldine Irvine: it has been in their family since the '60s. Guests come to enjoy solitude and wild scenery in the daytime and in the evening experience the cooking of Michelin-starred chef Chris Firth-Bernard, Scottish Chef of the Year 1998. Bar meals are also available. Accommodation is in four distinct categories: rooms in the main house (ask for one facing the sea); the turf-roofed log cabins (lots of country charm but no view but priced accordingly); cottage rooms (very attractively decorated with four rooms offering views of the sea across the fields); and the boathouse suite (fireplace in the sitting room and spectacular view from the bedroom atop a spiral staircase). You can take a local boat round the islands to see seals and birds. *Directions:* Achiltibuie is 85 miles from Inverness. Take the A835 for 10 miles beyond Ullapool and turn left for Achiltibuie.

SUMMER ISLES HOTEL
Owners: Gerry & Mark Irvine
Achiltibuie
Wester Ross IV26 2YG, Scotland
Tel: (01854) 622282, Fax: (01854) 622251
Email: summerisleshotel@aol.com
13 rooms
Double: £104–£130, Suite: £180–£220
Open Easter to Oct
Credit cards: MC, VS
Children over 6
www.karenbrown.com/ews/summer.html

Ardsheal House has a fabulous location on a bluff overlooking Loch Linnhe and the Morvern Mountains. A 1½-mile driveway and an 800-acre estate give an off-the-beaten-track feel to a house that is excellently situated for sightseeing. The Sutherlands are extremely enthusiastic about their lovely home, which dates back to the 1760s. When Neil inherited the estate the house had been sold to pay the inheritance tax but he and Philippa bought it back in 1994. It had been a hotel for many years and was rather large as a home for two people, so they decided to open it up to guests, offering dinner, bed, and breakfast. The heart of the house is the oak-paneled entry hall with its cheery open fire and sitting nook overlooking the garden. Dinner is served under the watchful eye of Neil's ancestors, though often in the summer meals are enjoyed in the spacious conservatory. Interesting furniture abounds as Neil's grandfather was a trader in Java, and Phillippa and Neil have lived in Hong Kong. Discuss your sleeping requirements when booking since there are bedrooms to suit all tastes, from a Javanese four-poster to a family room with a double and two single beds. Ardsheal House is a splendid base for exploring the Western Highlands, visiting Glencoe and Glenfinnan (where Bonnie Prince Charlie raised the Scottish standard at the start of the Jacobite rebellion), and making day trips to the islands of Mull, Staffa, and Iona. *Directions:* Ardsheal House is 17 miles south of Fort William and 30 miles north of Oban, located on the A828 5 miles south of Ballachulish Bridge between Glencoe and Appin.

ARDSHEAL HOUSE   New
Owners: Philippa & Neil Sutherland
Kentallen of Appin
Argyll PA38 4BX, Scotland
Tel: (01631) 740227, Fax: (01631) 740342
Email: info@ardsheal.co.uk
6 rooms, Double: £110
Open Feb to Nov, Credit cards: MC, VS
Children welcome
www.karenbrown.com/ews/ardsheal.html

After twenty years of farming south of the border and eight years as a banker in London, David returned to his native Scotland with his wife Kay and their white bull terrier Louis. They found Fascadale House (literal translation: "sheltered haven"), built by a local minister as his private home in 1863, set in 6 acres of gardens and woodlands on the shore of Loch Fyne. Incorporating designer fabrics and antiques, it has been tastefully redecorated in a style that thoroughly complements its Victorian architecture. A sweeping staircase leads upstairs from the paneled entrance hallway to three comfortable bedrooms, two with en-suite bathrooms, one with its private bathroom across the hall. To relax, guests can enjoy a game of billiards or simply watch the proceedings from a comfortable leather chair. The drawing room, with its open fire and view across the loch to the Cowal Hills beyond, is available for those preferring a more serene atmosphere. A short à-la-carte menu is available for dinner. One- and two-bedroom self-catering accommodations are available for weekly rentals. There are many lovely gardens to visit in area—Crarae Gardens are full of rare plants and shrubs that are at their best in May and June. Trace Loch Fyne south to the Mull of Kintyre and spend a day exploring its sandy coves, rocky headlands, and charming fishing villages. *Directions:* From Oban take the A816 for 35 miles to Lochgilphead and the A83 towards Campbeltown to Ardrishaig where you find Fascadale House on your right at the south end of the village.

FASCADALE HOUSE   New
Owners: David & Kay Cameron Davies
Tarbert Road, Ardrishaig, Lochgilphead
Argyll PA30 8EP, Scotland
Tel: (01546) 603845, Fax: (01546) 602152
Email: info@fascadale.com
3 rooms, 3 cottages
Double: £80, Cottage: £175–£345 per week
Open all year, Credit cards: MC, VS
Children welcome
www.karenbrown.com/ews/fascadale.html

234   *Hotels in Scotland*

A convenient resting place north or south on the "Road to the Isles," Arisaig House lays a sumptuous trap for unwary travelers that, once entered, may delay their onward progress for days. Built as an imposing holiday home for a wealthy English industrialist in 1864, the house was badly damaged by fire and subsequently rebuilt in the mid-1930s, a fact reflected in the handsome paneling and plasterwork of the public rooms. A splendid hand-carved staircase leads from the inner reception hall to the second floor and the majority of the expansive and recently refurbished bedrooms, named for Scottish lochs. Since Ruth and John Smither acquired the property in 1982, the number of bedrooms has been gradually reduced to twelve and the room sizes increased. All rooms have sparkling bathrooms with deliciously warmed white towels and, with one exception, views to the ocean or the hills nearby. The terraced Victorian walled garden is the source of fresh fare for the kitchen where it is artfully combined with local meat, fish, and game to produce award-winning cuisine. After dinner, guests can retire to the comforts of the drawing room, the bar, or the cozy fireside lounge. Stroll though the gardens and down to the sea. Take a day trip to the isles of Rhum, Muck, and Eigg from the adjacent village of Arisaig. *Directions*: From Fort William take the A830 towards Mallaig for the 30-mile drive to Arisaig House, found on your left 3 miles before the village of Arisaig.

ARISAIG HOUSE   New
Owners: Ruth & John Smither, Andrew Smither
Beasdale, by Arisaig
Inverness-shire PH39 4NR, Scotland
Tel: (01687) 430622, Fax: (01687) 450626
Email: arisaighse@aol.com
12 rooms
Double: £175–£295
Open Mar to Nov, Credit cards: MC, VS
Children over 8
Relais & Châteaux Member
www.karenbrown.com/ews/arisaig.html

The Reid family, wealthy industrialists who built steam locomotives, had a yen for grandeur when they built Auchterarder in the 1830s as their country residence. It boasts vast rooms with lofty ceilings, lavishly paneled halls and reception rooms, and a winter-garden conservatory leading to an ornate sitting room—a tremendous amount of craftsmanship went into this magnificent house. This is truly a house of the age of Scottish baronial architecture, an era of grandeur, which the management have gone to great lengths to keep and enhance with the use of ornate wallpapers and elaborate furnishings. The six very large master bedrooms have high ceilings, tall windows, and very spacious bathrooms. The Graham Room has a particularly impressive array of fitted furniture. The Stuart Room sports a huge Victorian bathroom with marble floor and walls and a large claw-foot tub with a dinner-plate-sized showerhead. Turret and courtyard rooms are, by comparison, small rooms with much quieter decor. Perth, the ancient capital of Scotland, is only a few miles away, as are Stirling Castle, Drummond Castle, and Crief. *Directions:* From Perth take the A9 (Stirling road) to Auchterarder. From The center of the village take the B8062 (Crief road) for 1½ miles and the hotel is on your right.

AUCHTERARDER HOUSE
Manager: Ian Fleming
Auchterarder
Perthshire PH3 1DZ, Scotland
Tel: (01764) 663646, Fax: (01764) 662939
Email: auchterarder@wrensgroup.com
15 rooms
Double: £170–£295
Open all year
Credit cards: all major
Children over 12
www.karenbrown.com/ews/auchterarder.html

Five years of hard work by owners Wendy and Don Matheson have seen Boath House transformed from a "house beyond economic repair" to a magnificent example of a fully restored, grade-A-listed Georgian mansion set in 20 acres of grounds with its own Victorian walled garden and trout-stocked lake. Six spectacular bedrooms are just the beginning. My favorite has a view of the lake and a bathroom with a free-standing, centrally located tub that begs you to soak in it. Two of the smaller rooms can be converted into a family-sized suite. Guest facilities include a comfortable sitting room with fireplace, an award-winning dining room (the five-course dinner menu changes daily), and, conveniently located in the basement, a gymnasium, sauna, and aromatherapy spa. Contemporary art from local artists is displayed throughout the house and the Mathesons encourage guests to move selected items to their room on a "try before you buy" basis. A separate double-bedded guest cottage reached by a short walk through the grounds provides a secluded hideaway. Golfers head to the championship courses at Nairn and Dunbar but Don urges them not to overlook the local courses, which provide very good value for money. Just outside the nearby seaside town of Nairn you can visit the massive sand dunes that swallowed the village of Culbin two centuries ago. Loch Ness and Cawdor Castle are great attractions. *Directions:* From Inverness take the A96 towards Aberdeen. Go through Nairn and Boath House is on your left after 2 miles.

BOATH HOUSE   New
Owners: Wendy & Don Matheson
Auldearn, Nairn
Inverness-shire IV12 5TE, Scotland
Tel: (01667) 454896, Fax: (01667) 455469
Email: wendy@boath-house.demon.co.uk
7 rooms
Double: £150–£200, Suite: £200
Closed last 2 weeks in Jan, Credit cards: all major
Children welcome
www.karenbrown.com/ews/boath.html

Royal Deeside is an area of outstanding beauty and "royal" because the Royal Family have their summer home, Balmoral, here. Sitting at the end of a quiet lane with its gardens looking over Ballater golf course to the distant hills of Glen Muick, this sturdy Edwardian-style house was skillfully converted to a hotel by Priscilla and John Finnie. Guests have a small sitting room with lots of magazines and interesting books on local castles, which adjoins a convivial, cozy bar. Little tables are spaciously arranged in the large dining room where a four-course dinner is served—there are no hidden extras and canapés, coffee, and petits fours are included. The first floor (second in America) bedrooms are spacious and furnished in traditional style while the four that nestle under the eaves are more contemporary in their decor and snugger in size. Ballater is a perfect location for exploring castles. There are numerous castles to explore: Drum, Crathes, Dunnottar, Fraser, Corgarff, Balmoral, and Craigievar. Golf, gardens, and art galleries round out the list of local attractions. *Directions:* From Aberdeen take the A93 for 40 miles to Ballater. Continue on A93 through the village towards Braemar, and Braemar Place is the last street on the left before you begin to climb the hill to leave the village.

BALGONIE HOUSE
Owners: Priscilla & John Finnie
Braemar Place
Ballater
Grampian AB35 5NQ, Scotland
Tel & fax: (013397) 55482
Email: balgonie@lineone.net
9 rooms
Double: £116–£120
Closed mid-Jan to mid-Feb
Credit cards: all major
Children over 5
www.karenbrown.com/ews/balgonie.html

With lush lawns stretching beside the confluence of the Dee and Feugh rivers, Banchory Lodge has a magnificent setting. There has been a hostelry here since the 16th century when the mail coach halted at Banchory to change horses. Over the years the hostelry has evolved in to a pleasing, rather rambling country house hotel. The first thing I always notice at Banchory House is the abundance of flower arrangements, from little posies on coffee tables to grand floral arrangements alongside splendid oil paintings. Log fires and oversized chairs set the relaxed, comfortable atmosphere of the place. Dinner is served in the grand dining room, which has a comfortable formality, with guests both in jacket and tie and casual attire. Country-house fare is the order of the day here, but if you wish to dine more simply, just choose one or two courses from the menu. Bedrooms are delightfully old-fashioned: room 9 with its semi-circular window was a particular favorite—though I would settle for any of the rooms that face the tumbling river. Fishing (the hotel has four beats), golfing, and walking are popular pastimes. Nearby Crathes Castle (an L-shaped tower house) has an early-18th-century formal garden, while Drum Castle has a magnificent rose garden. Farther away lie Fyvie and Craigievar. *Directions:* From Aberdeen take the A93 for 17 miles to Banchory. Turn left at the traffic lights and left just before you cross the river.

BANCHORY LODGE
Owner: Margaret Jaffray
Banchory, near Aberdeen
Grampian AB31 3HS, Scotland
Tel: (01330) 822625, Fax: (01330) 825019
Email: banchorylodgeht@btconnect.com
22 rooms
Double: £90–£130, Suite: £130–£145
Open Mar to Dec
Credit cards: all major
Children welcome
www.karenbrown.com/ews/banchory.html

The Sutherland family made a fortune in jute manufacturing and in 1840 built Kinloch House, an impressive baronial-style mansion, as their country home. Under the ownership of Sarah and David Shentall, Kinloch has emerged as a luxurious country house hotel while maintaining all the atmosphere of a grand Scottish country home. The golden-oak-paneled entry hall rises to a first-floor gallery lit by an intricate leaded-light ceiling. Here the hall fire blazes a welcome to this lovely hotel, which marries all the style and elegance of days gone by with the amenities of a first-class hotel. Bedrooms off the gallery are generally large and spacious (one is smaller). Several have lovely old four-poster beds and one a half-tester. Rooms at the front of the house offer lovely views across a field of highland cattle to the rolling Sidlaw Hills and glimpses of nearby lochs. All the spacious bedrooms with their large bathrooms in the east wing capture the same lovely countryside view. David, in his clan Sinclair kilt, is happy to advise you on which malt whisky to select—he has over 160 of them—or which of his many vintage brandies to enjoy. Enjoy the pool and fitness center and choose from over 40 golf courses within an hour's drive. Blair Castle and Scone Palace are popular with visitors. *Directions:* From Perth take the A9 (Inverness road) for 10 miles to Dunkeld and the A923 (Blaigowrie road) for 8 miles.

KINLOCH HOUSE
Owners: Sarah & David Shentall
By Blairgowrie
Tayside PH10 6SG, Scotland
Tel: (01250) 884237, Fax: (01250) 884333
Email: reception@kinlochhouse.com
20 rooms
Double: £155–£172, Suite: £195–£225
Closed Dec 18 to 29
Credit cards: all major
Children welcome
www.karenbrown.com/ews/kinloch.html

Originally the house of the local laird, Hobsburn dates back to the 17th century. Set in its 75-acre estate and connected to the village by a long driveway, it has now become home to Christopher and Jacqui McLean May, their two dogs, Moscow and Findlay, and their award-winning herd of pedigree Highland cattle. Guests have the run of the home, including the formal drawing room complete with paintings of family forbears and an extremely comfortable sitting room with log-burning stove. Breakfast is served in the expansive country kitchen or, weather permitting, outside on the patio. A four-course dinner with complimentary drinks is available with advanced reservations, though guests often walk down the drive to the Horse and Hounds pub. Two spacious, tastefully decorated bedrooms (one in vivid orange and aquamarine and the other in rose pink and blue) each have a twin and a double bed and their own private bathroom across the hall. An additional small double-bedded room is available to rent with either of these rooms. Situated just north of the border with England, with easy access (one and a half hours by car) to both Newcastle and Edinburgh, Hobsburn is surrounded by local history, with abbeys at Jedburgh and Melrose, and castles at Floors and Mellerstain. Shoppers head for the nearby wool and cashmere factory shops. *Directions:* Cross the border on the A68. Turn left on the A6088 towards Hawick for the 8-mile drive to Bonchester Bridge where you find the entrance to Hobsburn on your left almost opposite the Horse and Hounds pub.

HOBSBURN   New
Owners: Jacqui & Christopher McLean May
Bonchester Bridge, Hawick
Roxburghshire TD9 8JW, Scotland
Tel: (01450) 86072, Fax: (01450) 860330
Email: kb@mcleanmay.com
3 rooms
Double: £80
Open all year, Credit cards: MC, VS
Children over 16
www.karenbrown.com/ews/hobsburn.html

There has been a fortified tower house beside the sea on the Beauly Firth since the 16th century. Simon Frazer, the eighth lord of Lovat, incorporated the tower into his home when he married Jean Stewart in 1621—you can see their stone marriage lintel above the drawing-room fireplace and see the tower walls with their arrow slits behind the paneling. Janet and Graham Cross now offer guests a warm Scottish welcome here. Bunchrew's position on the banks of the Beauly Firth is magnificent—even if you do not secure a room with a water view, you are assured of enjoying the view at dinner. Bedrooms and bathrooms are comfortable rather than luxurious and Janet and Graham set the highest of standards, so improvements are constantly being made. Three new rooms were added in 2001, one being the old nursery in a tower room. Some guestrooms have charming old furniture, while others have reproduction furniture, and all is spotlessly clean and well cared for. Hot-water pipes running through rooms and along corridors are an unusual feature of the older part of the house. You can take a trip to visit the large school of bottle-nosed dolphins that reside in the firth, go hill walking, and play golf. Inverness and Loch Ness with its famous resident are just down the road. *Directions:* Arriving in Inverness, follow signposts for the city center and the A82 Fort William road for a short distance to the A862 Beauly road, which takes you along the Beauly Firth for 3 miles to the little village of Bunchrew. Bunchrew House is on your right.

BUNCHREW HOUSE   New
Owners: Janet & Graham Cross
Bunchrew, Inverness
Inverness-shire IV3 6TA, Scotland
Tel: (01463) 234917, Fax: (01463) 710620
Email: welcome@bunchrew-inverness.co.uk
14 rooms
Double: £140–£200
Open all year, Credit cards: MC, VS
Children welcome
www.karenbrown.com/ews/bunchrew.html

Callander is such an attractive, bustling little town. I selected Brook Linn for its lovely location, and outstanding warmth of welcome. Built as a private home for a wealthy wool merchant, this solid Victorian home is set high on the hill well away from the bustle of the town but close enough for a ten-minute walk to find you at its heart. A hearty Scottish breakfast is the only meal served, and Fiona and Derek are happy to recommend restaurants nearby. Brook Linn is furnished in a clean and tidy manner appropriate to the house. The principal bedrooms have small shower rooms tucked into the corner and two are large enough to have a double and a single bed. A tiny single room does not have en-suite facilities so is let at a reduced rate. The Trossachs with their rolling pasture and heather moors, mountains, and glens are on your doorstep. The Wallace Monument Museum and Stirling Castle are just a short drive away. *Directions:* Take the A84 into Callander going north through the town and turn right just beyond Pinewood Nursing Home into Leny Feus. Follow the road up the hill and right into Brook Linn's driveway.

BROOK LINN
Owners: Fiona & Derek House
Leny Feus, Callander
Perthshire FK17 8AU, Scotland
Tel & fax: (01877) 330103
Email: derek@blinn.freeserve.co.uk
7 rooms
Double: £54
Open Easter to Oct
Credit cards: MC, VS
Children welcome
No-smoking house
www.karenbrown.com/ews/brooklinn.html

We defy you not to wax lyrical over the Three Chimneys and The House Over-By, an outstanding restaurant with rooms. The Three Chimneys restaurant, which serves some of the finest food in Scotland, is housed in an historic croft packed with all the old-world charm of thick walls, low beams, and cozy dining nooks, while the six exquisite bedrooms are found in The House Over-By, a contemporary building built to echo the historic restaurant. The Spears have run the restaurant for almost two decades and in this time Shirley has gained a worldwide following for her food. Incorporating as much fresh local produce as possible from Skye and the Highlands, many of her dishes are based on traditional ideas but given a modern slant. Accommodation in the adjacent House Over-By is stylishly chic. The large luxurious bedrooms are decorated in soft, earthy Highland colors, and each has a sparkling, state-of-the-art shower room and views across Loch Dunvegan to the Waternish Peninsula. In the mornings a generous buffet is served in the breakfast room. For sightseeing, you are just 5 country miles from Dunvegan with its ancient castle. Narrow lanes wind you round the Outer Hebrides with its bays, beaches, and spectacular views then, continuing up the peninsula, the road leads to the most westerly point of Skye at Neist Point lighthouse. *Directions:* From the outskirts of Dunvegan take the B884 towards Glendale for 4 miles to Colbost where you find Three Chimneys and The House Over-By on the left beside the Croft Museum.

THREE CHIMNEYS & THE HOUSE OVER-BY   *New*
Owners: Shirley & Eddie Spear
Colbost, Dunvegan
Isle of Skye IV55 8ZT, Scotland
Tel: (01470) 511258, Fax: (01470) 511358
Email: eatandstay@threechimneys.co.uk
6 rooms
Double: £175
Closed 2 weeks in Jan. Credit cards: all major
Children welcome
www.karenbrown.com/ews/threechimneys.html

Beyond a vast expanse of immaculately mown lawn stands Culloden House, a beautiful Georgian mansion built so as to incorporate the ruins of Culloden Castle, Bonnie Prince Charlie's headquarters before the fateful battle of 1746. Culloden House has always had a reputation for hospitality, a tradition that is continued today by Stephen Davies and his staff, who offer the warmest of welcomes. After canapés in the clubby bar, dine in the gracious dining room with its lofty ceiling, faux-marble columns, and original plaster medallions, enjoying dinner served by staff uniformed in the Culloden tartan. Finish the evening with coffee and homemade chocolates in the grand drawing room. Bedrooms and suites in the main house vary in size from vast to snug, with bathrooms that run the gamut from small and rather ordinary to large and luxurious. Several of the most elegant rooms have smaller bathrooms, so be sure to discuss your choice of room when you make reservations. With the rambling nature of the hotel, which has no elevator, it is considered unsuitable for those who have difficulty with stairs. Parties of friends traveling together may wish to stay in the luxurious Adam-style pavilion. Culloden battlefield, just down the road, is a "must visit," as are nearby Cawdor Castle and Loch Ness. *Directions:* Take the A9 south from Inverness to the A96 Aberdeen and Nairn turnoff. Go straight over the first roundabout and take the next right to Culloden. Go through two sets of traffic lights and take the next road left to the hotel.

CULLODEN HOUSE
Manager: Stephen Davies
Culloden
Inverness-shire IV2 7BZ, Scotland
Tel: (01463) 790461, Fax: (01463) 792181
Email: info@cullodenhouse.co.uk
20 rooms, 8 suites
Double: £190–£250, Suite: £250–£270
Open all year, Credit cards: all major
Children over 12
www.karenbrown.com/ews/culloden.html

Kinlochfollart was built as a manse, a vast home for the former minister, which dwarfs the tiny country church just up the road. The church chose an inspirational spot for the minister's home, giving him spectacular views straight up Loch Dunvegan. However, the upkeep of the place overwhelmed the parish, so the clergy was moved to snugger quarters and now Kinlochfollart is the lovely home of Rosemary and Donald MacLeod. Guests enjoy the kind of luxury that was totally unknown to earlier occupants and the MacLeods really go the extra mile to treat their guests as visiting friends. You are welcomed with a reviving cup of tea on arrival, enjoy pre-dinner drinks together before dinner, then eat your evening meal with Rosemary and Donald round the dining-room table (dinner reservations must be made in advance). Visitors have the run of the house with the library, sitting room, and conservatory being open for their use. This is MacLeod country and the home of the MacLeod chief, Dunvegan Castle, the oldest inhabited castle in Scotland, is just up the road and well worth a visit. The island abounds in spectacular drives and you can take local boat excursions to view the nearby seal colonies. *Directions:* Arriving on Skye, take the A85 to Sligachan then the A863 to Dunvegan. Enter the village and take a small road to the left signposted Glendale (ignore the first Glendale turning). After half a mile Kinlochfollart is the white house to your right set in the trees beside the loch.

KINLOCHFOLLART   New
Owners: Rosemary & Donald MacLeod
By Dunvegan
Isle of Skye IV55 8WQ, Scotland
Tel & fax: (01470) 521470
3 rooms
Double: £78–£84
Closed Christmas & New Year
Credit cards: all major
Children welcome

Drumsheugh Gardens is a quiet square of Victorian townhouses grouped round a leafy garden just three minutes' walk from Princes Street. Three of these spacious townhouses have been beautifully restored as The Bonham hotel, which offers the elegance of an old exterior, a spacious interior, a tongue-in-cheek modern decor, and the most up-to-date plumbing and communications. You feel like Alice standing before the enormous looking glasses in the dining room, while in the sitting room there's the Cheshire cat sculpture sitting beside the fire, inviting you to sit on the circular cherry-red couch that swirls upward to an enormous light fixture. Bedrooms range in size from petite to grand suites and range in their decor from sedate to vibrant. Those at the back on the upper floors enjoy lovely views over the Firth of Forth. A great many have whimsical touches such as a mural of a parrot in a porthole in a room with a nautical theme and an ornate chimney pot painted on the bedhead in a spacious room overlooking the rooftops. Bedrooms are in the forefront of new technology, with an integrated system that turns the TV into a computer screen and provides CD audio, DVD, and full Internet access. Beds are large, bathrooms gleamingly modern. *Directions:* Take George Street (parallel to Princes Street) through Charlotte Square (Hope Street) and onto Queensferry Road. Just as the road goes downhill, turn left into Chester Street and first right into Drumsheugh Gardens. Double-park on arrival.

THE BONHAM
Owner: Peter Taylor, Manager: Fiona Vernon
35 Drumsheugh Gardens
Edinburgh EH3 7RN, Scotland
Tel: (0131) 223 6060, Fax: (0131) 226 6080
Email: reserve@thebonham.com
46 rooms, 2 suites
Double: £165–£240*, Suite: £325*
*Continental breakfast
Closed Christmas, Credit cards: all major
Children welcome
www.karenbrown.com/ews/bonham.html

A brisk, fifteen-minute walk from Princes Street brings you to Channings, a delightful country-house-style hotel encompassing five large Edwardian townhouses whose front parlors are now quiet sitting rooms. Its public areas are decorated with the greatest taste and fireplaces and new blue carpeting give a very restful feeling. A recent refurbishment of half the bedrooms, one a four-poster, has given them a smart new look—all are individually decorated with lovely fabrics and provide every amenity such as satellite TV, direct-dial phones with voice mail, modem point, and trouser press. Some bathrooms have Jacuzzis or slipper roll-top baths. One of the garden-level Club Rooms even has its own private garden. Our "superior" bedroom was a beautifully decorated twin with comfortable armchairs, an alcove with desk and chair, and an enormous, gleaming bathroom with bidet, slipper bath, and separate shower. Rooms tucked under the eaves have pine furniture and sloping ceilings, which give them a pleasant cottage-cozy ambiance. Channings' warm and traditional restaurant, which serves first-class food, contrasts strikingly with the light and contemporary wine bar and conservatory. *Directions:* Take George Street (parallel to Princes Street) through Charlotte Square (Hope Street) and onto Queensferry Road. Cross the river and take the second right (beside Learmonth Hotel) and follow South Learmonth Gardens to Channings. Double-park on arrival.

CHANNINGS
Owner: Peter Taylor
Manager: Marco Truffelli
12–16 South Learmonth Gardens
Edinburgh EH4 1EZ, Scotland
Tel: (0131) 332 3232, Fax: (0131) 332 9631
Email: reserve@channings.com
43 rooms, 3 suites
Double: £160–£210, Suite: £250
Closed Christmas, Credit cards: all major
Children welcome
www.karenbrown.com/ews/channings.html

Danube Street was built in 1826 as one of the most fashionable streets in Stockbridge, an area of Edinburgh that lies a ten-minute walk from Princes Street and the heart of the city. Towards the middle of this lovely terrace is number 7, home to friendly Fiona and Colin Mitchell-Rose, who have the most delicious sense of humor. It's very much a comfortable family home, with dogs Millie and George (the official greeters) in their basket in the hall. Breakfast comes complete with homemade jam and scones, fruit salad, and traditional cooked breakfast served at the long dining table. Guestrooms, all beautifully decorated and with pretty bedlinens, are below stairs: a spacious four-poster room overlooks the garden and has its tea- and coffee-making tray set atop the old kitchen range (this was once the home's kitchen), while a large twin-bedded room and snug single room face the street. Guests have their own private entry and can come and go as they please. Just round the corner Fiona and Colin have a lovely two-bedroom apartment with a well-equipped kitchen, a queen-sized four-poster room, a twin-bedded room, and a living room with pull-out sofa. This provides excellent and luxurious accommodation for family and friends who want to stay three or more days. *Directions:* From Princes Street take Frederick Street north across George Street, through Circus Place to the bottom of the hill. Cross the bridge and turn left into Leslie Place. Danube Street is the second turning to the left.

SEVEN DANUBE STREET
Owners: Fiona & Colin Mitchell-Rose
7 Danube Street
Edinburgh EH4 1NN, Scotland
Tel: (0131) 332 2755, Fax: (0131) 343 3648
Email: seven.danubestreet@virgin.net
3 rooms, 1 2-bedroom apartment
Double: £95–£115, Apartment: £140
Closed Christmas, Credit cards: MC, VS
Children welcome, No-smoking house
www.karenbrown.com/ews/danube.html

The wide cobbled streets of Edinburgh's New Town with their regular layout, crescents, squares, and gardens are in sharp contrast to the narrow, winding, medieval streets of Edinburgh's Old Town. Just a five-minute walk from either Princes Street or Waverley Station you find 27 Heriot Row, Andrea and Gene Targett-Adams' lovely Georgian home overlooking the trees of Queen Street Gardens. Gene specializes in the restoration of Georgian houses and has done a lovely job on his own. Guests are welcome to use the upstairs drawing room, a grand room overlooking Queen Street Gardens, saved from formality by a bright-pink decor (if you want to stroll through these private gardens, Andrea and Gene will lend you their key). Breakfast is a social occasion round the dining-room table in the little lemon dining room. Guests are introduced to one another and a convivial atmosphere prevails. Bedrooms are found "below stairs" and have their own private entry. The three lovely rooms (queen, twin, and single) are beautifully decorated—the Garden Room queen bed has pretty coronet drapes, while the single's bathroom has lovely blue wallpaper with underwater scenes. *Directions:* Coming from the south turn left from Princes Street into Charlotte Square (no choice) and stay in the left-hand lane. Keep going until you are forced to turn right (still keeping in the left-hand lane), take the second left down Frederick Street and then first left into Heriot Row. No. 27 is halfway along.

27 HERIOT ROW
Owners: Andrea & Gene Targett-Adams
27 Heriot Row
Edinburgh EH3 6EN, Scotland
Tel: (0131) 225 9474, Fax: (0131) 220 1699
Email: t.a@blueyonder.co.uk
3 rooms
Double: £100
Open all year, Credit cards: MC, VS,
Children welcome
No-smoking house
www.karenbrown.com/ews/heriot.html

The location is absolutely perfect—just a ten-minute stroll from Princes Street in the heart of Georgian Edinburgh. Three townhouses have been combined to form this luxury hotel, which has the air of a private club. No expense has been spared to create the look and feel of a sumptuous home. Beautiful fabrics, antiques, gorgeous furniture, and lots of flowers set an elegant mood. The drawing room centers on an elaborate crystal chandelier. There is no bar: guests order from the butler. Each bedroom has a different decor and color scheme. A great many of the bathrooms are especially grand, several with claw-foot tubs, others with a bath and separate shower, and the suites have luxurious steam showers. Three terrace suites have their own private terrace and entrance to Great King Street. Edinburgh has some excellent restaurants from formal to funky and many of them are within easy walking distance. *Directions:* From the west end of Princes Street (with the castle on your right) turn left into Charlotte Square then turn right into Queen Street. Turn third left into Queen Street Gardens East, which becomes Dundas Street, then take the third right onto Great King Street. The Howard is on the right with a car park to the rear.

THE HOWARD
Owner: Shaune Ayers
Manager: Dairin Murphy
34 Great King Street
Edinburgh EH3 6QH, Scotland
Tel: (0131) 315 2220, Fax: (0131) 557 6515
Email: reserve@thehoward.com
15 rooms
Double: £275–£295, Suite: £355–£475
Closed Christmas
Credit cards: all major
Children welcome
www.karenbrown.com/ews/howard.html

Susie and Andrew Hamilton are only the fourth family to call 16 Lynedoch Place home since it was built almost 180 years ago. This classical Georgian townhouse is packed with architectural features (cantilevered staircase, roof cupola, bow-walled dining room), but one of the beauties of the place is that it has both a front and back garden—a most unusual feature for an Edinburgh townhouse. Guests have their own front-door key and come and go as they please, often seeking out Susie in the kitchen (and along the way saying hello to Gerty and Holly, the resident pets) to discuss their sightseeing or dining plans. A breakfast that will set you up for the entire day is served in the elegant dining room. Below stairs you find three absolutely delightfully decorated guestrooms (a double, a twin, and a single), each equipped to the highest of standards. On this level guests also have a cozy little sitting nook supplied with a selection of reference books, a pay phone, and decanter of whisky for a nightcap. For planning explorations of the Highlands and islands of Scotland, Andrew has two itineraries (two-night and five-night) that he is happy to share with guests. *Directions:* Take Queens Street (parallel to Princes Street) onto Randolph Crescent then turn right onto Queensferry Road. As the road goes downhill, bear left into Lynedoch Place (if you go across the river you have gone too far). Park to unload and Susie will direct you to street parking (a five-minute walk) where you can leave your car for the duration of your stay.

16 LYNEDOCH PLACE
Owners: Susie & Andrew Hamilton
16 Lynedoch Place
Edinburgh EH3 7PY, Scotland
Tel: (0131) 225 5507, Fax: (0131) 226 4185
Email: susie.lynedoch@btinternet.com
3 rooms
Double: £70–£100
Closed Christmas, Credit cards: MC, VS
Children welcome
www.karenbrown.com/ews/lynedoch.html

Leith, a bustling, modern seaport ten minutes from the center of Edinburgh, with an old quarter dating back to the 15th century, is fast being redeveloped into a vibrant and fashionable neighborhood. Here the chic and stylish Malmaison hotel sits directly on the waterfront facing a large cobbled courtyard. You realize that this is no ordinary hotel as soon as you enter the light and spacious lobby with its eye-catching decor—mushroom- and cream-colored squares on the walls echo the geometric theme found in the original Malmaison, built by Napoleon for Josephine; custom-made, high-backed sofas and chairs lend a certain panache; and doors have lovely wrought-iron detailing. Guestrooms, which are surprisingly inexpensive for a city hotel, are spacious and comfortable, with excellent amenities such as CD players, well-stocked mini bars, and satellite TVs. Color schemes vary, but all the rooms are designed with imagination and flair. There are four four-poster rooms and an especially charming corner suite with a small bedroom and large sitting room, which is full of delightful nooks and crannies and has enchanting views. No need to leave the hotel to eat—you can choose between the café-bar with its short menu and daily specials and the classic, atmospheric brasserie. *Directions*: From Princes Street follow signs for Leith/Docklands (A900)—this brings you to Leith Walk. Go straight and onto Constitution Street through two sets of traffic lights, turning left into Tower Street (just before the dock gates). The hotel is at the end of the street with a large car park to the rear.

MALMAISON
Manager: Andrew Spearman
One Tower Place
Leith, Edinburgh EH6 7DB, Scotland
Tel: (0131) 468 5000, Fax: (0131) 468 5002
60 rooms, Double: £115–£125, Suite: £165**
*Breakfast not included: £8.75–£10.75
Open all year
Credit cards: all major
Children welcome

A long, tree-lined drive leads to the 17th-century Prestonfield House Hotel, located in 13 acres of gardens and parkland just ten minutes' drive from the city center. Peacocks strut gracefully on a circular lawn directly in front of this grand, white stone manor, setting a delightful scene. Public rooms, in the original part of the building, are dignified and impressive—I was particularly struck by the Leather Room whose walls are covered with stunning, red, 17th-century Spanish leather. You dine in the almost circular restaurant watched over by massive portraits then climb a worn stone staircase to the beautiful tapestry room where, beneath the most ornate plasterwork ceiling, you enjoy coffee, chocolates, and after-dinner drinks. In 1997 26 luxury bedrooms were added in a well-thought-out extension to this historic house. Our bedroom was a real treat, with windows overlooking the park, two armchairs, and fluffy bathrobes in the luxurious bathroom. The bedrooms in the old house, not all en suite, have a very old-fashioned feel to them. The breakfast room in the new section is charming—light and airy, with hand-painted pale-green-silk Chinese wallcoverings and lovely views of the grounds. From April to October a "Taste of Scotland" evening with dinner, song, dance, and bagpipes is held in the adjacent stables. *Directions:* From the city center take the A68 (A7). Turn left at the lights after passing the Commonwealth swimming pool.

PRESTONFIELD HOUSE HOTEL
Owners: Stevenson family
Manager: Richard Scott
Priestfield Road
Edinburgh EH16 5UT, Scotland
Tel: (0131) 668 3346, Fax: (0131) 668 3976
Email: info@prestonfieldhouse.com
31 rooms
Double: £145–£225, Suite: £325–£400
Open all year
Credit cards: all major
Children welcome
www.karenbrown.com/ews/prestonfield.html

Windmill House has the feel of a country estate with a city address. There's a family of resident badgers by the tree stump, an ancient windmill, and acres of grounds stretching down to the Water of Leith—all just a mile as the crow flies from the center of Edinburgh. A remarkable setting with a remarkable home that looks hundreds of years old, though it was actually built just a few years ago—Michael is a builder and Georgian home restorer who combined both of his passions in his home. It's a home so lovely that you are thrilled to stay there—or is it just that the Scotts put you in a euphoric mood? Judge for yourself. Pinch yourself as you sip tea in the drawing room or put your feet up and watch the television in the sitting room. Climb the elegant staircase to the spacious bedrooms, each beautifully decorated in sunny Georgian colors and accompanied by a top-of-the-line bathroom. One bedroom has an adjacent room for a child. Self-catering accommodation is sometimes available in the old windmill. Go through the garden gate and you are in the grounds of the Museum of Modern Art whence a path leads you along the river and into the heart of the city. Those who prefer to ride will find the bus stop an eight-minute walk away. There are plenty of local restaurants for dinner. *Directions:* Going down Princes Street (castle on left) follow signs for Glasgow (go straight at the end of Princes Street). Follow the road for a mile until just before the BMW showroom (on left)—turn right and immediately right into Colbridge Avenue, which leads to Colbridge Gardens.

WINDMILL HOUSE   New
Owners: Vivien & Michael Scott
Colbridge Gardens
Edinburgh EH12 6AQ, Scotland
Tel & fax: (0131) 346 0024
Email: windmillhouse@hoppo.com
3 rooms, Double: £90–£110
Closed Christmas & New Year, Credit cards: MC, VS
Children welcome
www.karenbrown.com/ews/windmill.html

The Isle of Eriska is a 300-acre private island off the west coast of Scotland linked to the mainland by a decorative wrought-iron bridge. In 1884 the splendidly named Hippolyte Blanc designed a grand baronial mansion, now a hotel and home to the welcoming Buchanan-Smith family, with son Beppo in charge of the day-to-day running of the hotel. A grand paneled hall, complete with blazing log fire, sits at the center of the house and it is here that morning coffee and a traditional afternoon tea are served, which you can enjoy in the comfortable drawing room overlooking the grounds. Wild badgers come to the library steps at night to be fed, oblivious to guests enjoying a drink—perhaps one of the hotel's excellent assortment of malt whiskies. Bedrooms come in all shapes and sizes, with Kerrera, Lismore, Skye, and Glensanda providing the most spacious quarters. Eriska is a splendid base for exploring the Western Highlands, visiting Glencoe, and making day trips to the islands of Mull, Staffa, and Iona. However, there are also many attractions on the island, including a magnificent indoor swimming pool, a six-hole golf course, a tennis court, clay-pigeon shooting, or tramping round the island to find the donkeys. *Directions:* From Crianlarich take the A85 towards Oban. At Connel take the bridge towards Fort William (A825) for 4 miles to the village of Benderloch. Turn left and left again following signposts to the Isle of Eriska for the 4-mile drive to the hotel.

ISLE OF ERISKA
Owners: Buchanan-Smith family
Manager: Beppo Buchanan-Smith
Ledaig, Oban
Argyll PA37 1SD, Scotland
Tel: (01631) 720371, Fax: (01631) 720531
Email: office@eriska-hotel.co.uk
17 rooms
Double: £220–£280
Closed Jan, Credit cards: all major
Children welcome
www.karenbrown.com/ews/eriska.html

Ettrickshaws, a former hunting lodge, is my idea of a blissful county house hotel: tucked away in a peaceful valley far enough from the beaten path to ensure quiet repose but close enough for interesting sightseeing forays; five bedrooms—the perfect size to ensure lots of attention; and owners who cook and take care of you. A log fire warms the hallway sitting room and the clubby bar is manned in the evening by the amiable Graham, who is also your sommelier. Jenny does the cooking and changes her set menu every day, offering four choices of starters and desserts with a set main course (a vegetarian alternative can be provided). Ask about the dinner, bed, and breakfast rates when making a reservation—these offer very good value for money. Of the five bedrooms I particularly enjoyed room 1, decorated in sunny shades of yellow, and room 2, the premier room with a large sleigh bed and bay window sitting nook with views across Ettrick Water to the countryside. Fishing for salmon and brown trout is available on the hotel's own beats. Horse riders (horses are available) head for the Buccleuch Country Ride, a three- to four-day ride through lovely countryside on bridleways, private tracks, and quiet roads. Selkirk, Galashiels, and Hawick produce tweed, wool, and cashmere and all have their own mill shops. Locally there are a great many abbeys, castles, and historic houses to visit. *Directions:* From Selkirk town square follow the A708 Moffat road for ½ mile and turn left on the B7009 to Ettrickbridge. Go through the village and Ettrickshaws is on your left in 1 mile.

*ETTRICKSHAWS   **New***
Owners: Jenny & Graham Oldfield
Ettrickbridge, by Selkirk
Selkirkshire TD7 5HW, Scotland
Tel & fax: (01750) 52229
Email: jenny@ettrickshaws.co.uk
5 rooms, Double: £90–£110
Open all year, Credit cards: MC, VS
Children over 12
www.karenbrown.com/ews/ettrickshaws.html

For those who wish they could afford to stay at Inverlochy Castle, perhaps the next best thing to staying there is to stay just down the driveway at The Factor's House (formerly the Inverlochy estate manager's home), which is owned and operated by the castle. Guests can walk through the extensive grounds to the castle for dinner and may use the tennis courts and fish in the loch. A homey mixture of sofas and chairs graces the main lounge and blackboards outline the various offerings for main courses and desserts on the dinner menu. It's a cheerful, relaxed kind of place without any pretensions of grandeur. Upstairs, the bedrooms are nicely decorated with coordinated wallpaper, drapes, and bedspreads and each has its own bathroom. Several are large enough to accommodate a sitting area. Just across the drive Heather Cottage provides five additional smaller bedrooms, with the ground-floor room specifically equipped to handle a wheelchair. Because it has a kitchen and sitting room the cottage is very suitable as an exclusive longer-stay rental for those who want self-catering accommodation. Popular sights include Loch Ness where you might catch a glimpse of the monster and the Glenfinnan monument to Bonnie Prince Charlie at the head of Loch Sheil. *Directions:* The Factor's House is 3 miles out of Fort William on the A82 Inverness road, on the left.

THE FACTOR'S HOUSE   New
Inverlochy Estate
Torlundy, by Fort William
Highland PH33 6SN, Scotland
Tel: (01397) 702177, Fax: (01397) 702953
Email: infor@inverlochy.co.uk
10 rooms
Double: £65–£110*
*Breakfast not included £10
Closed Nov to Feb
Credit cards: MC, VS
Children welcome
www.karenbrown.com/ews/factors.html

Set on a quiet road high above Loch Linnhe with its gardens terracing down to a terrific view across the loch to distant mountains, The Grange has a countryside feel to it, yet you are just a few minutes' walk from the center of Fort William. Built for a wealthy lady in 1884, The Grange, with its gracefully sloping roofs, has a decidedly feminine feel to it, a feeling that is continued indoors where Joan and John Campbell have decorated their home throughout in a light, airy decor. A very comfortable sitting room is there for you to enjoy and breakfast, the only meal offered, is served in the dining room. The lovely bedrooms are decorated to the highest of standards and have the advantage of all having loch views. If I had to choose a favorite, it would be the delicious ground-floor room with its patio and luxurious bathroom with both a claw-foot tub and a shower. Guests often walk down to the pier to enjoy a seafood dinner at the Cranogg Restaurant or sometimes they take the scenic 12-mile drive to the Old Station at Spean Bridge. Countless possibilities exist for touring by car, while a favorite non-car excursion is to take the steam train from Fort William to Mallaig through some of Scotland's most fabulous scenery (summer only). *Directions:* Arriving in Fort William from the south with the loch on your left, turn second right into Ashburn Lane and left into Grange Road. The Grange is on the corner of Ashburn Lane and Grange road.

THE GRANGE
Owners: Joan & John Campbell
Grange Road
Fort William
Highland PH33 6JF, Scotland
Tel: (01397) 705516, Fax: (01397) 701595
Email: jcampbell@grangefortwilliam.com
4 rooms, Double: £78–£95
Open Mar to mid-Nov
Credit cards: MC, VS (for confirmation only)
Children over 12, No-smoking house
www.karenbrown.com/ews/grange.html

Nestling in the foothills of the mighty Ben Nevis, Inverlochy Castle sits amongst some of Scotland's finest scenery. Its magnificence does not appear to have altered since Queen Victoria visited in 1873. In her diaries she wrote, "I never saw a lovelier nor more romantic spot." Surrounded by landscaped gardens overlooking its own private loch, the turreted and gabled house was built to resemble a castle. Central heating and modern plumbing appear to be the only 21st-century additions. The two-storied Grand Hall with its frescoed ceiling sets the tone of this memorable hotel and the furnishings and decor throughout are luxurious. Dinner is an experience to savor in any of the three dining rooms, each decorated with period and elaborate furniture given as gifts by the King of Norway. The staff outnumbers the guests and attention to detail ensures that things are done properly. Inverlochy Castle is a very grand, very expensive, and most outstanding hotel. The small number of rooms and the hotel's popularity mean that early reservations are necessary. There are various outdoor activities available to guests including fly fishing for brown trout in the private loch, clay-pigeon shooting, guided walks, and grouse stalking. From Fort William you can take the Road to the Isles, a lovely, dead-end drive that brings you to Mallaig where you can take ferries to the isles of Skye, Rhum, Eigg, Canna, and Muck. *Directions:* The castle is on the A82, Inverness road, 3 miles north of Fort William.

INVERLOCHY CASTLE
Manager: Michael Leonard
Torlundy, Fort William
Highland PH33 6SN, Scotland
Tel: (01397) 702177, Fax: (01397) 702953
Email: info@inverlochy.co.uk
17 rooms
Double: £250–£380, Suite: £390–£480
Open all year, Credit cards: all major
Children welcome
Relais & Châteaux Member
www.karenbrown.com/ews/inverlochy.html

How can you describe a Malmaison hotel without overusing the word "stylish"? It's quite a challenge! The Glasgow Malmaison, an architecturally interesting former church, offers excellent accommodation at down-to-earth prices in classic contemporary surroundings. The atmosphere is relaxed and informal, the staff attentive and upbeat, and the décor original and chic. A wrought-iron staircase depicting scenes from Napoleon's life (Malmaison was the home he built for Josephine) leads from the lobby to the bedrooms. These are handsomely simple rooms very smartly decorated in a tailored, uncluttered fashion, each equipped with CD player, satellite TV, two-line telephone, and mini bar, and accompanied by a gleaming bathroom with heated towel rail and power shower. In the "balcony" rooms (double-glazed for soundproofing) looking onto the Café Mal you can open up the windows to let the music drift in—great fun. For a special treat, choose one of the mezzanine suites with living room below a balcony bedroom and skylight views over the city. Below street level is a moody and jazzy brasserie partitioned into intimate little dining nooks. Breakfast, either a Continental buffet or a cooked meal, is served in the glass-roofed atrium in the cheerful Café Mal, a Mediterranean-style pizzeria, open to the public for lunch and dinner, where everything is made from scratch. *Directions*: From the west, exit the M8 at junction 19. Turn left at the traffic lights, go through the next set, and the hotel is on your left. Ask the hotel to send you directions if you are arriving from any other point.

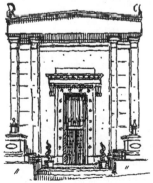

MALMAISON
Manager: David Moth
278 West George Street
Glasgow, G2 4LL, Scotland
Tel: (0141) 572 1000, Fax: (0141) 572 1002
72 rooms, Double: £120*, Suite: £145–£165*
*Breakfast not included: £8.75–£10.75
Open all year
Credit cards: all major
Children welcome

In a fashionable Glasgow suburb three adjoining grand Victorian mansions, once the homes of wealthy industrialists, now form a small luxury hotel. The houses are not interconnected, so you pop in and out between buildings, under wide umbrellas when it's raining. The dining room, bar, and one drawing room are in number 1, The Boardroom meeting room is in 2, and the reception and second drawing room are in 3. Spectacular features of 2 and 3 are the enormous, two-story stained-glass windows in the stairwells. The well-equipped bedrooms, generally very spacious and high-ceilinged, all have comfortable seating areas and some have large dressing areas. All but twin rooms have king-sized beds. Many rooms have four-posters swathed in yards of striking, dark-colored fabric—one room is dramatically done entirely in black. Since some guestrooms have very bold decor while others are quieter and more traditional in style, state your preference when booking. Public areas are delightful: number 3's comfortable drawing room reflects its Victorian heritage, with beautiful moldings, coal fire, overstuffed furniture, and lots of paintings, while number 1's is tailored and soothingly elegant in creams and browns. The dining room, serving very fine cuisine, looks light and fresh, papered in blue and cream stripes, and the bar is dark and cozy. *Directions*: Leave the M8 at junction 17 onto the Great Western Road (A82), which you follow to Hyndland Road. Turn left, then first right, right at the mini-roundabout, and right again at the end of the road.

ONE DEVONSHIRE GARDENS
Manager: Mark Calpin
Devonshire Gardens
Glasgow G12 0UX, Scotland
Tel: (0141) 339 2001, Fax: (0141) 337 1663
27 rooms, Double: £185–£275*, Suite: £345*
*Breakfast not included: £10.50–£14.50
Open all year
Credit cards: all major
Children welcome

Nestled in a secluded glen at the foot of the loch for which it is named, Mullardoch House is well worth the 8-mile drive required to reach it up a winding single-track road. Originally built in 1912 as a hunting lodge, it has been recently renovated by owner Andy Johnston and now provides seven very nicely appointed bedrooms and the opportunity for total peace and quiet in a beautiful Highland setting. Downstairs you find a bar, dining room, and comfortable sitting room with crackling fire, interesting books, and resident black Labrador, Toby, who spends the bulk of his day patiently awaiting the appearance of after-dinner chocolates. Guests can walk in the surrounding hills, go fishing and boating (a local boatman will take you out) on the loch or river, or simply relax and enjoy the magnificent views across Loch Scalbanach to the Affric Mountains. Beyond this peaceful glen lies Loch Ness where you can indulge in a bit of monster spotting on your way to Cawdor Castle, which Shakespeare featured in *Macbeth*, and Culloden Battlefield, where Bonnie Prince Charlie and his Highlanders made a last stand against the English. *Directions:* From Inverness take the A82 along Loch Ness towards Fort William. At Drumnadrochit turn right on the A831 to Cannich where you go straight at the crossroads in the village for the 8-mile drive on a single-track road to Mullardoch House at the head of the glen.

MULLARDOCH HOUSE   New
Owner: Andy Johnston
Glen Cannich, by Beauly
Inverness-shire IV4 7LX, Scotland
Tel & fax: (01456) 4155460
Email: andy@mullhousel.demon.co.uk
7 rooms
Double: £90–£102
Closed Nov to Mar, Credit cards: MC, VS
Children welcome
www.karenbrown.com/ews/mullardoch.html

Golf players will be enchanted with Greywalls because it is on the very edge of the Great
Muirfield golf course founded in 1744. Even if you have no interest in the game, you will
love this most beautiful of houses built in 1901 by Sir Edwin Lutyens and you will adore
the gardens laid out like a series of rooms by Gertrude Jekyll. It was the Weaver family
home until 1948 when they turned it into a hotel—family photos and letters decorate the
ladies' loo (perhaps they also adorn the gents' too—I did not visit) and photos of famous
guests, particularly golfers, are grouped around the reception area. The dining room
overlooks the tenth tee. The lounges are especially attractive, particularly the paneled
library with its interesting pictures, shelves of books, and open fireplace. The bar is most
convivial. Edward VII used to stay here and, because he admired the view, a special
outside loo-with-a-view was built for him near the garden wall: now it's a suite called
King's Loo. Guests can choose it or from an array of bedrooms which overlook either the
flower-filled gardens or the golf course. Golfers have Muirfield as well as ten other
courses nearby. Eighteen miles to the west lies Edinburgh. *Directions:* From Edinburgh
take the city bypass to the A198, go through Gullane, and the hotel is on your left.

GREYWALLS
Owners: Ros & Giles Weaver
Manager: Sue Prime
Muirfield, Gullane
East Lothian EH31 2EG, Scotland
Tel: (01620) 842144, Fax: (01620) 842241
Email: hotel@greywalls.co.uk
23 rooms
Double: £190–£230
Open Apr to Oct
Credit cards: all major
Children welcome
www.karenbrown.com/ews/greywalls.html

Dunain Park Hotel is a lovely country home overlooking the famous Caledonian Canal, which joins Loch Ness to the Moray Firth. The large sitting room all decorated in shades of green with its crackling, open fire provides a snug retreat on stormy days. Ann Nicoll loves to cook, using vegetables from the garden and lamb, beef, venison, and salmon fresh from local suppliers, mixing traditional Scottish cooking with modern Continental. The bedrooms are all very attractive. Room 1 overlooks the back garden and has an elegant, four-poster canopy bed and a delicate writing desk tucked into one corner. Room 11 is a particularly pretty upstairs corner suite with lovely views across the garden. A suite consists of a very large bedroom, a small adjacent sitting room where the sofa can be made into a child's bed, and an immaculate, modern bathroom. You find a small heated swimming pool in a log cabin almost hidden by tall bushes in the extensive grounds. A very pleasant drive leads around Loch Ness to Fort Augustus and back on the other bank. The Monster Research Centre is on the north bank near Drumnadrochit. *Directions:* Dunain Park Hotel is just off the A82, 2 miles southwest of Inverness.

DUNAIN PARK HOTEL
Owners: Ann & Edward Nicoll
Dunain Park
Near Inverness
Inverness-shire IV3 8JN, Scotland
Tel: (01463) 230512, Fax: (01463) 224532
Email: dunainparkhotel@btinternet.com
11 rooms, 2 cottages
Double: £138–£198, Suite: £158, Cottage: £198
Closed Jan
Credit cards: all major
Children welcome
www.karenbrown.com/ews/dunainpark.html

Overlooking the romantic ruins of Kildrummy Castle and surrounded by acres of lovely gardens and woodlands, Kildrummy Castle Hotel is a grand mansion house. The richly paneled and tapestried walls and ornately carved staircase give a baronial feel to this grand house, a feel that is echoed in the lounge and bar whose large windows overlook the romantic castle ruins and the gardens. Yet this is not a stuffy, formal hotel: the smiling, friendly staff does a splendid job, offering people a really warm welcome. Dinner in the richly furnished dining room is a delight. The bedrooms (named after various pools in the hotel's trout stream) are tastefully decorated and traditionally furnished. Their size ranges from a snug attic bedroom with a private balcony to a grand corner room with enormous windows framing the countryside. Guests are given a card which gives them complimentary access to the adjacent Kildrummy Castle Gardens which present an idyllic picture at all times of the year. From Kildrummy you can join the Speyside Whisky Trail and enjoy a wee dram. At Alford lies Craigiever, a fairy-tale castle unchanged since it was built in 1626. Nearby Ballater is a busy resort surrounded by wooded hills. Between Kildrummy and Braemar, home of the September Royal Highland Gathering, lies Balmoral Castle whose grounds are open in June and July when the Royal Family is not in residence. *Directions:* From Aberdeen take the A944 through Alford to the A97 where you turn right for Kildrummy Castle.

KILDRUMMY CASTLE HOTEL
Owners: Mary & Thomas Hanna
Kildrummy by Alford
Aberdeenshire AB33 8RA, Scotland
Tel: (019755) 71288, Fax: (019755) 71345
Email: bookings@kildrummycastlehotel.co.uk
16 rooms
Double: £135–£180
Closed Jan, Credit cards: all major
Children welcome
www.karenbrown.com/ews/kildrummycastlehotel.html

The tree-lined drive winds through a vast estate to the parklike lawns surrounding Cromlix House. Little rabbits hop gaily around—they're so tame that you can approach within a few yards of them before they disappear into the surrounding woodlands. The heavy Victorian exterior of the building hides an absolute jewel of an interior. Cromlix House, converted in 1981 from the Eden family home, was named as Andrew Harper's Hideaway Hotel of the Year for 1999/2000. It retains much of the original furniture designed for the house, along with family paintings and porcelain and all the old fittings dating back to when this grand house teemed with servants. The tone of an elegant Victorian home is set by the stately front hall with its wooden ceiling and richly paneled walls and is carried through into the inviting morning room, peaceful, well-stocked library, and garden conservatory. There is a private chapel with its organ pipes along one of the staircases—the perfect venue for a wedding. Upstairs are six luxurious rooms and eight very spacious, beautifully decorated and furnished suites. Serene countryside walks to little lochs where you may see swans and their young or a visit the family and pet cemeteries offer the chance for utter peace and quiet. The Trossachs with their lovely lakes, Stirling Castle, and Bannockburn are close at hand. Golf at Gleneagles is a 20-minute drive away. *Directions:* Take the A9 out of Dunblane, turn left onto B8033, go through Kinbuck village, and take the second left turn after a small bridge.

CROMLIX HOUSE
Owners: Ailsa & David Assenti
Kinbuck by Dunblane
Perthshire FK15 9JT, Scotland
Tel: (01786) 822125, Fax: (01786) 825450
Email: reservations@cromlixhouse.com
6 rooms, 8 suites
Double: £230–£245, Suite: £275–£345
Open all year, Credit cards: all major
Children welcome
www.karenbrown.com/ews/cromlixhouse.html

Ballathie House is a large turreted, Victorian, Scottish country estate home on the banks of the River Tay, surrounded by lawns, fields, and woodlands. While the house is imposing, it has a wonderfully warm atmosphere and a homey feel as well as glorious views over the river. A grand sweep of staircase leads up from the enormous hallway where sofas and chairs are grouped around a blazing fire. The drawing room, with its tall windows framing views across the lawn to the river, is made more intimate by cozy groupings of tables and chairs. My favorite accommodations are the spacious bedrooms with turret bathrooms and the smaller bedrooms with river views. Beyond the kitchen there is a ground-floor suite equipped for the handicapped. For complete peace and quiet request a riverside room in the adjacent building—upstairs rooms have balconies. The bar is a lively place, and dinner is delicious—chef Kevin MacGillivray was Scottish Chef of the Year 1999/2000. Red squirrels are found on the Ballathie estate, and you may be fortunate and catch a glimpse of one of these rarely seen animals. Nearby is Dunkeld, a delightful town with a ruined cathedral set in expansive lawns. Scone Palace, where Scottish kings were once crowned, has fine furniture, clocks, porcelain, and needlework. *Directions:* From Perth take the A9 towards Inverness for about five minutes to the B9099, Stanley road. Go through Stanley and take a right-hand fork towards Blairgowrie, following signs for Ballathie House.

BALLATHIE HOUSE
Manager: Christopher Longden
Kinclaven near Perth
Perthshire PH1 4QN, Scotland
Tel: (01250) 883268, Fax: (01250) 883396
Email: email@ballathiehousehotel.com
43 rooms
Double: £150–£200, Suite: £220–£240
Open all year
Credit cards: all major
Children welcome
www.karenbrown.com/ews/ballathie.html

It was a relief to be told by Carol that the ancient turret entrance hall is holding up the entire castle, as it has for over a millennium. I arrived to find rooms shrouded with dustsheets and oil paintings stacked in hallways—Carol and John were in the midst of a total revamp due to an almost catastrophic chimney fire. The Steels are expansive hosts who are really interested in giving their guests a slice of Scottish life in their castle. Carol is an excellent cook, offering dinner (with advance notice) in the grand dining room. Guests have the entire upper level of the main wing, reached by a grand staircase embellished with two of John's hunting trophies (he's just as happy to talk about his hunting exploits as he is to discuss the wonders of the huge yellow backhoe/excavator that he received as a Christmas present from Carol). Each branch of the staircase leads to a bedroom with its adjacent private bathroom (one has a grand piano on the landing and another has an extra bedroom for older children or traveling companions). The vast estate provides you with lots of opportunities for walking and you are surrounded by the most magnificent Highland scenery. An excellent day out combines visiting Pitlochry, Blair Castle, and The House of Bruar (the Harrods of the north). *Directions:* From the south take the A93 through Blairgowrie towards Bracmar and Glenshee. Fork right at the Bridge of Cally. After 5 miles turn left, towards Kirkmichael and Pitlochry. The 2-mile long driveway is on the right after nearly 2 miles.

ASHINTULLY CASTLE   New
Owners: Carol & John Steel
Kirkmichael, Blairgowrie
Perthshire PH10 7LT, Scotland
Tel: (01250) 881237, Fax: (01250) 881490
2 rooms
Double: £76
Open Apr to Oct
Credit cards: MC, VS
Children over 12

Set at the foot of the Black Isle (a sheltered spit of land just north of Inverness), The Dower House was built as the retirement home for the owners of baronial Highfield House. While Highfield fell into disrepair, The Dower House flourished and was remodeled into a cottage orné, an adorable, single-story doll's house. The cute exterior belies a more spacious interior. The dining room and sitting room open up from the entrance hall where Sweep the springer spaniel adds his tail-wagging greeting to Mena's warm welcome. Mena has played on the interesting architecture and decorated the house in a most appealing, flowery, feminine way, adding attractive Victorian furniture and all the special touches that make you feel you are staying with friends. Robyn's delectable food has earned him a red star from Michelin. As an alternative to rooms in the house, consider staying in the lovely, three-bedroom gate lodge. An enjoyable day trip is to explore the villages of the Black Isle of which the historic port of Cromarty with its fine old buildings is a highlight. You can enjoy magnificent Highland scenery on the train journey from nearby Dingwall to Kyle of Lochalsh. The local distillery at Glen Ord offers tours and samples. Traditional Scottish tweeds and woolens are available in nearby Beauly. *Directions:* Take the A862 from Inverness through Beauly to Muir of Ord. The Dower House is on the left, 1 mile beyond the town on the Dingwall road.

THE DOWER HOUSE
Owners: Mena & Robyn Aitchison
Highfield
Muir of Ord
Ross-shire IV6 7XN, Scotland
Tel & fax: (01463) 870090
Email: rooms@thedowerhouse.co.uk
5 rooms, 1 cottage
Double: £120–£130, Cottage: £150
Open all year, Credit cards: MC, VS
Children welcome
www.karenbrown.com/ews/dowerhouse.html

Clifton House is a unique hotel which reflects the character of its owners, the Gordon Macintyre family, and their love of the theatre. As a highlight during the winter months, (September to May) several plays, concerts, and recitals are staged in the hotel dining room which steps up on several levels—just like a small theater. The overall decor is flamboyantly Victorian, abounding in flowers, masses of pictures, rich colors, and draped curtains. A log fire lures you into the warmth of the main drawing room with its ornate, hand-blocked wallpaper, which was used in the robing room of the Palace of Westminster in 1849—it is very elaborate and marvelously Victorian. Each of the bedrooms has its own flavor and personality, and one must appreciate the imagination and interest behind each scheme. The bedrooms tend to be decorated dramatically (such as 7 with its red chandelier hanging in a red-velvet-draped four-poster-bed) so it is as well to ask to see several rooms to decide which suits you best. Small, artistic, and colorful, the Clifton is personally managed by family members and a very conscientious staff, and is interesting and fun to stay in. Nairn is an old fishing/seaside town on the Moray Firth. There are castles to visit (Cawdor, Brodie, Balvenie, and Grant) and whisky distilleries to tour. *Directions:* From Inverness take the A96 (15 miles) to Nairn, turn left at the only roundabout in town and Clifton House is on your left after half a mile.

CLIFTON HOUSE
Owner: Gordon Macintyre
Viewfield Street
Nairn
Nairnshire IV12 4HW, Scotland
Tel: (01667) 453119, Fax: (01667) 452836
Email: macintyre@clifton-hotel.co.uk
12 rooms
Double: £100–£107
Open mid-Jan to mid-Dec, Credit cards: all major
Children welcome
www.karenbrown.com/ews/clifton.html

This 1760s former manse sits surrounded by acres of lawns and trees in the heart of the picturesque seaside town of North Berwick, just a half-hour train ride from Edinburgh. The Scotts' furniture complements their lovely home perfectly. Gwen has a real eye for design and color and has done the most stylish job of decorating. From the front hallway a door opens to the downstairs wing, a suite of rooms with two bedrooms, two bathrooms, and a cozy sitting room—absolutely perfect for families or friends traveling together. Upstairs are two more lovely bedrooms and bathrooms. Breakfast is the only meal served round the long dining-room table but there is no shortage of restaurants and pubs to walk to for dinner. Golfers are in heaven staying here for there are 18 courses within a 20-minute drive, including those at Gullane and Muirfield. A half-hour train ride finds you at the bottom of Edinburgh Castle, which makes for hassle-free day trips to all the shopping and historic sights. North Berwick's beach is a two-minute walk away as is the High Street with its shops and restaurants. Bass Rock, an important nesting site for sea birds, can be visited by boat from the harbor. There are castles, museums, and a whisky distillery nearby. *Directions:* From Edinburgh take the A1 towards Berwick-upon-Tweed for 10 miles. Exit onto the A198 for North Berwick, keeping to the A198 through the town. Turn left on Law Road and The Glebe House is on your left after 100 yards.

THE GLEBE HOUSE   New
Owners: Gwen & Jake Scott
Law Road
North Berwick
East Lothian EH39 4PL, Scotland
Tel & fax: (01620) 892608
Email: j.a.scott@tesco.net
4 rooms
Double: £60–£80
Closed Christmas & New Year, Credit cards: none
Children welcome
www.karenbrown.com/ews/glebe.html

Oban, with its broad sweep of sheltered harbor, is the gateway to the islands—from here ferries ply their way to the isles of Mull, Iona, Coll, Staffa, Tiree, Colonsay, and Lismore. On a quiet street right on the bay, just beyond the bustling ferry terminal, sits The Manor House, built in 1780 as the principal home of the Duke of Argyll's Oban estate. Today this stylish hotel is the perfect place to stay to enjoy various day trips to the Western Isles. Bedrooms are not large but each is accompanied by a snug bath or shower room, and all are most attractively decorated. It is well worth the few extra pounds to secure a room with a sweeping water view across to Mull, Lismore, and the hills of Morvern. The most popular day trips are to Mull, Staffa, and Iona. Walk to the nearby ferry terminal for the 10 am boat to Mull and pick up a scenic bus tour of the island in Craignure. Alternatively, venture onwards to Iona, the historic cradle of Christianity and burial place of many Scottish kings, including the infamous Macbeth, or to Staffa to explore Fingal's Cave, immortalized by Mendelssohn. Remember to wear sensible footwear and waterproof clothing for trips to Iona and Staffa. On the mainland Glencoe is a popular destination. *Directions:* Arriving in Oban, enter the one-way system following signposts for the ferry and Gallanach. Do not turn for the ferry but continue towards Gallanach—The Manor House is on the right after 300 yards.

THE MANOR HOUSE
Manager: Gabriella Wijker
Gallanach Road
Oban
Argyll PA34 4LS, Scotland
Tel: (01631) 562087, Fax: (01631) 563053
Email: manorhouseoban@aol.com
11 rooms
Double: £140–£160
Closed Mon & Tues Nov to Mar
Credit cards: all major, Children over 12
www.karenbrown.com/ews/themanor.html

This turreted, baronial-style mansion stands on the site of the home of Colonel Alexander Murray who accepted the surrender of Quebec. A traditional lounge bar decorated in soft shades of beige, leads to a lovely Victorian-style conservatory offering magnificent long views down the Tweed Valley. The gracious, tall-ceilinged dining room with its frescoed ceiling is found up the dramatic, sweeping staircase. Table settings are immaculate and the staff young and helpful. The food is especially good and attracts a great deal of local patronage. The fruit and vegetables are home grown in the large walled kitchen garden. Bedrooms come in all shapes and sizes; all are quietly colorful and each has a modern bathroom. On the grounds you find a good all-weather tennis court; putting green; acres of lush, green lawns; and flowerbeds leading to a 2-acre walled kitchen garden. Cringletie's location, just half an hour's drive from Edinburgh, makes it a convenient spot from which to visit the city and return to peaceful countryside surroundings. Other attractions include Traquair, the oldest inhabited house in Scotland, and Abbotsford, the house that is now the memorial to Sir Walter Scott. *Directions:* Cringletie House is on the A703, 3 miles north of Peebles and 20 miles south of Edinburgh.

CRINGLETIE HOUSE HOTEL
Manager: Kellie Bradford
Peebles
Peeblesshire EH45 8PL, Scotland
Tel: (01721) 730233, Fax: (01721) 730244
Email: cringletie@wrensgroup.com
13 rooms
Double: £180–£200
Open all year
Credit cards: all major
Children welcome
www.karenbrown.com/ews/cringletie.html

Surrounded by the peace and quiet of the countryside, yet only a few minutes' drive from the center of Pitlochry, Auchnahyle is a complex of cottages and farm buildings set round a farmyard. The largest cottage is Penny and Alastair's home and inside everything is cottage-cozy, brimming with a charming array of antiques. You enter the cottage beside a spacious conservatory to find a snug dining room and sitting room opening off either side of the steep, narrow staircase, which leads to two snug bedrooms tucked under the eaves with rambling roses peeping in at the windows. If you have difficulty with stairs, ask for the ground-floor bedroom, all bright and cheerful in red and white. Penny cooks as though she is giving a private dinner party and guests are encouraged to bring their own wine. Across the farmyard Rowan Tree Cottage is rented for family vacations: parents often tuck their children in bed and slip across the farmyard for a meal. Guinea fowl and two friendly dogs, Pixie, and Woofa, complete the rural picture. Pitlochry is a delightful town absolutely stuffed with woolen shops—you can spend a day just choosing a selection of sweaters. The Festival Theatre is a great draw and Blair Castle is only a ten-minute drive away. *Directions:* Enter Pitlochry from the south (A9). Pass under the railway bridge, turn right on East Moulin Road, and take the fourth turning right (by the letter box) down Tomcroy Terrace. Continue to the end.

AUCHNAHYLE
Owners: Penny & Alastair Howman
Pitlochry
Perthshire PH16 5JA, Scotland
Tel: (01796) 472318, Fax: (01796) 473657
Email: howmanA@aol.com
3 rooms
Double: £70–£80
Closed Christmas & New Year
Credit cards: MC, VS
Children over 12
www.karenbrown.com/ews/auchnahyle.html

Pitlochry developed in the latter half of the 19th century as a Highland health resort and remains today an attractive town of sturdy Victorian houses standing back from the wooded shores of Loch Faskally. Knockendarroch House sits above the rooftops of the town, isolated by its own little hill and surrounding garden. Tony and Jane Ross run their hotel with great enthusiasm and warmth. Dinner guests are treated to a glass of sherry as they peruse the four-course menu. Intertwining flowers decorate the stained-glass windows which filter sunlight onto the staircase leading up to the simply furnished, spacious, high-ceilinged bedrooms—two of the snug attic bedrooms have little balconies overlooking the town's rooftops. All the crisply decorated rooms have shower rooms and are equipped with telephones, color televisions, and coffee- and tea-makings. If you have difficulty with stairs, request the ground-floor bedroom. Pitlochry and the surrounding countryside have much to keep visitors occupied for several days. During the summer season the Pitlochry Festival Theatre has a repertoire of plays, which makes it possible for you to see as many as four plays in a three-night stay. *Directions:* Enter Pitlochry from the south (A9). Pass under the railway bridge, turn right on East Moulin Road and take the second turning left onto Higher Oakfield (the hotel is on your left).

KNOCKENDARROCH HOUSE
Owners: Jane & Tony Ross
Higher Oakfield
Pitlochry
Perthshire PH16 5HT, Scotland
Tel: (01796) 473473, Fax: (01796) 474068
Email: info@knockendarroch.co.uk
12 rooms
Double: £108–£130*
*Includes dinner, bed & breakfast
Open Feb to Nov
Credit cards: all major
Children over 12, No-smoking house
www.karenbrown.com/ews/knockendarroch.html

Pool House has occupied its riverside location at the head of Loch Ewe for over 300 years. Starting life as a fishing lodge and once owned by Osgood MacKenzie, the founder of nearby Inverewe Gardens, it was also headquarters to the Royal Navy for North Atlantic and Murmansk convoy operations during World War II. It was purchased in 1991 by its current owners, the Harrisons, who have since wrought changes that belie its somewhat plain exterior. All the bedrooms have magnificent bathrooms, with two featuring amazing, enormous, antique canopied shower tubs. Victoriana abounds in the form of brass and four-poster beds, porcelain, and paintings, and has been combined with antique French and Edwardian furniture and unique decorator touches to yield amazing results. Unlike the single room at the back of the property, all the suites enjoy sweeping views across the loch, as do the comfortable lounge and dining room. Truly a family operation, Peter and Margaret are assisted by their two daughters Liz and Mhairi, whose husband John is the chef responsible for the delightful food, which makes special use of local seafood. In the low season (October to April) the price of dinner is included in your room rate. The great attraction of the area is the adjacent world-famous Inverewe Gardens. *Directions:* Poolewe is a 72-mile drive from Inverness. From Inverness take the A9 to Tore and the A432 towards Ullapool to Garve where you take the A832 to Poolewe (portions of this last road are single-track).

POOL HOUSE   New
Owners: Margaret & Peter Harrison,
* Liz Miles, Mhairi & John Moir*
Poolewe
Wester Ross IV22 2LD, Scotland
Tel: (01445) 781272, Fax: (01445) 781403
Email: poolhouse@inverewe.co.uk
5 rooms
Double: £220–£280
Closed Jan & Feb, Credit cards: MC, VS
Children not accepted
www.karenbrown.com/ews/pool.html

The Airds Hotel, a long, low, white ferry inn, looks down on the shore of Loch Linnhe, the Isle of Lismore, and the green Morvern Mountains. Here Eric and Betty with their son Graeme and his wife Anne have created a delightful, intimate country house hotel that provides a haven of perfect tranquillity in a stunningly beautiful area. Betty and Graeme's food has earned a coveted Michelin star and dining is a divine, evening-long occasion. The two large lounges have lots of comfortable chairs. All the bedrooms are cottagey in size, but beautifully appointed, with lovely fabrics, quality furniture, and luxury bathrooms. My favorites are the snug attic rooms that look out over the loch, but it is a tight squeeze getting large bags up the final flight of stairs, so you may want to request a main-floor room—with loch view. The suite of two small rooms enjoys loch views both from the bedroom and the sitting room and has an immaculate, large bathroom. The road runs in front of the hotel, but this is not a problem since there is not much traffic in this quiet part of the world. A small passenger ferry sails from Port Appin to the Isle of Lismore. *Directions:* Port Appin is 2 miles off the A828, 25 miles north of Oban.

THE AIRDS HOTEL
Owners: Betty & Eric Allen
 Anne & Graeme Allen
Port Appin
Argyll PA38 4DF, Scotland
Tel: (01631) 730236, Fax: (01631) 730535
Email: airds@airds-hotel.com
12 rooms
Double: £205, Suite: £225
Closed Jan
Credit cards: MC, VS
Children welcome
Relais & Châteaux Member
www.karenbrown.com/ews/airdshotel.html

Viewfield House has always been home to the Macdonald family and there have always been Macdonalds on Skye. At the end of the 19th century this prosperous family remodeled Viewfield House adding a huge extension of large, grand rooms and completing the refurbishment with a baronial tower. Continuing a tradition begun by his grandfather, Hugh and Linda welcome guests to their home. Trophies of hunts and safaris (along with a smattering of British wildlife specimens) decorate the vast entrance hall and guests enjoy the large living room and the grand dining room hung with Macdonald family portraits. In the evenings guests enjoy four-course dinners shared around the long dining room table in a true dinner-party atmosphere. Bedrooms come in all sizes from spacious to cozy depending on whether you are in the Victorian or Georgian wing of the house or tucked under the eaves in the old nursery. There are telephones in all rooms and washers and dryers for the use of guests. Portree is the only town on the island, built round a natural harbor where colorful cottages line the port and houses rise steeply up to the main streets of the town. It is a bustling, lively town, which hosts Skye week in June, a folk festival in mid-August, Highland Games in August, and a fiddlers' rally in September. *Directions:* From Kyle of Lochalsh take the bridge to Skye, then the A87 to Portree. Just as you enter the town, Viewfield House is on your left-hand side.

VIEWFIELD HOUSE
Owners: Linda & Hugh Macdonald
Portree
Isle of Skye IV51 9EU, Scotland
Tel: (01478) 612217, Fax: (01478) 613517
Email: info@viewfieldhouse.com
12 rooms
Double: £110–£135*
*Includes dinner, bed & breakfast
Open Easter to mid-Oct, Credit cards: MC, VS
Children welcome
www.karenbrown.com/ews/viewfield.html

Hotels in Scotland

Originally built as a hunting lodge in 1820 and subsequently expanded in 1880, Finnart Lodge, the home of Annie and Archie Boyd, offers an idyllic lochside retreat. The recently completed "Millennium" folly and the splendid conservatory are lovely spots for enjoying the stunning views across the water to the surrounding hills. Two twin-bedded rooms, Blue and Green, offer en-suite bathrooms, and Blue boasts its own private view down the loch. A third twin-bedded room, Trellis, is equipped with a washbasin and has a private bathroom with shower just a few steps down the hallway. For those who simply must have a double bed, a different bedroom can be substituted in combination with the Trellis bathroom. Advance reservations must be made for dinner, which features local produce and homegrown vegetables in season. Tastefully and comfortably furnished throughout and with a liberal sprinkling of antiques and curios, the house provides a great base for walking and fishing. Archie will happily provide the use of a boat and fishing gear. If you fancy a day out on the train, consider visiting Oban or Mallaig from nearby Ranoch station. *Directions:* From the A9 Perth to Inverness road exit for Calvine (11 miles north of Pitlochry). Drive through Calvine then turn right to Kinloch Rannoch via Trinafour (13 miles from the A9). In Kinloch Rannoch follow signs for Rannoch school, which brings you onto the south shore of the loch. After 5 miles pass Rannoch school and the gates to Finnart Lodge are on the loch side of the road after another 5 miles.

FINNART LODGE   New
Owners: Annie & Archie Boyd
Rannoch
Perthshire PH17 2QF, Scotland
Tel: (01882) 633366, Fax: (01882) 633232
Email: finnartlodge@cs.com
3 rooms, Double: £80
Closed Christmas & New Year, Credit cards: none
Children over 12
www.karenbrown.com/ews/finnart.html

Shieldaig has an overwhelmingly beautiful location facing a small, tree-covered island on the shores of Loch Torridon. Here single-track roads wind you through spectacular, rugged scenery of mountains rising straight from the sea and sea lochs penetrating far inland. A wonderful place to stay in Shieldaig is Tigh an Eilean, an 18th-century house converted to a hotel and personally run by Cathryn and Christopher Field. The decor is quiet and soothing with soft beiges and warm pastels. Dinner is taken in the airy dining room overlooking the loch and there are snug little lounges and an honesty bar. Bedrooms are cozy and very comfortable—be sure to request a loch view. The hotel will pack you a picnic lunch or you can obtain supplies from the Fields' little shop next door. Walking, birdwatching, and fishing are popular pastimes with the Beinne Eighe Nature Reserve and the 15,000-acre National Trust estate nearby. Guests often drive around the Applecross peninsula with its awesome, twisting pass of Bealach-na-Bo and its views of Skye and the Outer Hebrides. Tigh An Eilean is an excellent place to stop if you are traveling between Skye (Kyle of Lochalsh) and Ullapool and do not want to rush through all this magnificent scenery in one day. *Directions:* Shieldaig is 68 miles from Inverness. Take the A832 (Ullapool road) to Garve and then on to Kinlochewe where you turn left on the A896 (single-track road) to Shieldaig. The hotel is on the waterfront.

TIGH AN EILEAN (House by the Island)
Owners: Cathryn & Christopher Field
Shieldaig by Strathcarron
Wester Ross IV54 8XN, Scotland
Tel: (01520) 755251, Fax: (01520) 755321
Email: tighaneileanhotel@shieldaig.fsnet.co.uk
11 rooms
Double: £112.50
Open Apr to mid-Oct, Credit cards: MC, VS
Children welcome
www.karenbrown.com/ews/tighaneilean.html

On a rocky spit of land almost surrounded by water, the whitewashed Eilean Iarmain hotel, a Harris Tweed shop, and a huddle of cottages face Isle Ornsay, a tiny island whose lighthouse was built by Robert Louis Stephenson's grandfather. Across the sound mountains tumble directly into the sea, adding a wild, end-of-the-earth feel. The Eilean Iarmain (pronounced "Ellen Earman") is a hotel with a lot of style. Chintz chairs add a homey touch to the cozy parlor and in the dining room you find that the menu is in Gaelic, thankfully with an English translation (the staff speaks Gaelic and English). A tartan-patterned carpet leads up the pine stairs to six bedrooms. All have the same tariff but there is a great variety of size and decor: room 2 has a canopied half-tester bed that once resided in Armadale castle; the turret room is paneled in mellow pine and has a seating area in the turret. More rooms are found in the cottage across the road. In addition there are four luxurious suites with sitting room and bathroom downstairs and bedroom upstairs. Step out of the front door of the hotel and round the side and you find yourself in the old-fashioned pub (bar meals are served) where locals gather—on Thursday evenings they often bring their instruments. Be sure to visit the Armadale Castle. *Directions:* From Kyle of Lochalsh take the bridge to Skye, then the A850 to the A851, a single-track road with passing places, towards Armadale: turn left to Eilean Iarmain.

EILEAN IARMAIN (Isle Ornsay)
Owners: Sir Iain & Lady Noble
Manager: Morag MacDonald
Sleat
Isle of Skye IV43 8QR, Scotland
Tel: (01471) 833332, Fax: (01471) 833275
Email: hotel@eilean-iarmain.co.uk
12 rooms, 4 suites
Double: £120–£150, Suite: £150–£200
Open all year, Credit cards: all major
Children welcome
www.karenbrown.com/ews/eileaniarmain.html

"Even the food is eclipsed by your openheartedness," a guest wrote in the visitor's book, a thoughtful summing up of how Sukie and Bill Barber run Old Pines, their home and a restaurant with rooms. It is one of those special places where food and your enjoyment are taken seriously yet in a very relaxed way. Sukie is a master chef and the Barbers' food, hospitality, and housekeeping have received a string of awards. Ingredients are sourced as locally as possible and much is organic. Salads and herbs are grown on site on a pick-and-eat basis and the bread is baked twice a day. Books, sofas, chairs, and a log fire crowd the sitting room and guests often elect to eat together in the dining room. The single-story building is well suited to those with mobility problems and several bedrooms are designed for wheelchair guests. Likewise, children are especially welcome (there are two family rooms and a family suite), joining the Barbers' children for high tea and then amusing themselves in the playroom while parents enjoy a relaxed evening. Bedrooms are cozy and rustic and each has a shower room. Walks start at the front door and just up the road you can take the gondola for a close-up look at Ben Nevis. Sukie's favorite drive takes you to the most westerly point on the mainland, offering you spectacular Highland scenery and views of the islands of Rhum, Muck, and Eigg. *Directions:* From Fort William take the A82 for 10 miles through Spean Bridge towards Inverness. At the war memorial, at the edge of the village, turn left—Old Pines is on your right after 400 yards.

OLD PINES RESTAURANT WITH ROOMS   *New*
Owners: Sukie & Bill Barber
Spean Bridge, by Fort William
Inverness-shire PH34 4EG, Scotland
Tel: (01397) 712324, Fax: (01397) 712433
Email: kb@oldpines.co.uk
8 rooms
Double: £140–£150 (£10 extra Fri & Sat nights)*
Includes dinner, bed & breakfast
Closed Christmas & 2 weeks end of Nov
Credit cards: MC, VS, Children welcome
www.karenbrown.com/ews/oldpines.html

The Creggans Inn stands next to the shore of Loch Fyne on the doorstep of some of the most remote and unspoiled countryside in Scotland. Previously owned by Sir Fitzroy McLean (thought to have been the role model for Ian Fleming's James Bond, otherwise known as "007"), the property is now in the hands of the Robertson family who are bringing years of experience in hotel ownership on the Isle of Mull to its renovation and upgrading. Scheduled for completion in late 2001, the work was well in hand when we visited and the rooms that we inspected had been finished to a very high level of comfort. Guest facilities include a private second-floor sitting room, lounge areas, and restaurant, all with expansive views across the loch to the low, rolling hills beyond. A small but lively public bar at the end of the inn also serves as headquarters to the local shinty (hockey) team whose photographs adorn the walls. Here you have the opportunity to take a "wee dram" or sample some fine Scottish ale in the company of the locals. Strachur is easily accessible and well located as a base for touring and walking on the west coast. Nearby sights include castles (Inverary is home to the Duke of Argyll) and gardens (Younger botanical gardens, an offshoot of the better-known Edinburgh gardens, were established on the west coast to benefit from the milder climate). *Directions:* From Glasgow take the M8 to Gourock, cross the Clyde by ferry to Dunoon, and take the A815 to Strachur where you find The Creggans Inn across the road from the loch.

THE CREGGANS INN   **New**
Owners: Onny, Alex & Thomas Robertson
Strachur
Argyll PA27 8BX, Scotland
Tel: (01369) 860279, Fax: (01369) 860637
Email: info@creggans-inn.co.uk
14 rooms
Double: £100–£156, Suite: £156–£176
Open all year, Credit cards: MC, VS
Children welcome
www.karenbrown.com/ews/creggans.html

Kilcamb Lodge Hotel occupies a picture-perfect remote location on the shores of Loch Sunart. The house itself, a former hunting lodge, has been meticulously converted to a country house hotel and its interior is as delightful as the surrounding scenery. Try to secure one of the loch-facing rooms. Rooms 6, 7, and 8, with either a king or twin beds, offer spectacular loch views in rooms large enough to accommodate spacious sitting areas. Room 5 also shares the same lovely view but is smaller, with a double bed. The dining room with its fine cuisine and the sitting room also overlook the loch. Apart from the utter peace and quiet of the place, the surrounding scenery is a tremendous attraction—a paradise for lovers of wildflowers, animals, and birds. To the south are the Morvern Hills and Mull is an enjoyable day trip from the hotel. To the west is the Ardnamurchan Peninsula, the most westerly point in the British mainland. The scenery here varies from stark glens and soaring hills to lush valleys, and the little inlets with their white-sand beaches overlooking the distant islands of Rum, Muck, Eigg, and Skye are unforgettable. *Directions:* From Glasgow take the A82 north to the Corran ferry (7 miles before Fort William)—the ferry runs every half-hour and reservations are not necessary. Leaving the ferry, turn left and follow the A861, a narrow two-lane road, for 12 miles to Strontian where you find the hotel on your left beside the loch.

KILCAMB LODGE HOTEL
Owners: Anne & Peter Blakeway
Strontian, Ardnamurchan
Highland PH36 4HY, Scotland
Tel: (01967) 402257, Fax: (01967) 402041
Email: kilcamblodge@aol.com
11 rooms
Double: £80–£130*, Suite: £130*
*Breakfast not included: £8.50–£12.50
Closed Jan, Credit cards: MC, VS
Children welcome
www.karenbrown.com/ews/kilcamb.html

Originally constructed in 1720 as a dower house by the McLeods of Dunvegan Castle, Talisker House lies in a secluded valley nestled beneath the imposing rock mass of Preshal Mhor. It was purchased by Jon Wathen's parents in the early 1960s as a family retreat and he and Ros returned from Australia in 1995 to restore and refurbish the property, complete with many family antiques and heirlooms. Paintings of Jon's Norfolk relatives are hung in the stairway. The four guest bedrooms (two conveniently located on the ground floor) are elegantly furnished, two with imposing four-poster beds. The focal point of guest facilities is the sitting room, situated on the first floor. Window seats afford expansive views over the garden and out towards the coast; logs crackle in the fireplace; and a grand piano completes the aura of relaxed elegance. Good food is high on the list of reasons to visit. Ros uses a host of homegrown vegetables and herbs to create her very own breads, soups, and desserts. Accessed by a private driveway and set in a 2-acre garden, the house is a short walk from the ocean. Local activities focus on walking and fishing. A visit to the nearby Talisker distillery provides an interesting diversion. *Directions:* Turn left off the A863 onto the B8009 to Carbost. At the top of Carbost village veer left and follow signs for the 4 miles to Talisker (a single-lane road).

TALISKER HOUSE   New
Owners: Jon & Ros Wathen
Talisker
Isle of Skye IV47 8SF, Scotland
Tel: (01478) 640245, Fax: (01478) 640214
4 rooms
Double: £86
Open mid-Mar to Oct
Credit cards: MC, VS
Children welcome

Quite the most impressive building that you see for many a mile along the breathtakingly beautiful, rugged coast of Wester Ross is the Loch Torridon Hotel, a grand shooting lodge built by the Earl of Lovelace in 1887. The Earl picked an isolated spot where the mountains descend almost to the lochside, leaving just enough room for this imposing building and its sweep of lawn to the water's edge. The public rooms are huge: an enormous bay window frames the idyllic view of loch and mountains and the pretty pink-and-navy damask sofas and chairs seem almost lost in the vastness of the sitting room. The large pine-paneled entry and the dining room have a tribute to the 50th anniversary of Queen Victoria's reign painted just below the ceiling as a border encircling the rooms. The principal bedrooms are very large and enjoy magnificent bathrooms—I particularly admired the turret bathroom in room 2 and the grand tub sitting center stage in room 1. Smaller bedrooms are tucked cozily under the eaves. Be sure to request a room with a view. The area is renowned for its beautiful Highland scenery and you can take a spectacular drive by following the southern shore of Loch Torridon to Applecross, over the hair-raising Pass of the Cattle, and returning to Torridon via the A896. *Directions:* Torridon is 64 miles from Inverness. Take the A832 (Ullapool road) to Kinlochewe where you turn left on the A896 (single-track road) to Torridon.

LOCH TORRIDON HOTEL
Owners: Geraldine & David Gregory
Torridon by Achnasheen
Wester Ross IV22 2EY, Scotland
Tel: (01445) 791242, Fax: (01445) 791296
Email: stay@lochtorridonhotel.com
20 rooms, 1 suite
Double: £132–£290, Suite: from £220
Closed Jan
Credit cards: MC, VS
Children welcome
www.karenbrown.com/ews/torridon.html

Ullapool is a fishing port, ferry terminal, and popular holiday resort set on the shores of Loch Broom, a broad sea loch. The Ceilidh Place has the façade of a whitewashed row of fishermen's cottages but the interior is anything but traditional: this is a somewhat Bohemian, very eclectic establishment and the nicest place in town. Ceilidh (pronounced "kaylee") is Gaelic for meeting socially—then maybe there could be a song and some impromptu music and that would make it a grand ceilidh. Jean Urquhart and her late husband opened a coffee shop, which grew to include music and the sale of pictures, then along came accommodation, a bookstore, an exhibition hall, a restaurant, and a snug pub. Accommodation is in the hotel with its modern extension to the rear or dormitory accommodation in the clubhouse across the road. The rooms are contemporary in their decor, often with a built-in desk and fitted furniture (but no TV). Guests tend to gravitate towards the upstairs sitting room with its homey mix of furniture arranged in cozy seating areas, tea- and coffee-makings, and honor bar. The coffee bar is a great place to enjoy a cappuccino or a meal or you might prefer the more up-market restaurant. Possible day trips include the Inchnadamph Caves, the ruins of Ardvreck Castle, and Lochinver with its heart-stopping views. *Directions:* Ullapool is 60 miles northwest of Inverness on the A835. West Argyll Street parallels the harbor one street back from the water.

THE CEILIDH PLACE
Owner: Jean Urquhart
14 West Argyll Street
Ullapool
Wester Ross IV26 2TY, Scotland
Tel: (01854) 612103, Fax: (01854) 612886
13 rooms
Double: £100–£130
Open all year
Credit cards: all major
Children welcome

Hotels in Wales

The Olde Bull's Head has a long and interesting history. The walls of its traditional beamed bar are decorated with antique weaponry and the town's ancient ducking chair provides a most unusual curio. Guests have the use of a large sitting room with flowery-chintz-covered chairs. Dine in the stylish new brasserie or à-la-carte restaurant situated upstairs in the former hayloft. David Robertson, one of the owners, takes care of the front of the house. Charles Dickens stayed here, hence most bedrooms are named after Dickens characters. Each room is decorated differently, with matching drapes and bedspread and coordinating wallpaper and armchair. All have modern bathrooms, television, and phone and either a lovely antique brass or iron bed. Castle Street leads to Beaumaris Castle, a squat, concentric fortification commissioned by Edward I. Nearby, the Marquis of Anglesey's house and gardens are open to the public. Past Bangor, on the mainland, is Caernarfon Castle where Prince Charles was invested as Prince of Wales. *Directions:* From Chester take the A55, coast road, to Anglesey and cross on the Britannia Road Bridge, then follow the A545 to Beaumaris.

THE OLDE BULL'S HEAD
Owners: David Robertson & Keith Rothwell
Castle Street
Beaumaris
Isle of Anglesey LL58 8AP, Wales
Tel: (01248) 810329, Fax: (01248) 811294
E-mail: info@bullsheadinn.co.uk
15 rooms
Double: £87–£100
Closed Christmas & New Year
Credit cards: all major
Children over 7
www.karenbrown.com/ews/oldebullshead.html

Tan-y-Foel, "the house under the hillside," sits high above the Conwy Valley, just outside Betws-y-Coed, within 8 acres of rugged woodland and pasture on the edge of the Snowdonia National Park. This small country house, owned and run by Janet and Peter Pitman and their daughter Kelly, has a contemporary rather than a traditional style, with the interior decor featuring bold and vibrant modern designs. Rooms 4, 5, and 6 enjoy spectacular countryside views—room 6 with its lime-green-and-lemon four-poster bed was a particular favorite. Rooms 1 and 9 (a converted hayloft) are external annex rooms providing extra privacy. All rooms are furnished with thoughtful touches such as toiletries, bathrobes, and ironing equipment. Janet, a master chef of Great Britain, uses organic and fine local produce and takes pride in her menu, which changes daily. Dinner is served in a delightful little room that in past years was the dairy. The rugged grandeur of the Snowdonia mountain passes is in complete contrast to the pretty countryside around Tan-y-Foel where miles of public footpaths allow you to enjoy the peace and quiet of the countryside. Just down the road you find Bodnant Gardens, the finest in Wales. Castle lovers head for nearby Conwy and Caernarfon. *Directions:* From the Llandudno roundabout on the A55 take the A470 towards Betws-y-Coed through Llanrwst and continue for 2 miles. Turn left at the signpost for Capel Garmon and Nebo (do not take the single-track road) and Tan-y-Foel is on your left after 1½ miles. Manchester airport is about an hour and a half's drive away.

TAN-Y-FOEL
Owners: Pitman family
Capel Garmon, near Betws-y-Coed
Conwy LL26 0RE, Wales
Tel: (01690) 710507, Fax: (01690) 710681
Email: enquiries@tyfhotel.co.uk
6 rooms
Double: £99–£150
Closed Christmas, Credit cards: all major
Children over 7, No-smoking house
www.karenbrown.com/ews/tanyfoel.html

Sitting high above the River Conwy, with glorious views of Snowdonia and overlooking the ramparts of Conwy Castle across the broad river estuary, The Old Rectory Country House offers guests friendly hospitality and the chance to learn a little about the Welsh and their culture: in summer a harpist often plays for guests before they go in to dinner. The dining tables are elegantly set with crystal and silver, the polished wood floors are covered with lovely patterned carpets, and fine watercolors hang on the walls. Dinner here is a highlight as Wendy is a Master Chef of Great Britain. After dinner, coffee is served in the pine-paneled drawing room. Michael will help to plan sightseeing routes. Bedrooms, though not large, are well equipped with an iron and small ironing board, television, telephone, mineral water, fruit and flowers. Walnut, Mahogany, and the coach-house rooms have splendid garden views. Mahogany has a half-tester bed and a bathroom with a large, bright, peacock-blue corner tub. Glorious Bodnant Gardens, best know for its azaleas and rhododendrons, is just down the road while also nearby is the medieval town of Conwy with its dramatic castle. Beyond lie all the rugged delights of Snowdonia. *Directions:* The Old Rectory is half a mile south of Conwy on the A470, just a one-and-a-half-hour drive from Manchester airport.

THE OLD RECTORY COUNTRY HOUSE
Owners: Wendy & Michael Vaughan
Llanrwst Road
Llansanffraid Glan Conwy
Conwy LL28 5LF, Wales
Tel: (01492) 580611, Fax: (01492) 584555
Email: info@oldrectorycountryhouse.co.uk
6 rooms
Double: £119–£199
Open Feb to Nov 20
Credit cards: MC, VS
Children over 7, No-smoking house
www.karenbrown.com/ews/theoldrectory.html

Ynyshir Hall shares its location on the Dovey river estuary with a 1,000-acre bird reserve, home to herons, oystercatchers, curlews, and cormorants. Nestled in acres of gardens full of azaleas and rhododendrons, the hall was built in the 16th century, its most illustrious owner being Queen Victoria. Now it is home to professional artist Rob Reen and his wife Joan who have done the most wonderful job of decorating their country house hotel in rich colors, with each room accented by Rob's oils, acrylics, and watercolors. Relax round the fire in the elegant blue drawing room, enjoy a drink in the richly decorated bar, and dine on country-house fare in the turquoise-blue dining room. Bedrooms are named after famous artists. Monet, a ground-floor suite has a conservatory sitting room. A frieze of wispy clouds adds whimsy to the bathroom in the Renoir suite, which has particularly lovely views of the garden. Ynyshir Hall's central location makes it an ideal base for exploring the rugged Snowdonia National Park to the north and coastal paths to the south. Outstanding castles in the vicinity include Harlech, Powys, and Chirk. In nearby Machynlleth a traditional Welsh street market is held every Wednesday. *Directions:* From Aberystwyth take the A487 for 11 miles (towards Machynlleth) to Eglwysfach. Turn left in the village and Ynyshir Hall is on your right after half a mile.

YNYSHIR HALL
Owners: Joan & Rob Reen
Eglwysfach, Machynlleth
Powys SY20 8TA, Wales
Tel: (01654) 781209, Fax: (01654) 781366
Email: info@ynyshir-hall.co.uk
10 rooms
Double: £130–£205, Suite: £190–£210
Closed Jan 5 to15, Credit cards: all major
Children over 9
Relais & Châteaux Member
www.karenbrown.com/ews/ynyshir.html

From taking bed-and-breakfast guests to helping to get the farm on its feet, through expanding the traditional slate-hung farmhouse, to leasing the land and hiring a chef, Ty'n Rhos is Nigel and Lynda Kettle's Welsh success story. Over the years guests have become friends, returning year after year for a countryside holiday in this exceptionally beautiful part of Wales. I was particularly impressed by the very good-value-for-money prices and the genuine warmth of welcome that Lynda and Nigel extend to new and old friends. Dinner is either a set, four-course meal or à-la-carte, except on Sunday evenings when the set menu, the only one available, offers two choices for each course. All the bedrooms are beautifully appointed—request a room with a view of wonderful open countryside across the Menai Straits to the island of Anglesey. I particularly liked the ground-floor rooms whose patio doors open onto the garden. Ty'n Rhos is located between the sea and the wild mountains of Snowdonia National Park. Caernarfon Castle is close at hand as is the Snowdon mountain railway, the little steam train that ascends Mount Snowdon. *Directions:* From Chester take the A55. Just before Bangor turn left on the A5 (signposted Betws-y-Coed) and immediately right on the B4366 (signposted Llanberis). After 4 miles cross the roundabout and take the first right towards Seion. Ty'n Rhos is on your left after half a mile.

TY'N RHOS
Owners: Lynda & Nigel Kettle
Llanddeiniolen, Caernarfon
Gwynedd LL55 3AE, Wales
Tel: (01248) 670489, Fax: (01248) 670079
Email: enquiries@tynrhos.co.uk
14 rooms
Double: £80–£110, Suite: £150
Open all year
Credit cards: all major
Children over 6
www.karenbrown.com/ews/tynrhos.html

Tyddyn Llan is a delightful gray-stone country house set in the peaceful Vale of Edeyrnion. It was once a shooting lodge for the Dukes of Westminster and converted into a friendly hotel by Peter and Bridget Kindred in 1983. Inside is roomy and comfortable with antiques and interesting paintings by Peter who runs painting weekends in November and March. Bridget and Peter are on hand to see that everything runs smoothly. Bedrooms are lovely, decked out in country-house style—rooms on the first floor (second in America) are more spacious than those tucked under the eaves. Fishing (with a ghillie if required) is available on the Kindreds' own 4 miles of the nearby River Dee. You can hike the old drovers' roads and tramp into the nearby Berwyn Mountains. (Llandrillo was an important point on the drovers' route, which was used for hundreds of years for driving livestock from Welsh farms to the markets in England.) Steam trains run on a narrow track down one side of the lake. A more scenic train ride is from Blaenau Ffestiniog, a slate town where slate crags overhang the houses, to Porthmadog on the coast. On the way to the train visit Llechwedd slate caverns. Many visitors head into the walled city of Chester with its half-timbered shops. *Directions:* Tyddyn Llan is near Llandrillo, on the B4401 between Corwen (A5) and Bala.

TYDDYN LLAN
Owners: Bridget & Peter Kindred
Llandrillo
Near Corwen
Denbighshire LL21 0ST, Wales
Tel: (01490) 440264, Fax: (01490) 440414
Email: tyddynllanhotel@compuserve.com
10 rooms
Double: £105–£140
Open all year
Credit cards: all major
Children welcome
www.karenbrown.com/ews/tyddynllan.html

I always hope that a beautiful region and a beautiful hotel will coincide and such is the case here. Snowdonia provides the most beautiful of Welsh scenery and Bodysgallen Hall provides the most beautiful of Welsh hotels. Built around a 13th-century watchtower and overlooking Conwy Castle, this large, rambling hotel looks surprisingly uniform, considering six centuries of additions, alterations, and restorations. The mellow elegance and character of the house are preserved throughout. The spacious, dark-oak-paneled Jacobean entrance hall and the drawing room on the first floor have large fireplaces, mullioned windows, and comfortable furniture that create a warm, relaxed atmosphere. Nineteen beautiful bedrooms are found in the main house: none of the rooms are large, neither are their bathrooms, but they are all decorated to the highest of standards—I particularly enjoyed my stay in room 8, which has a sitting nook and the loveliest of views of the gardens. Sixteen suites are located in adjoining little cottages. Bodysgallen Farm has undergone a skillful conversion to a spa with a spacious indoor swimming pool, gym, and beauty salons. The grounds are an absolute delight and include a 17th-century knot garden, an 18th-century walled rose garden, and a woodland walk that offers spectacular views of Conwy Castle. *Directions:* Take the A55 from Chester to the roundabout on the outskirts of Conwy where you turn right on the A470. The hotel entrance is on your right after 1 mile.

BODYSGALLEN HALL
Manager: Matthew Johnson
Llandudno LL30 1RS, Wales
Tel: (01492) 584466, Fax: (01492) 582519
Email: info@bodysgallen.com
35 rooms
Double: £160–£250*, Suite: £185–£240*
*Breakfast not included: £14.50
Open all year, Credit cards: all major
Children over 8
Relais & Châteaux Member
www.karenbrown.com/ews/bodysgallen.html

This hotel has a superb location high in the mid-Wales mountains at the head of Lake Vyrnwy overlooking miles and miles of pine-forested mountaintops. A decidedly old-fashioned feeling permeates the building, from the pine-paneled entrance hall to the drawing room with its ornate ceiling, grand piano, and large windows opening up to views of the lake stretching into the distance with pine-forested hills rising from its shore. The bar and conservatory dining room share the same stunning view: sunsets are dramatic. Bedrooms face either the lake or the driveway behind the hotel—it is well worth the extra pounds to secure a bedroom with a lake view (room 1 is quite the loveliest and rooms 31 to 38 have lake-view terraces). The tavern that lies adjacent to the hotel offers a cozy pub full of locals and a casual dining room serving traditional pub meals. Walking and relaxing are the most popular pastimes. The lake is stocked with trout every year and over 10,000 pheasants are released during the shooting season. Tennis, biking, and sailing are available for guests. *Directions:* Lake Vyrnwy is a one-hour drive from Shrewsbury—take the A458 towards Welshpool and just after Ford take the B4393 to Lake Vyrnwy. The hotel's driveway is on the right 400 yards after the dam.

LAKE VYRNWY HOTEL
Manager: Anthony Rosser
Lake Vyrnwy
Llanwddyn
Powys SY10 0LY, Wales
Tel: (01691) 870692, Fax: (01691) 870259
Email: res@lakevyrnwy.com
35 rooms
Double: £110–£182, Suite: £182
Open all year
Credit cards: all major
Children welcome
www.karenbrown.com/ews/vyrnwy.html

This grand and dignified house was designed by Sir Clough Williams-Ellis (of fanciful Portmeirion) and rescued from ruin by Sir Bernard Ashley (of Laura Ashley fame). The lounging rooms are a delight: a great hall with an open fire, antiques, huge sofas, and interesting pictures, a flowery sitting room, and a book-filled library with leather chairs and a snooker table. Each bedroom or suite is individually planned and quite different from the next—some are very flowery, others very masculine. The suites are up two long flights of stairs under the eaves. The smaller rooms of the north wing are most attractive—several have small four-poster beds and Welsh mineral water, sherry, and fluffy robes are provided. Since opening, the hall has collected a plethora of awards including a Michelin star for its cuisine. The Wye river valley offers several places of interest and nearby are the ruins of Tintern Abbey, celebrated by Wordsworth. You can visit Hereford, a lovely, sleepy, medieval city astride the River Wye, its cathedral built in several styles from the 11th century, and Hay-on-Wye with its many bookstores. There is an abundance of pretty countryside, from the stark beauty of the Brecon Beacons to the soft prettiness of the Wye valley. *Directions:* Llangoed Hall is on the A470, midway between Buith Wells and Brecon.

LLANGOED HALL
Llyswen, Brecon
Powys LD3 0YP, Wales
Tel: (01874) 754525, Fax: (01874) 754545
Email: llangoed-hall-co-wales-uk@compuserve.com
23 rooms
Double: £155–£280, Suite: £310–£335
Open all year
Credit cards: all major
Children over 8
www.karenbrown.com/ews/llangoed.html

A soft pink colorwash brightens the exterior of this spacious home in the village of Newport. Cnapan House is very much a family-run affair, with John and Eluned Lloyd, their daughter Judith, and her husband Michael Cooper extending a warm welcome. John and Michael are your genial hosts while Eluned and Judith work together in the kitchen. Lunchtime fare emphasizes whole-food cooking with old-fashioned, hearty soups and puddings (vegetarian dishes available). Tables are covered with lace cloths for dinner, adding a romantic touch to a special meal where the main course is always served with five or six vegetables. Guests can enjoy before-dinner drinks in either the sitting room or the bar, both snug rooms filled with country antiques and overflowing with charm. The bedrooms are superb, artfully decorated in a light, airy style and immaculately furnished, with every nook and cranny filled with old family treasures. One guestroom is a family room with a small adjoining bunk-bedroom for the children. (Nursery teas are served in the early evening so that parents can put the children in bed or in front of the TV before coming down to dinner.) You will love the welcoming, free-and-easy atmosphere that pervades this home. Just down the lane you find Newport's pretty beach and a particularly lovely section of the Welsh coastal path. *Directions:* Newport is on the A487 11 miles west of Cardigan and 7 miles east of Fishguard (not to be confused with the other Newport near Cardiff).

CNAPAN HOUSE
Owners: Lloyd & Cooper families
East Street
Newport, near Fishguard
Pembrokeshire SA42 0WF, Wales
Tel: (01239) 820575, Fax: (01239) 820878
Email: cnapan@online-holidays.net
5 rooms, Double: £64
Closed Jan & Feb, Credit cards: MC, VS
Children welcome
www.karenbrown.com/ews/cnapan.html

Penmaenuchaf Hall is a lovely country house hotel with a quite unpronounceable name. According to owners Lorraine Fielding and Mark Watson, "pen mine ich av" is a somewhat accurate pronunciation. Lorraine, Mark, and daughter Lara moved here in 1989 and spent two years converting this beautiful old home into a hotel. Lorraine says the most enjoyable part was deciding upon the color schemes and choosing the fabrics— you'll be pleased with her choices: the decor throughout is absolutely delightful. From the log fire that warms the hallway sitting room through the comfortable lounge to the cozy dining room, the house exudes a welcoming ambiance. The principal bedroom, Leigh Taylor, is named after the wealthy Lancashire cotton magnate who built Penmaenuchaf as a grand holiday home. Today it can be your holiday home in northern Wales. Venture to explore Snowdonia National Park and the central Welsh coast and return in the evening to enjoy an <u>excellent dinner</u>. Of particular interest are the rugged scenery of Snowdonia, Portmeirion village with its Italianate houses, the narrow-gauge Ffestiniog railway, 13th-century Harlech Castle, Llechwedd Slate Caverns, and Bodnant, one of the world's finest gardens. *Directions:* From the Dollgellau bypass (A470) take the A493 towards Tywyn and Fairbourne. The entrance to Penmaenuchaf Hall is on the left after ¾ mile.

PENMAENUCHAF HALL
Owners: Lorraine Fielding & Mark Watson
Penmaenpool
Dolgellau
Gwynedd LL40 1YB, Wales
Tel: (01341) 422129, Fax: (01341) 422787
Email: relax@penhall.co.uk
14 rooms
Double: £110–£170, Suite: £170
Open all year, Credit cards: all major
Children over 6
www.karenbrown.com/ews/penmaenuchaf.html

Maes-y-Neuadd, a 14th-century manor nestled into the hillside 3 miles from Harlech Castle, translates as "the hall in the field," an apt description for this sturdy home. With its 16th-, 18th-, and 20th-century additions, this rambling country house hotel has lots of character. Four hospitable owners, June, Lynn, Michael, and Peter, are on hand to make you feel thoroughly at home in this relaxed, unstuffy, friendly hotel. Enjoy a drink in the convivial bar before dinner looking out over rolling countryside to the distant mountains of Snowdonia National Park. The set-price dinner offers choices for all courses and always has a tempting Welsh lamb dish on the menu. Bedrooms come in all shapes and sizes, with most containing queen or king/twin beds. I particularly enjoyed Wynne, decorated in soft pinks, and Moelwyn, a deluxe room in the coach house (just a few steps from the main building) with its roof rising to the rafters and a wood-burning stove. Apart from exploring castles and Snowdonia, one of the delights of staying here is to ride on the nearby Ffestiniog Railway with its steam train that takes you through spectacular countryside. On Friday evenings (summer only) you can enjoy "steam cuisine," a delicious Maes-y-Neuadd dinner, as you ride the rails. *Directions:* Maes-y-Neuadd is off the B4573, 3 miles north of Harlech.

MAES-Y-NEUADD
Owners: June & Michael Slatter
* Lynn & Peter Jackson*
Talsarnau
Harlech LL47 6YA, Wales
Tel: (01766) 780200, Fax: (01766) 780211
Email: maes@neuadd.com
15 rooms, 1 suite
Double: £143–£172, Suite: £159
Open all year
Credit cards: all major
Children welcome
www.karenbrown.com/ews/maesyneuadd.html

Key Map

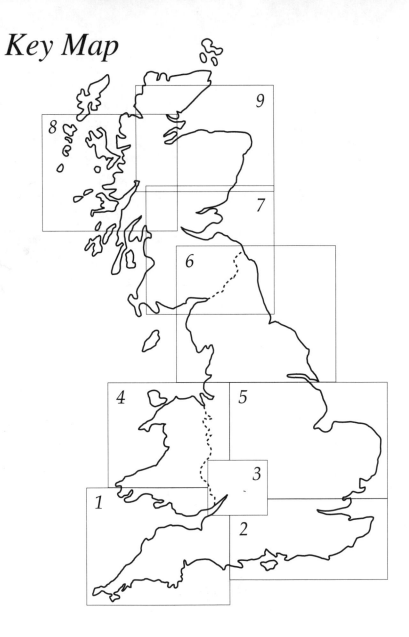

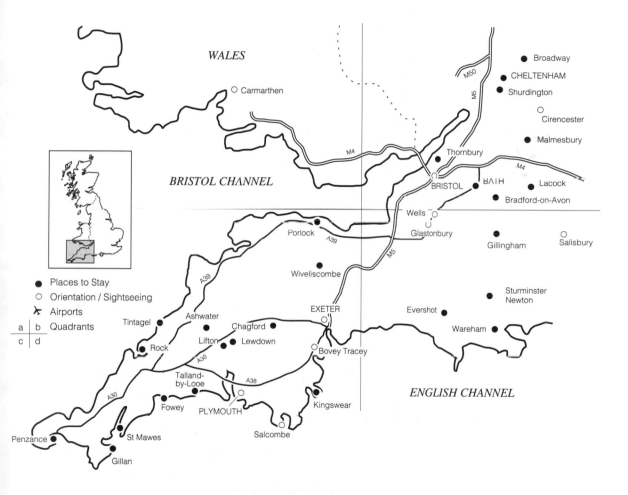

Map 1

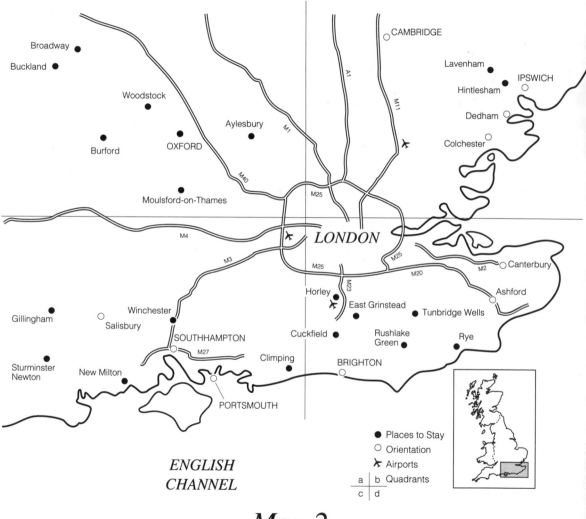

Broadway

Buckland

Woodstock

Aylesbury

CAMBRIDGE

Lavenham

Hintlesham   IPSWICH

Dedham

Colchester

Burford   OXFORD

Moulsford-on-Thames

LONDON

M25

M4

M3

Canterbury

Ashford

Gillingham

Winchester

Salisbury

SOUTHHAMPTON

M27

Sturminster
Newton

New Milton

Climping

PORTSMOUTH

Horley

Cuckfield

East Grinstead   Tunbridge Wells

Rushlake
Green   Rye

BRIGHTON

ENGLISH
CHANNEL

● Places to Stay
○ Orientation
✈ Airports

a	b	Quadrants
c	d	

Map 2

304

Map 3

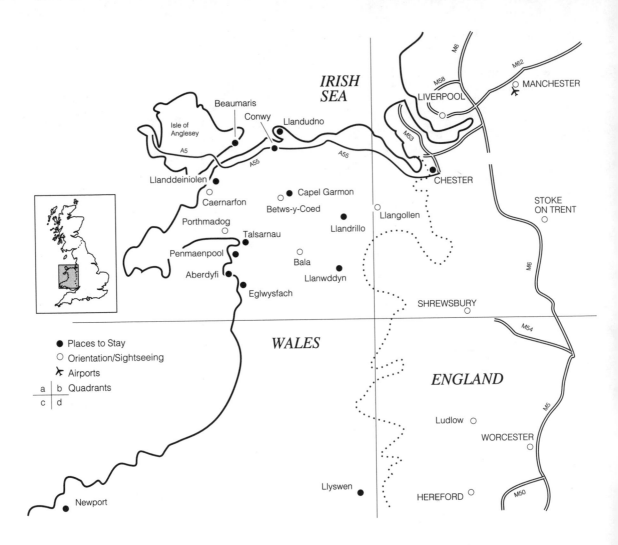

Map 4

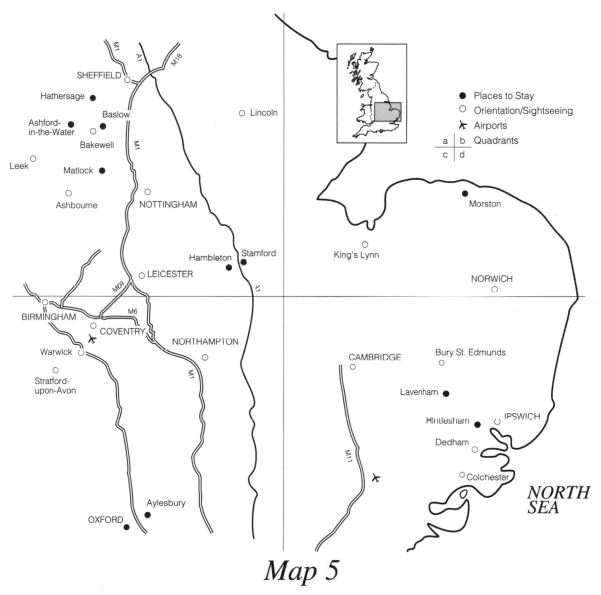

Map 5

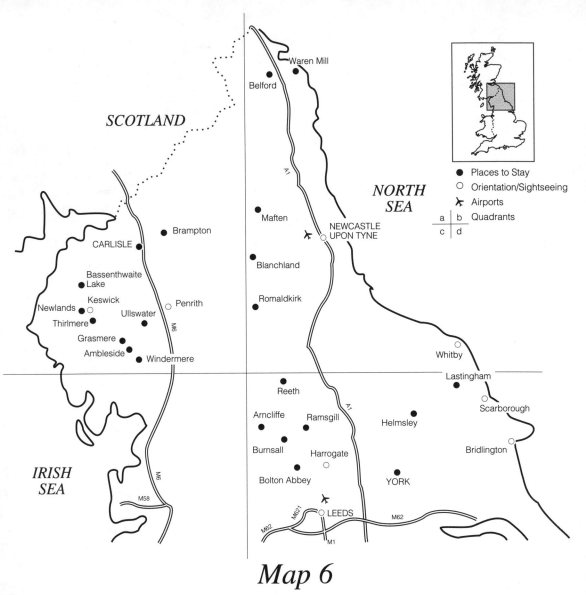

SCOTLAND

NORTH SEA

IRISH SEA

Waren Mill

Belford

Maften

NEWCASTLE UPON TYNE

Blanchland

Romaldkirk

Brampton

CARLISLE

Bassenthwaite Lake

Keswick

Newlands

Thirlmere

Ullswater

Penrith

Grasmere

Ambleside

Windermere

Reeth

Arncliffe

Ramsgill

Helmsley

Burnsall

Harrogate

Bolton Abbey

YORK

LEEDS

Whitby

Lastingham

Scarborough

Bridlington

A1

M6

M58

M62

M621

M1

M62

A1

● Places to Stay
○ Orientation/Sightseeing
✈ Airports

a	b
c	d

Quadrants

Map 6

308

Blairgowrie

Kinclaven

Perth

Dundee

Blairgowrie

A 82

A 9

A 94

A 929

A 85

A 85

A 83

Callander

Kinbuck

Auchterarder

A 85

A 9

Dunblane

A 84

A 82

Stirling

M 90

M9

Gullane

North Berwick

A 80

M9

A 8

M 8

M8

EDINBURGH

A 1

GLASGOW

A 78

A 80

Peebles

Ettrickbridge

A 77

A 76

A 7

A 68

Bonchester
Bridge

ENGLAND

Dumfries

A 701

A 74

A 75

● Places to Stay
○ Orientation/Sightseeing
✈ Airports

a	b	Quadrants
c	d

Map 7

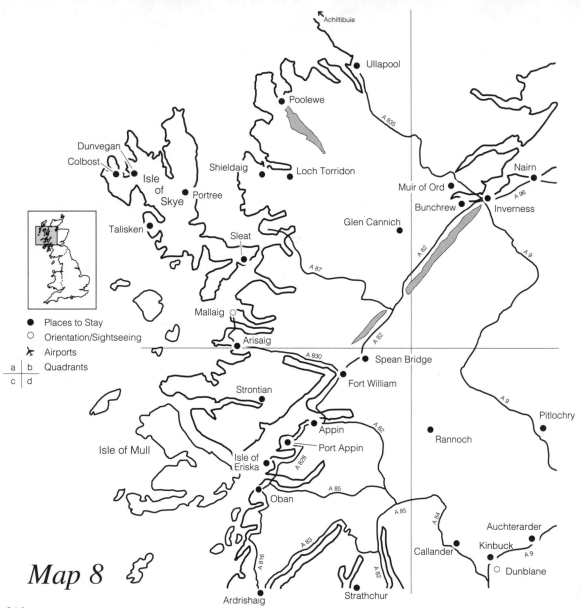

Map 8

Achiltibuie

Ullapool

Poolewe

Dunvegan
Colbost
Isle
of
Skye

Shieldaig

Loch Torridon

A 835

Nairn

Muir of Ord

A 96

Portree

Bunchrew

Inverness

Talisken

A 82

Sleat

Glen Cannich

A 9

A 87

Mallaig

Arisaig

A 830

Spean Bridge

A 82

● Places to Stay
○ Orientation/Sightseeing
✈ Airports

a	b
c	d

Quadrants

Strontian

Fort William

A 9

Pitlochry

Appin

A 82

Isle of Mull

Port Appin

Rannoch

Isle of
Eriska

A 828

Oban

A 85

A 85

A 84

Auchterarder

Kinbuck

Callander

A 9

A 816

A 83

Dunblane

A 82

Ardrishaig

Strathchur

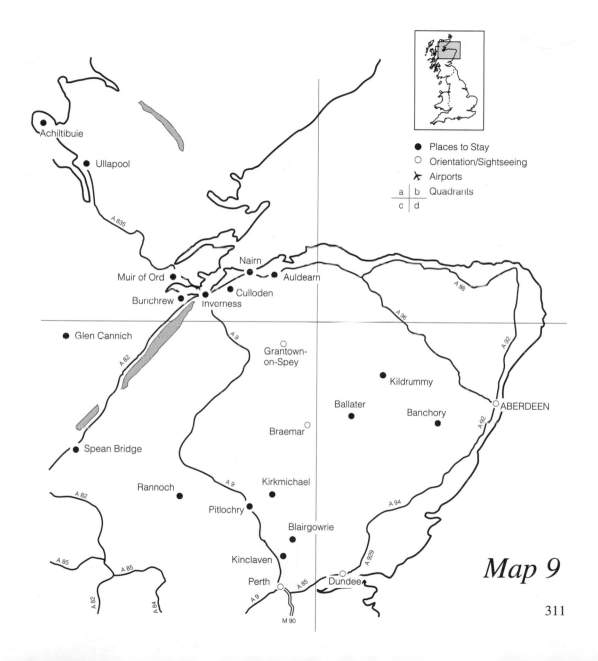

Achiltibuie

Ullapool

A 835

Muir of Ord
Nairn
Auldearn
Bunchrew
Culloden
Inverness

Glen Cannich

A 82

A 9

Grantown-
on-Spey

Kildrummy

Ballater
Banchory

Braemar

ABERDEEN

A 92

A 96

A 96

A 92

Spean Bridge

Rannoch

A 82

A 9

Kirkmichael

Pitlochry

Blairgowrie

A 94

A 85

A 85

Kinclaven

Perth

A 9

A 85

Dundee

A 929

A 82

A 84

M 90

Map 9

311

● Places to Stay
○ Orientation/Sightseeing
✈ Airports
a | b   Quadrants
c | d

Places to Stay with Handicap Facilities

We list below all the hotels that have ground-floor rooms, or rooms specially equipped for the handicapped. Please discuss your requirements with them to determine if they have accommodation that is suitable for you.

England

Ambleside, Rothay Manor
Ashford-in-the-Water, Riverside House
Aylesbury, Hartwell House
Baslow, Fischer's at Baslow Hall
Belford, The Blue Bell Hotel
Bolton Abbey, The Devonshire Arms
Broad Campden, The Malt House
Broadway, The Lygon Arms
Burford, Burford House
Evershot, Summer Lodge
Grasmere, White Moss House
Horley, Langshott Manor
Lacock, At the Sign of the Angel
Lewdown, Lewtrenchard Manor
London, The Cadogan
London, 22 Jermyn Street
London, Knightsbridge Green Hotel
London, The Leonard
Lower Slaughter, Washbourne Court Hotel
Moulsford, The Beetle & Wedge
New Milton, Chewton Glen
Oxford, The Old Bank Hotel

Reeth, The Burgoyne Hotel
Romaldkirk, The Rose & Crown
Shurdington, The Greenway
Sturminster Newton, Plumber Manor
Talland-by-Looe, Talland Bay Hotel
Thirlmere, Dale Head Hall
Ullswater, Sharrow Bay Hotel
Windermere, Holbeck Ghyll
York, The Grange

Scotland

Auchterarder, Auchterarder House
Edinburgh, The Bonham
Edinburgh, Prestonfield House Hotel
Fort William, The Factor's House
Fort William, The Grange
Glasgow, Malmaison
Isle of Eriska, Isle of Eriska Hotel
Inverness, Dunain Park Hotel
Kinclaven, Ballathie House
Muir of Ord, The Dower House
North Berwick, The Glebe House
Pitlochry, Auchnahyle
Pitlochry, Knockendarroch House

Portree, Viewfield House
Sleat, Eilean Iarmain Isle Ornsay Hotel
Spean Bridge, Old Pines Restaurant with
  Rooms
Talisker (Isle of Skye), Talisker House
Torridon, Loch Torridon Hotel

Wales
Eglwysfach, Ynyshir Hall
Llanddeiniolen, Ty'n Rhos
Talsarnau, Maes-y-Neuadd

314

Index

Index

Gunnerside, 77

H

H.M.S. Victory, 42
Haddon Hall, 63
Hadleigh, 51
Hambleton
    Hambleton Hall, 176
Handicap Facilities, Places with, 312
Hartington, 62
    Cheese Shop, 62
Hartwell House, Aylesbury, 140
Harvington
    The Mill at Harvington, 177
Hathersage, 67
    The George, 178
Hawes, 77
    Wensleydale Creamery, 77
Hawkshead, 55
    Beatrix Potter Gallery, 55
Hay-on-Wye, 106
Heligan, Lost Gardens of, 33
Helmsley, 74
    The Black Swan, 74, 179
Hever Castle, 37
Hidcote Manor Gardens, 19
High Peak Trail, 63
Hintlesham
    Hintlesham Hall, 180
Hobby Drive, 30
Hobsburn, Bonchester Bridge, 241
Holbeck Ghyll, Windermere, 226
Holkham, 48
    Holkham Hall, 48
Hope, 67

Horley
    Langshott Manor, 181
Horsehouse, 77
Hotel du Vin, Tunbridge Wells, 217
Hotel du Vin, Winchester, 223
Hotel Kandinsky, Cheltenham, 161
Hotel on the Park, Cheltenham, 162
Hotel Tresanton, St. Mawes, 208
Hotels (Introduction)
    About Hotels, 9
    Children, 9
    Christmas Programs, 10
    Credit Cards, 9
    Finding Hotels, 10
    Handicap Facilities, 10
    Rates, 10
    Relais & Châteaux, 11
    Reservations, 11
Howard, The, Edinburgh, 251
Hunters Inn, 30
Hutton-le-Hole, 73
    Ryedale Folk Museum, 74

I

Ilam, 62
Insurance, Trip Cancellation (Introduction), 11
Inverewe Gardens, 97
Invergarry, 90
Inverlochy Castle, Fort William, 260
Inverness, 90
    Dunain Park Hotel, 265
Isle of Anglesey, 108
Isle of Eriska, 256
Isle of Skye, 91
Isle Ornsay, 93

O

Oaks Hotel, The, Porlock, 201
Oare, 29
Oban
    The Manor House, 273
Ockenden Manor, Cuckfield, 167
Offa's Dyke, 105
Old Bank Hotel, The, Oxford, 198
Old Bell, The, Malmesbury, 192
Old Man of Storr, 92
Old Parsonge Hotel, Oxford, 199
Old Pines Restaurant with Rooms, Spean Bridge, 283
Old Rectory Country House, The, Conwy, 292
Old Scone, 85
Olde Bull's Head, The, Beaumaris, 290
One Devonshire Gardens, Glasgow, 262
Ornsay, Isle, 93
Oxford, 15
    Ashmolean Museum, 15
    Blackwell's, 15
    Botanical Gardens, 15
    Christ Church College, 15
    Information Centre, 15
    Magdalen College, 15
    Merton College, 15
    Old Parsonage Hotel, 199
    St. Mary's Church, 15
    The Bear, 15
    The Old Bank Hotel, 198

P

Parsley Hay, 63
Peak Cavern, 66
Peebles
    Cringletie House Hotel, 274
Pelham Hotel, The, London, 132

Penmaenpool
    Penmaenuchaf Hall, 300
Pennine Way, 67
Penrhyn Castle, 108
Penshurst Place, 38
Penzance, 31
    The Abbey Hotel, 200
Perth, 84
    Ballhousie Castle, 84
    Museum and Art Gallery, 84
    Museum of the Black Watch, 84
    St. John's Kirk, 84
Petworth, 42
    Petworth House, 42
Pheasant, The, Bassenthwaite Lake, 58, 143
Pilsey, 64
Pitlochry, 85
    Auchnahyle, 275
    Festival Theatre, 85
    Knockendarroch House, 276
    Tummel Dam Fish Ladder, 86
Plockton, 97
Plumber Manor, Sturminster Newton, 212
Poolewe
    Pool House, 277
Porlock, 29
    The Oaks Hotel, 201
Porlock Weir, 29
Port Appin
    The Airds Hotel, 278
Porthmadog, 110
Portloe, 32
Portmeirion, 111
Portree, Isle of Skye, 92
    Viewfield House, 92, 279
Portscatho, 32

Index

Woolley Grange, Bradford-on-Avon, 150
Wykeham Arms & The Saint George, The, Winchester, 224

Y

Ynyshir Hall, Eglwysfach, 293
York, 71
    Betty's Bakery and Tearooms, 71
    Castle Museum, 72

York (continued)
    Clifford's Tower, 72
    Jorvik Viking Centre, 71
    Middlethorpe Hall, 229
    Minster, 71
    National Railway Museum, 72
    National Trust Shop, 71
    The Grange, 228
    Treasurer's House, 71
Yorke Arms, The, Ramsgill, 202

Enhance Your Guides

Online

www.karenbrown.com

- Hotel News
- Currency Converter
- Corrections & Edits
- Meals, Wheels & Deals
- Links to Hotels & B&Bs
- Prints of our Favorite Covers
- Color Photos of Hotels & B&Bs

Visit Karen's Market

books, maps, itineraries,
and travel accessories
selected with our
KB travelers in mind.

Join the Karen Brown Club Online

Member benefits include an additional 20% discount in our
online store, access to new discoveries, special deals
negotiated with our travel partners, and more!

Join the Karen Brown Club

Why become a Karen Brown Club member? Savings! In no time at all members earn back their membership fee—in most cases, when they use just *one* of our membership discounts. Visit the Karen Brown website, *www.karenbown.com,* for details.

Karen Brown online store discount
A members-only discount worth an **additional 20%** off all orders in our store.

New discoveries: See our new hotels & B&Bs for next year as we find them
Receive early access to our newly discovered properties. If you cannot find a room in one of our currently recommended properties, these yet-to-be-published gems might be able to offer you alternative accommodation—a priceless benefit!

Discounts negotiated through our travel partners
Partners include participating recommended properties, such as Karen's own Seal Cove Inn. Benefits include condo rental upgrades in Mexico, airline discounts, auto rental discounts, and more!

A complete listing of member benefits can be found on our website:

www.karenbrown.com

Become a Member Today

SHARE YOUR COMMENTS AND DISCOVERIES WITH US

Please share comments on properties that you have visited. We welcome accolades, as well as criticisms.

Also, we'd love to hear about any hotel or bed & breakfast you discover. Tell us what you liked about the property and, if possible, please include a brochure or photographs. We regret we cannot return photos.

Owner _____ Hotel or B&B _____

Address _____ Town _____ Country _____

Comments on places that are in the book and/or recommendations for your own *New Discoveries*.

Your name _____ Street _____

Town _____ State _____ Zip _____ Country _____

Tel _____ E-mail _____ Date _____

Do we have your permission to electronically publish your comments on our website? Yes _____ No _____

If yes, would you like to remain anonymous? Yes ___No ___, or may we use your name? Yes___ No___

Please send report to: Karen Brown's Guides, Post Office Box 70, San Mateo, California 94401, USA
tel: (650) 342-9117, fax: (650) 342-9153, e-mail: karen@karenbrown.com, www.karenbrown.com

SHARE YOUR COMMENTS AND DISCOVERIES WITH US

Please share comments on properties that you have visited. We welcome accolades, as well as criticisms.

Also, we'd love to hear about any hotel or bed & breakfast you discover. Tell us what you liked about the property and, if possible, please include a brochure or photographs. We regret we cannot return photos.

Owner _____ Hotel or B&B _____

Address _____ Town _____ Country _____

Comments on places that are in the book and/or recommendations for your own *New Discoveries*.

Your name _____ Street _____

Town _____ State _____ Zip _____ Country _____

Tel _____ E-mail _____ Date _____

Do we have your permission to electronically publish your comments on our website? Yes _____ No _____

If yes, would you like to remain anonymous? Yes ____No ____, or may we use your name? Yes____ No____

Please send report to: Karen Brown's Guides, Post Office Box 70, San Mateo, California 94401, USA
tel: (650) 342-9117, fax: (650) 342-9153, e-mail: karen@karenbrown.com, www.karenbrown.com

SELECT REGISTRY™

DISTINGUISHED INNS OF NORTH AMERICA

Publishers of the best travel guide to nearly 400 of the finest country inns, B&Bs, and unique small hotels in North America.

Now, more than ever, the traveling public needs places where gracious hospitality and comfortable and uncomplicated settings provide a respite from daily life and its tensions. Select Registry…where the destination becomes part of the journey.

Please visit our web site at **www.selectregistry.com** or call **1-800-344-5244** and tell us that you saw this message in your Karen Brown Guidebook. We will send you a complimentary copy of the registry ($15.95 retail) for just $3.00 postage and handling.

KB Travel Service

❖ **KB Travel Service** offers travel planning assistance using itineraries designed by *Karen Brown* and published in her guidebooks. We will customize any itinerary to fit your personal interests.

❖ We will plan your itinerary with you, help you decide how long to stay and what to do once you arrive, and work out the details.

❖ We will book your airline tickets and your rental car, arrange rail travel, reserve accommodations recommended in *Karen Brown's Guides,* and supply you with point-to-point information and consultation.

Contact us to start planning your travel!

800.782.2128 or e-mail: info@kbtravelservice.com

Service fees do apply

KB Travel Service
16 East Third Avenue
San Mateo, CA 94401 USA
www.kbtravelservice.com

Independently owned and operated by Town & Country Travel
CST 2001543-10

Seal Cove Inn

Located in the San Francisco Bay Area

Karen Brown Herbert (best known as author of the Karen Brown's guides) and her husband, Rick, have put 23 years of experience into reality and opened their own superb hideaway, Seal Cove Inn. Spectacularly set amongst wild flowers and bordered by towering cypress trees, Seal Cove Inn looks out to the distant ocean over acres of county park: an oasis where you can enjoy secluded beaches, explore tidepools, watch frolicking seals, and follow the tree-lined path that traces the windswept ocean bluffs. Country antiques, original watercolors, flower-laden cradles, rich fabrics, and the gentle ticking of grandfather clocks create the perfect ambiance for a foggy day in front of the crackling log fire. Each bedroom is its own haven with a cozy sitting area before a wood-burning fireplace and doors opening onto a private balcony or patio with views to the park and ocean. Moss Beach is a 35-minute drive south of San Francisco, 6 miles north of the picturesque town of Half Moon Bay, and a few minutes from Princeton harbor with its colorful fishing boats and restaurants. Seal Cove Inn makes a perfect base for whale-watching, salmon-fishing excursions, day trips to San Francisco, exploring the coast, or, best of all, just a romantic interlude by the sea, time to relax and be pampered. Karen and Rick look forward to the pleasure of welcoming you to their coastal hideaway.

Seal Cove Inn • 221 Cypress Avenue • Moss Beach • California • 94038 • USA
tel: (650) 728-4114, fax: (650) 728-4116, e-mail: sealcove@coastside.net, website: sealcoveinn.com

KAREN BROWN wrote her first travel guide in 1976. Her personalized travel series has grown to sixteen titles which Karen and her small staff work diligently to keep updated. Karen, her husband, Rick, and their children, Alexandra and Richard, live in Moss Beach, a small town on the coast south of San Francisco. They settled here in 1991 when they opened Seal Cove Inn. Karen is frequently traveling, but when she is home, in her role as innkeeper, enjoys welcoming Karen Brown readers.

CLARE BROWN, CTC, was a travel consultant for many years, specializing in planning itineraries to Europe using charming small hotels in the countryside. The focus of her job remains unchanged, but now her expertise is available to a larger audience—the readers of her daughter Karen's country inn guides. When Clare and her husband, Bill, are not traveling, they live either in Hillsborough, California, or at their home in Vail, Colorado, where family and friends frequently join them for skiing.

JUNE BROWN'S love of travel was inspired by the *National Geographic* magazines that she read as a girl in her dentist's office—so far she has visited over 40 countries. June hails from Sheffield, England and lived in Zambia and Canada before moving to northern California where she lives in San Mateo with her husband, Tony, their daughter Clare, their German Shepherd, and a Siamese cat.

BARBARA TAPP, the talented artist who produces all of the hotel sketches and delightful illustrations in this guide, was raised in Australia where she studied in Sydney at the School of Interior Design. Although Barbara continues with freelance projects, she devotes much of her time to illustrating the Karen Brown guides. Barbara lives in Kensington, California, with her husband, Richard, their two sons, Jonothan and Alexander, and daughter, Georgia.

JANN POLLARD, the artist responsible for the beautiful painting on the cover of this guide, has studied art since childhood, and is well-known for her outstanding impressionistic-style watercolors which she has exhibited in numerous juried shows, winning many awards. Jann travels frequently to Europe (using Karen Brown's guides) where she loves to paint historical buildings. Jann lives in Burlingame, California, with her husband, Gene.

Travel Your Dreams • Order Your Karen Brown Guides Today

Please ask in your local bookstore for Karen Brown's Guides. If the books you want are unavailable, you may order directly from the publisher. Books will be shipped immediately.

_____ *Austria: Charming Inns & Itineraries* $19.95

_____ *California: Charming Inns & Itineraries* $19.95

_____ *England: Charming Bed & Breakfasts* $18.95

_____ *England, Wales & Scotland: Charming Hotels & Itineraries* $19.95

_____ *France: Charming Bed & Breakfasts* $18.95

_____ *France: Charming Inns & Itineraries* $19.95

_____ *Germany: Charming Inns & Itineraries* $19.95

_____ *Ireland: Charming Inns & Itineraries* $19.95

_____ *Italy: Charming Bed & Breakfasts* $18.95

_____ *Italy: Charming Inns & Itineraries* $19.95

_____ *Mid-Atlantic: Charming Inns & Itineraries* $19.95

_____ *New England: Charming Inns & Itineraries* $19.95

_____ *Portugal: Charming Inns & Itineraries* $19.95

_____ *Spain: Charming Inns & Itineraries* $19.95

_____ *Switzerland: Charming Inns & Itineraries* $19.95

Coming soon: Karen Brown's *Pacific Northwest* and Karen Brown's *Mexico*

Name _____ Street _____

Town _____ State_____ Zip _____ Tel _____

Credit Card (MasterCard or Visa) _____ Expires: _____

For orders in the USA, add $5 for the first book and $1 for each additional book for shipment. Overseas shipping (airmail) is $10 for 1 to 2 books, $20 for 3 to 4 books etc. CA residents add 8% sales tax. Fax or mail form with check or credit card information to:

KAREN BROWN'S GUIDES
Post Office Box 70 • San Mateo • California • 94401 • USA
tel: (650) 342-9117, fax: (650) 342-9153, e-mail: karen@karenbrown.com, www.karenbrown.com